DATE DUE

2007 6	

Good in
a Room

Good in a Room

HOW TO SELL YOURSELF

(AND YOUR IDEAS)

AND WIN OVER ANY AUDIENCE

Stephanie Palmer

CURRENCY

DOUBLEDAY

New York London Toronto Sydney Auckland

A CURRENCY BOOK
PUBLISHED BY DOUBLEDAY

Published in the United States by Doubleday, an imprint of The Doubleday Broadway
Publishing Group, a division of Random House, Inc., New York.

www.currencybooks.com

Book design by Chris Welch

Library of Congress Cataloging-in-Publication Data
Palmer, Stephanie.
Good in a room : how to sell yourself (and your ideas) and win over
any audience / by Stephanie Palmer.
p. cm.
"A Currency book."
Includes index.
I. Selling—Psychological aspects. 2. Success in business.
3. Persuasion (Psychology) 4. Success. I. Title.
HF5438.8.P75P35 2008
650.1—dc22
2007037918

ISBN: 978-0-385-52043-0

PRINTED IN THE UNITED STATES OF AMERICA

SPECIAL SALES
•
Currency Books are available at special discounts for bulk purchases for sales promotions
or premiums. Special editions, including personalized covers, excerpts of existing books,
and corporate imprints, can be created in large quantities for special needs. For more information, write to Special Markets, Currency Books, specialmarkets@randomhouse.com

I 3 5 7 9 I0 8 6 4 2

First Edition

To Jean, George, and Tim

Contents

Part I
How to Swim with Sharks

Contents

Part II
Titles, Teasers, and Trailers

Part III
Getting in the Room

Part IV
Inside the Room

Part V
Mini-Meetings

Part VI
Troubleshooting

Good in a room *adj.* **1.** *Hollywood:* Term used by agents and managers to describe their clients who pitch well. **2.** *Corporate:* Capable of making compelling presentations in meetings and persuading colleagues, clients, and decision makers. **3.** *Personal:* Able to connect with people easily and make a favorable impression.

Good in
a Room

Introduction

You walk through the revolving doors into a three-story lobby. The space is silent. The air is cool. It feels like a museum. You walk across the marble floor, each footstep producing an echo, until you reach the massive marble reception desk.

Behind the desk are four security guards in crisp navy suits. You tell one of the guards your name and whom you are going to see. The guard places a phone call and then gives you a security pass. Another security guard ushers you into a steel and mirror-paneled elevator. He presses the button for the top floor.

You exit the elevator into the luxurious reception area. In front of you is a mahogany reception desk staffed by a strikingly attractive assistant. She welcomes you by name and says, "Please have a seat. I'll let them know you're here."

A slight chill runs up your spine. *Them?* You had expected to meet only with the chief operating officer (COO). But before you can sit down in one of the club chairs in the waiting area, another assistant emerges from the hallway and leads you into a private conference room with a rectangular marble table surrounded by twelve Aeron chairs. The assistant gestures toward rows of bottled water on a buffet table against the wall. "Smartwater, Fiji, or Perrier?" he asks.

Then you wait for thirty minutes. The calm façade you brought in with you starts to evaporate. You fantasize about what could happen if they say yes. You worry about what could happen if they say no. You might never get in this room again.

You start to sweat.

Then you remember what you learned from reading this book, *Good in a Room*. You have a comprehensive strategy for each of the five stages of the meeting. You know how to avoid the secret traps that take most people out of the running. And when the time comes to pitch your idea, you know exactly what to say and how to say it.

Suddenly the COO enters. Following the COO is the CEO, the vice chairman, and the president of the company. Everyone takes their seats and the meeting begins. . . .

Twenty minutes later, the meeting ends smoothly. The room is warm with enthusiasm and the executives smile as they shake your hand. The COO sees you out the door. He says, "We'll talk it over and get back to you soon."

The next day, you get the call: "Yes." A wave of relief washes over you and the muscles in your shoulders begin to relax. You did it. You got in the right room with the right people and delivered a winning pitch.

Best of all, your confidence has grown substantially. With this experience under your belt, you'll be better positioned for the next high-stakes meeting and decision makers will be more inclined to say yes to your ideas.

You've broken through to the next level in your professional life. You're excited about your future. You know that you'll be hearing the word *yes* a lot more often.

That's what it's like to be good in a room.

CHAPTER 1

Why You Should Read This Book

The reason you should read this book is because the strategies and tactics that people use to sell ideas in Hollywood work in the rest of the business world. I have worked with entrepreneurs, executives, and professionals in industries such as real estate, financial services, retail sales, law, advertising, marketing, video games, and more. The techniques used to sell ideas in Hollywood not only work in other industries, they often work *better*.

As you already know, "good in a room" is a Hollywood term referring to creative people who excel at pitching in high-stakes meetings. I've had—literally—thousands of these meetings. During my time as a studio executive at MGM, I had over three thousand pitch meetings where writers, directors, stars, and producers would try to persuade me to buy their ideas.

Most of the time, ideas are pitched poorly. However, there are some people who succeed all the time. Over a period of years, I paid attention to what worked and what didn't. I identified the techniques that were being used in all of the successful meetings—regardless of who was pitching. I also found a considerable number of ways that the person pitching could break the deal, often without knowing it.

Many studio executives, or "suits," have backgrounds in sales, marketing, or finance. My degree is in theatrical directing from Carnegie Mellon. So when I started hearing pitches, I wasn't just thinking about whether to say yes or no. I was seeing the meeting as a theatrical performance.

Unfortunately, most writers, like most people, do not have a comprehensive strategy to deliver a great performance. When the time comes to pitch in a high-stakes situation, even someone experienced can stumble and ruin a golden opportunity without a solid meeting technique.

When someone with a great idea doesn't present it effectively, it not only hurts them, but all of us as well. Why? Because mediocre ideas will get purchased and produced if superior ideas aren't pitched well enough.

The fact is that when it comes to making a buying decision, buyers can more easily evaluate the information on the surface, i.e., the pitch. It's harder to evaluate what's inside. As you know, this is true beyond Hollywood. In a grocery aisle, success is determined more by the design and copywriting on the packaging than by the quality of the product. In job interviews, hiring decisions tend to look past differences in work experience and focus on how the candidates perform in the room. My point is not that pitching is everything. Rather, it's that good products deserve good packaging and great ideas deserve a great pitch.

Even shy, awkward, introverted people can learn to pitch well. One of my highlights from MGM was when I found a new writer named Mike who was pitching a high school comedy with a unique angle. His script was great, but his pitch was a disaster. He didn't know how to handle the small talk, he pitched too soon and with way too much detail—he broke the deal in a dozen different ways. Ordinarily I would just pass on his project, but I was frustrated with the quality of the movies we were making and I didn't want to send this great script back to the slush pile. So I coached Mike on how to perform in each stage of the meeting and told him exactly what to say when my boss asked, "So, what's your project about?"

The next day, Mike pitched his idea beautifully to my boss, and it sold right there in the meeting. Afterward, he told me that he'd been staying on his brother's couch for the last three months and was preparing to move back in with his parents. With this one sale, his career was on an entirely new trajectory. And for me, in a job where so much of my time was spent surviving cutthroat politics and producing mediocre ideas, helping Mike succeed was really gratifying. I realized then that I wanted to focus on pitching, not production.

A year later, I left my executive job and started my own company, also called Good in a Room, to help writers and directors with quality ideas get the attention and financing they deserve. Then I did an interview with National Public Radio and I started getting some remarkable calls. A fashion designer wanted help bringing out his summer collection. A marketing exec wanted to get promoted to VP. A financial advisor wanted to find new clients and expand her business.

Soon enough, my non-Hollywood clients were landing million-dollar accounts, doubling their client rosters, launching successful small businesses, increasing their revenue, and getting promoted. Sure, some of my clients were skeptical at first. William, for example, was a sixty-something financial advisor from Texas. We met at the Merrill Lynch campus in New Jersey. I was there to give the concluding presentation at the annual conference for top producers.

William was already quite successful. He didn't need to change how he was doing business. As well, he was in a conservative business in a conservative part of the country, so anything that came out of a liberal place such as Hollywood was immediately suspect.

Still, he wanted to take his business to the next level, and he was smart enough to realize that unless he wanted to simply put in more hours and work harder, he was going to have to try something new. I consulted with him the next morning before we went to the airport and suggested that he modify his standard approach in a few significant ways. He was doubtful, but he said he'd give it a shot when he got back to Texas.

When I landed in LA, William had already left me a message. Turns out the guy sitting next to him on the plane had just sold his business and needed a financial advisor he could trust. Rather than trying to "sell" him, as so many financial advisors do, my client practiced the Good in a Room techniques and signed him rather effortlessly.

Meeting a client on a plane is practically a cliché (though in reality, it doesn't happen very often), and all of the credit belongs to William. Still, the idea that a sixty-something financial advisor in conservative Texas could, with one consultation, master and successfully apply what works for thirty-something writers in liberal Los Angeles? Very cool.

Whether you work in Hollywood or not, the fact is that selling ideas is really difficult to do. The reason the pitching secrets of the most successful writers and directors are relevant is that these people have evolved an advanced method for selling ideas.

Whether you're a screenwriter, a journalist with an idea for a story, an entrepreneur with a business plan, an inventor with a blueprint, or a manager with an innovative solution, if you want other people to invest their time, energy, and money in your idea, you face an uphill battle.

First, ideas aren't tangible—no one can kick the tires of your idea. Second, ideas aren't quantifiable—the decision maker can't reliably estimate the value of your idea in monetary terms. As my boss at MGM used to say, "If we knew which ideas would be hits, we would only make hits." Third, ideas are risky—there can be millions of dollars on the line and reputations at stake when a buyer says yes to an idea. Fourth, people who buy ideas hear so many pitches that getting their attention and actually convincing them is exceptionally difficult. Finally, the more original your idea is, the tougher it is to pitch effectively. Any groundbreaking idea will be harder to sell simply because there isn't a precedent to show it will work.

As risks increase and buyers become more difficult to persuade, people who sell ideas must clear an even higher bar. We must get in the right rooms with the right people. We need a comprehensive strategy and the most advanced tactics. Then we can present ourselves and our ideas with confidence.

CHAPTER 2

Who This Book Is For

In your professional life, sometimes you're the *seller* (one who pitches an idea) and sometimes you're the *buyer* (one who is being pitched). I'm assuming that you're reading this book because you want to become a more effective seller, that is, you want to get better at persuading other people to invest their time, energy, and money in your ideas.

While the techniques in this book apply to any situation where a seller is pitching an idea to a buyer, there are subtle differences depending on the type of seller you are. You may be more than one type of seller (so don't feel boxed in), but over time, I've found that my clients tend to belong in one of the following categories:

- *Corporate:* salespeople, executives, managers
- *Entrepreneurial:* small business owners, inventors
- *Expert:* lawyers, financial advisors
- *Creative:* writers, designers, artists

Corporate

Two years into my tenure at MGM I was given a rare promotion from assistant to executive. Suddenly, I was supervising the assistants who used to be my colleagues. I was managing a team of script readers twice my age. I was pitching ideas to committees of people who used to give me their coffee and sandwich orders.

To keep my job (let alone do it well and be eligible for advancement) I needed to get others on board with my ideas. I had to prevent other people from piling my desk full of their work. Most important, I needed friends, alliances, and some political capital of my own.

Whether you work in sales, marketing, human resources, customer service, or management, you are enmeshed in a complex social system. You must effectively manage the people "below." You must please the people "above." You must cooperate with your colleagues and, if you want to get promoted, compete against them at the same time.

Corporate goal: To rise through the ranks (get raises, bonuses, and promotions)

Entrepreneurial

I understand the desire to be your own boss. It took me five years of planning and preparation before I felt I was ready to take the plunge and open my consulting firm. Even then, I was scared—but I wasn't alone.

In the last few years, two of the fastest-growing segments of the U.S. economy have been microbusinesses (companies run by only one person) and small businesses (with just a few employees).

What gets in the way of achieving your entrepreneurial dream is believing that if you are good at meeting the needs of your customers, you'll be successful. This classic mistake is why most small businesses fail.

Initially, your job isn't to serve the needs of your customers. Your job is to market and sell yourself in a concise, compelling, and accurate way so that you *have* customers.

Entrepreneurial goal: To position your business for maximum marketing effectiveness

Expert

Many of my clients are people who had to get a professional degree to be certified to do their job. These lawyers, financial advisors, and accountants (among others) tend to have one primary concern: bringing in business.

As you may know, the key to bringing in business is not just being good at what you do. Finding, courting, and signing new clients takes a different set of skills. For example, lawyers don't typically spend much time in law school learning about marketing strategy. However, finding new clients is often essential to making partner. In my experience, no matter your profession, the ability to generate new business is a crucial component to advancing in your company.

Expert goal: To find new clients and increase revenue

Creative

Creative professionals want to do original work. They also want to be successful. This creates a natural tension between the muse, who wants to create without limitations, and the ego, who wants to be recognized (and paid).

One of the things that surprised me the most about starting my consulting business is that even at the highest levels, this tension between muse and ego doesn't go away. Writers who have impressive resumes, millions of dollars, Emmys, Oscars—they still struggle like everyone else. They want to be groundbreaking and innovative, but they also want people to love (and pay for) their material.

Creative goal: To sell without "selling out"

Four Protagonists

I've created four characters, each of whom represents one of the above categories and faces an interesting challenge in his or her professional field. They are based on my clients and the issues that many of them have had in common. Let's get to know them and the typical (but serious) problems they face.

Liz—A Sales Executive (Corporate)

At age ten, in the sandbox of her backyard, Liz prevented a war from breaking out among her five younger siblings by negotiating The Big Wheel Peace Accords. At eighteen, she planned the most famous senior prom in her high school's history because she made the event a benefit for People for the Ethical Treatment of Animals (PETA) and got a famous vegetarian rapper to headline. In college, she helped the newspaper and the radio station increase circulation and listeners by cross-promoting their top stories. When she graduated she had a degree in art history and no idea what to do with it.

From a connection through a family friend, she started working as a salesperson at Tall People Furniture. Even though she's only five feet two, her friendly manner and ability to listen endeared her to customers. After two years on the sales floor, Liz is one of the top producers.

Recently, the owner of the company, George, told everyone that he plans to expand the sales force and promote one of the current salespeople to a managerial position. Liz would love to be promoted, but the other salespeople also want the job and they are all older and have more seniority. They're male, too. It shouldn't be an issue, but in the real world it is.

Still, Liz knows she could handle the responsibility and would love the challenge. She believes that if she could show George that she has fresh ideas and the ability to lead the team, he would consider her for the position.

Unfortunately, Liz doesn't have much available time. She's the newest member of the sales team and so she bears the brunt of the busywork. Increasingly, the other salespeople delegate more of their work to her. This way, they have more time on the floor to sell (and show their worth to George). If Liz wants to be considered for the promotion, she's going to have to change this trend, and fast.

J.J.—A Computer Consultant (Entrepreneurial)

Armed with a degree in computer science, J.J. got a job right out of college working for a prestigious game development company. He thought it was his dream come true. He was wrong.

Sure, he got to keep his dreadlocks, wear tie-dye, and come to work at 10 A.M., but with ten programmers competing for two design jobs, the environment was fiercely competitive. J.J. hid in his cubicle to avoid the company politics and wrote freeware for his beloved Macintosh, "Zelda."

Recently he'd had enough. He gave two weeks' notice, sublet his apartment, and moved in with his mom. Now he works the Kinko's night shift and spends his spare time fixing his friends' computers via remote desktop. Fixing machines is just something he's always been able to do, and it gives him a way to pass the time during the long nights.

Last night J.J. woke up at 2 A.M. with a vision: He would open a company that would focus exclusively on fixing Macs. He would help people understand that computers are people, too, each with their own distinct personality. He would provide regular checkups and preventive care as well as emergency tech support.

He would work for $50 an hour! He would move into his own apartment! Get a girlfriend!

There's only one problem: His friends can't afford $50 an hour. Besides, it might not even be possible to run a business that competes with all of the existing tech-support businesses, especially if he focuses only on Macs. What's an entrepreneur to do?

Fangxiao—A Financial Advisor (Expert)

When Fangxiao (pronounced "fang zhow") told her father that she wanted to trade stocks for a living, he wasn't pleased. He had talked to her since she was a child about entering one of the more stable "expertise" professions, such as medicine, law, or accounting. He felt that only those professions would justify the sacrifices her parents had made working multiple jobs to send her to college. Then Fangxiao explained that she'd won her collegiate stock market contest three years in a row, and her dad's mind began to change.

Fangxiao traded for a few years, bought her parents a Prius and started their retirement portfolios, then took a job as a financial advisor for one of the big brokerage firms. She had an easy time finding overseas clients because she spoke English as well as Mandarin and Cantonese. Ten years later she was managing a team of financial advisors as well as the portfolios of her own clients.

Then the laws governing international trading changed and suddenly Fangxiao wasn't allowed to trade on behalf of people who were not American citizens. The majority of her practice dried up, and her career trajectory took a dive.

Fangxiao was still pretty busy managing her team and could focus on that. She would probably accumulate clients slowly over time. However, she wouldn't make nearly as much money because the bonus structure at her company relied heavily on bringing in new business.

Moreover, her Asian heritage, formerly an asset in working with overseas clients, seemed to put her at a disadvantage in a profession where most of the market was used to working with white males. How can she develop her marketing and sales propositions to find a new niche?

Elliot—A Budding Screenwriter (Creative)

Elliot is shy. He only wears black. He doesn't like "people." He's a New Yorker at heart and LA's been a little hard to get used to. He tends not to leave the house unless it's to see his girlfriend (also an introvert) or to complete an assignment for *Prime Numbers*, the magazine for the technically savvy that employs him as a freelance journalist.

When he's not writing about what's hot in the kingdom of geek, Elliot works on his screenplay. It's a mystery inspired by his summer experiences at Camp Appaloosa called *The Last All-Nighter*.

Camp was the best time of Elliot's life. It's where he learned how to swim, sail, and fish. It's also where he made his closest friends. Elliot would love to be able to go back and visit for a weekend, but unfortunately Camp Appaloosa mysteriously closed after his last summer.

He's taken some writing classes, has the right software, and knows that if he wants to sell his script, he needs to get an agent or a manager. However, he doesn't know anyone in the business. He made copies of the script (at eight bucks a copy) and sent them to every literary agent in town. The total response to his mailing was . . . zip. How can Elliot get his work read by the right people, find an agent or manager, and sell his script?

Tune In Next Time . . .

While some of these stories may seem more applicable to your life than others, I hope you get something valuable out of each one. My goal is to structure all of the material in a commonsense way so you will have an easy time finding what you need. Let's get a bird's-eye view in the next chapter, "What's in This Book and How to Use It."

CHAPTER 3

What's in This Book and How to Use It

This book is designed chronologically. If you start at the beginning (which I recommend), you'll see the entire meeting process evolve from beginning to end. There will be helpful suggestions and exercises to guide you along the way.

In the section "How to Swim with Sharks," I'll help you develop the mind-set and habits of the best of the best. Don't worry, this will not be a rehashing of messages like "Work harder than the competition, be optimistic, and stay organized." Rather, this will be a simple and clear explanation of the strategies that will help you distinguish yourself from the competition.

Then, "Titles, Teasers, and Trailers" will give you a step-by-step approach for creating unique, memorable answers for the most common buyer questions, including "What do you do?" and "What's your project about?" After you read this section, you will never again use an elevator pitch—you'll have something far better.

In "Getting in the Room," I'll show you how to meet, engage, and develop relationships with the right people in your industry. This will not be a boring section on networking. In fact, I don't like traditional networking. I don't do it and I don't recommend it. I've got a different strategy based on the only networking principle that means any-thing—and I'll tell you all about it.

The section "Inside the Room" pulls back the curtain on meeting dynamics. You'll learn the five stages of every successful meeting. You didn't know there were five stages? Well, you will soon enough. This one concept will dramatically change the way you approach formal pitches, informal meetings, and even water-cooler conversations.

"Mini-Meetings" will give you practical examples of how to be more effective on the phone, in e-mail, and in person—because so much of the work happens in the communication before and after the meeting. Finally, "Troubleshooting" is a road map for handling the inevitable pitfalls and unexpected developments, so no matter what happens, you're ready.

On a Personal Note

When I was at MGM, the hardest part of my job was not cutthroat studio politics or grueling production schedules. The toughest part of my job was whenever I had to say no to an idea that was *almost* there.

I had to say no a lot. Every buyer does. The buyer's work is to say yes to projects that are ready, not almost ready. And no matter how good the idea is, if the seller can't pitch it in a compelling way, how can the buyer see the potential? How can he get his colleagues on board? How can he recommend the seller to his superiors? The fact is that poor pitches doom good projects.

It happens all the time. The ideas, products, and services that are pitched more effectively win. That's just how the game is played. No sense getting upset over it. Instead, let's accept the challenge and learn the strategies and tactics that will allow us (and our ideas) to succeed.

I'm writing this book because there are those of you out there who are doing your best to come up with creative ideas, innovative businesses, and superior products. You're devoting yourself to becoming good at whatever it is you do. My goal is to help you present your-self and your ideas so that your hard work pays off. I want you to be able to walk into any room with confidence. I want your clients, cus-tomers, co-workers, and bosses to have an easy time seeing that what you have is what they need.

My approach may be different from what you've heard before. But I've got to tell you, my clients hear the word *yes* a lot. You can, too.

Part I

.

How to Swim with Sharks

The famous military strategist Carl von Clausewitz said, "Business is war." I prefer "Business is like high school." In my experience, the business world has a great deal in common with the world of fourteen-to-eighteen-year-olds. Sure, some high school kids try to excel academically, but the real game is social. It's about who's in what clique, who gets invited to what party, who's in and who's out. In high school, a great deal depends on how well you are *liked*.

In the business world, it's the same way. Buyers prefer to work with people they like. They buy from people they like. They hire people they like. They promote people they like. And they tend to like people who are a lot like them.

If this bothers you, good. You would probably prefer to live in a world where people value competence and where rewards are based on merit. I feel the same way.

In my Hollywood jobs, all I wanted to do was make good movies. I had no idea how much time I would have to spend developing relationships and finding ways to work with difficult people. I was surprised at the lengths to which some people would go to satisfy their anger, jealousy, or pure competitive instinct.

For a while, I thought this was true only in Hollywood. Then, as I moved into the broader corporate world, I found the same behaviors. I've met people in every industry who are prima donnas, game players, turf defenders, and power grabbers—in other words, sharks.

Sharks are common. They are part of any business ecosystem. Thus, we must find a way to conduct ourselves that allows us to deal successfully with everyone, including them.

I believe that the solution is simple. If you want to be able to handle yourself in any situation, even in shark-infested waters, you must develop your most important asset—your ability to bond with other people.

CHAPTER 4

Secrets of Rapport

One of the notes studio executives are constantly giving to screenwriters is, "How can the hero be more *likeable?*" The reason for this note is that so much of the success of the project depends on whether or not the audience is willing to watch a protagonist struggle for two hours. If we like the character, then we're invested in seeing the character succeed. If we don't, we're not.

Likeability is so essential that in many movies an early scene is included for the sole purpose of getting the audience to know and like the hero. Blake Snyder, a friend of mine and a prolific Hollywood writer, calls this scene "Save the Cat."

The "Save the Cat" scene in a movie is where the hero does something that shows warmth and understanding. Sometimes, literally, the hero saves an animal. You may recall that in *Lethal Weapon*, Riggs saves a wounded dog. In *The Incredibles*, Mr. Incredible saves a cat. In *Back to the Future*, Marty throws his father out of the way of a moving car. In *Sea of Love*, Detective Frank Keller sees a criminal with his young son and, rather than arresting the perp in front of his kid, allows him to escape. These are the kinds of characters we want to spend time with.

Likeability is important in the movies. Likeability is important in real life, too, because it's a crucial ingredient in building *rapport*.

> **Rapport** (ra | pôr) *n.*: a close, harmonious relationship characterized by warmth, mutual understanding, and good communication.

When you have rapport with someone, they are paying attention to what you have to say. Without rapport, they are not. Thus, developing rapport quickly is the first and most important ingredient of being good in a room.

Likeability

Of course, you're not likely to get the chance to rescue a potential client's golden retriever from an oncoming train. So you're going to have to develop your rapport-building abilities.

Aside from whatever other likeable qualities you may have, the keys to being likeable are to be *empathic* and *interested*. Empathy means that you care. You can step into the other person's shoes, understand her feelings, and share her perspective. Interest means that you're curious about her; you want to get to know her better. If it is clear to the other person that you care about her and that you are intrigued by her, she will want to spend time with you and will have an easier time trusting you.

Many people try to be likeable by being entertaining. They make it a high priority to keep the other person's attention and maintain a fun atmosphere.

If you tell great stories and have a sense of humor, that's a tremendous asset. However, it doesn't inspire trust—and trust is essential to rapport.

Secret 1: Allow yourself to really care about the other person and to be curious about who he or she is. Empathic interest creates trust.

Common Ground

Common ground can take many forms. You and another person may have all sorts of things in common: opinions, friends, interests, experiences, and values. What's important in gaining rapport is to be on the same side of the issue.

For example, you may discover in talking with a potential buyer that you both love rock climbing. However, if you love rock climbing because it's a way of experiencing the beauty of nature and if the buyer loves it because of the competition between climbers, you don't really have common ground. In fact, that topic can become the exact opposite: a *friction point*.

Friction points are often found in areas such as religion and politics. These topics tend to be avoided for precisely this reason. Friction points are so dangerous that many of us avoid them by simply pretending to take the buyer's side, even if we don't agree. It seems harmless enough to fudge our beliefs a little to continue the conversation, right?

Wrong. Forgive me for being so blunt, but I see well-intentioned people make this mistake all the time. If you pretend to be interested when you are not, if you pretend to like something you don't, you cannot build the kind of rapport that pays dividends. At best, you can fool someone for a short period of time. That's bad ethics and ineffective strategy simultaneously.

When you're talking with another person, it's normal to find many places where you don't entirely agree or where you frankly disagree. Avoiding these topics means you can't get to know someone. Agreeing with the other person (when you really don't agree) means she can't get to know you. The solution is to be *curious*. In the above conversation about rock climbing, a question like "What about competing with the other climbers do you like?" might lead to an answer about bonding and camaraderie between fellow athletes. And while you may climb just to experience nature, perhaps you played a sport in high school or college and can resonate with the importance of team bonding. Now the conversation is on a different path with far more potential for common ground.

S e c r e t 2: Common ground cannot be faked or fudged. Rapport requires honesty.

Connection

You know you're building rapport when you feel a sense of connection. Connection happens when you and the other person (or the audience) let your defenses down. It can happen quickly, but it can also take time; many of us do not reveal ourselves so easily. This is why empathy, interest, and common ground are so important. They create the conditions necessary to establish a connection.

Some people try to force connection. This is especially true among people who style themselves as "people" people. There should be a sign on the door before you go to an annual meeting or conference: *Beware of "People" People.* These tend to be people who believe that they can connect with anyone but who really love to hear themselves talk.

"People" people tend to come at you with their charisma engines in overdrive. They give you a big smile as if you're their reason for being alive. They shake your hand with the double-hand grasp, or worse, the handshake–elbow grab, or worst of all, the handshake–shoulder clasp. The conversation feels like it's being drowned in false sincerity. Before long they've hit you with, "So, what's your *passion?* I mean, what are you really *passionate* about?"

Ugh.

Hey, if you're really interested in getting to know someone, you don't proceed like this. It's tacky and carries with it a tinge of disrespect. It's a way of saying, "I don't know you, but I've made the effort to pretend that you're my long-lost friend. In return, I require that you reveal yourself to me quickly so that I can move on to my next networking opportunity."

Warmth evolves over the course of a conversation as people learn to trust each other, find common ground, and communicate on the same wavelength.

Secret 3: The warmth that signifies true rapport is not something you can force.

Stay in Sync

To the extent that a conversation is like a dance, it's important to let the buyer "lead." This means staying in sync with the buyer in the following ways:

1. *Pace.* If the buyer speaks more slowly and casually, adjust your pace accordingly. If she's getting out a lot of words per minute, you can match her—just make sure to pause after she's finished speaking. Replying too soon often indicates (correctly) that instead of listening, you were formulating your reply.

2. *Depth.* If the buyer wants to talk about the weather or other traditional small-talk topics, that's fine. Start there. Don't jump the gun and ask about her off-work interests or family. That may be where the ideal common ground is, but the buyer may not be comfortable enough with you just yet. Allow the conversation to develop; when the buyer says something more personal, you can respond in kind.

3. *Tone.* If the buyer starts out low-key, it's a good idea for you to be low-key, too. Don't try to amp up the conversation or change the buyer's mood. It doesn't work. What does work is to meet the buyer at his energy level and shift into higher gears when he does.

Keep the Buyer in the Spotlight

When the buyer is talking, the spotlight is on him and he is giving you signals and clues about what he wants. When you are talking, the spotlight is on you and the buyer is likely losing interest.

The way to keep the spotlight on the buyer is to give him your full attention. Don't just hear the content of what he has to say. Pay attention to his word choices, inflections, and gesticulations as well. Maintain 100 percent outward focus and envelop the buyer with your attention. You will stand out in his memory and be the kind of person he looks forward to seeing again.

Secret 4: Keep the spotlight shining on the buyer.

Everyone Is Interesting

When you know you can create personal warmth in a business situation, your confidence will be apparent from the moment you walk in the room. No matter how irritating or boring someone seems, you'll be able to find common ground and build rapport. One of the keys to finding common ground, however, is being familiar with the buyer's home turf. That's the subject of the next chapter, "It's What You Know."

CHAPTER 5

It's What You Know

About once a month I get a phone call from a friend of a friend, or a friend of a friend's friend—you know, someone two to four degrees of separation away. "I'm thinking about moving to LA so I can work in Hollywood," they say. "Do you have any advice for me?"

"I'll do my best," I reply. Then after we've made small talk and gotten to know each other, I'll say, "So, have you read any books about moving out to Los Angeles?"

"Um . . . no."

"Have you read any books about Hollywood?"

"No. Not really."

"Okay. Well, in that case, here's my advice. Hollywood is a complex industry and there are many different paths you can take. It might help to read a couple of books that seem interesting to you. You can find a list on my Web site. Then call me back and I'll be happy to help you take the next step."

Not everyone calls me back, but those who do have undoubtedly learned some useful things. Plus, they've earned my respect by doing their homework. Finally, and most important, by reading the books that so many Hollywood professionals have read, they have a head start on finding common ground with anyone they meet in the industry. This gives them a distinct advantage when it comes to building rapport.

It's what you know that helps you develop relationships with whom you know.

I'm pretty sure this isn't news to you. You know that there are things that you don't know as well as you probably should. You may have a stack of books or magazines in your "I'll get to this eventually" pile, but you're doing fine and you just don't have time to catch up on *everything*. Believe me, I understand. I used to have that pile, too.

Information Is More than a Tool

Most of us think of information as something that we'll access when we need it, like getting a tool from our toolbox. If we get to a point where we need to know something, we check the Internet. We look it up. We call someone who read the book that we wish we had time to read in the first place.

However, when you understand the crucial importance of connecting with other people quickly, information becomes more important than just a tool. Shared knowledge is a bridge between your mind and the buyer's mind. It's a starting point for a conversation and the foundation for finding common ground.

I understand that trying to learn every bit of information relevant to your work could take the rest of your life. I'm not advising that. I am suggesting that you develop your knowledge base so that you can increase the speed at which you find common ground and build rapport.

Know Your Own Industry

You may know your own industry well, but if you deepen your expertise, you can comfortably speak on topics that are important to the buyer and pick up on any references.

- *Know the canon of your industry.* Your business has been shaped by the men and women who came before you, many of whom wrote about their experiences. Reading their books will increase your understanding of present-day issues and will ensure that when someone makes a reference, you're familiar with the source.
- *Stay on top of current trends.* Keep abreast of new developments by reading the popular books and magazines that focus on your profession. Also, if you're attempting to develop a relationship with someone in a different industry, read the magazines that you think *they* are reading.
- *Get up-to-the-minute information.* Bookmark the most popular Web sites in your industry and give them a quick scan every day. More than ever, news breaks online. It helps to be among the first to be in the know.

Know Your Specific Buyer

A year after *Legally Blonde* was released, a writing team came into my office and pitched me, quite literally, another version of *Legally Blonde*. The ideas were the same, beat for beat and character for character, save that instead of going to law school, she went to medical school. It was called *Blonde, M.D.,* I believe. I asked them if they knew that MGM had made *Legally Blonde.* They did not. I asked them if they knew that I was one of the executives who supervised the movie. They did not. I asked them if they had anything else to pitch. They did. They had a version in which she becomes a spy, titled *James Blonde.*

This is an extreme example, but I hope you take my point. Before you walk into the room, you need to know as much as possible about the people involved. Every scrap of information will help you figure out what's going on in their minds. This will make the process of building rapport easier and increase your ability to create a presentation that hooks them.

- *Research the buyer's company.* What has been written about her company? What position does it occupy in the industry? What are its recent projects?
- *Understand the buyer's role at the company.* Has your buyer ever been in the news? What does she do at the company? Where does she fit in the organizational hierarchy?
- *Be sensitive to the buyer's professional environment.* Who else works at that company at or above the buyer's level? Can you discover anything about them?

Broaden Your Base of General Knowledge

Often we only know enough about a topic to be able to ask one question, maybe make a comment or two. From there, we resort to smiling and nodding while we plan for a change of subject. That's a lost opportunity. If you can continue the conversation on a deeper level, it's more likely that you'll be able to bond with someone.

- *Read magazines you wouldn't normally read.* If you read *The Economist,* try *Wired.* If you read *The New Yorker,* try *Fast Company.* If you read *Maxim,* try *Cosmo.* Get a taste of the other side. Read what interests you, but be open to being engaged by a wide variety of topics. It can be useful to rip out things you like and file them.
- *Get a digital video recorder (DVR) and take control of your television.* I know that some people frown on watching TV and think it's a waste of time. Hey, I grew up in a house without a TV until I was seven-

teen. However, with modern technology and the wide variety of programming available through cable and satellite, TV can be an efficient way to explore any number of topics, from business to science, news, and sports.

- *Listen to radio and podcasts.* Because of how cheap it is to produce in an audio format, there are incredibly diverse arrays of programs to sample while you're driving, exercising at the gym, or taking a walk.

You're probably thinking this sounds like a lot of work. It is. However, this part of the work can be fun. In fact, it *should* be fun. If you follow your curiosity and focus on what interests you, you'll manage to find the time in your busy schedule. You'll become one of the few people who actually knows what's going on in your industry. Best of all, you'll be able to develop rapport with decision makers more quickly and more easily than ever before.

CHAPTER 6

Go Back to Square One

S quare One is a series of three very simple, very important
questions. I refer to these questions as Square One because they
are the starting point for developing a compelling pitch or
presentation.

You start at Square One when preparing your meeting strategy. You
return to Square One when you are confused or unsure. You will spend
a lot of time asking yourself these questions:

1. What do I want?
2. What do they want?
3. What do they expect?

What Do I Want?

This question is about goals, but it's not about your long-term professional or personal objectives. Those are your dreams, they're personal,
and I leave them to you.

The question "What do I want?" is about goals that can reasonably be achieved *in the meeting.* In my experience, successful people choose attainable goals. For example, less experienced people are the ones who think, "Even though it's a first meeting, my goal is for the buyer to say yes and finance the entire project." That's not likely. Professionals think, "For this first meeting, my goal is to be asked back for another meeting."

Having said that, I believe that when you walk into the room, you have three goals:

1. *To learn.* Learning is a great goal because whether you learn something or not is almost entirely within your control. Plus, having learning as a goal tends to reduce anxiety because you're focused on the process of the conversation, not the eventual outcome. Finally, if you learn from every meeting, your skills will continue to increase and so will your chances of getting what you want.

2. *To build rapport with the buyer.* As you know, rapport is the foundation for everything that follows. If you find common ground and build rapport with the buyer, even if he doesn't say yes, his door will still be open to you down the road.

3. *To get the buyer to agree to one (and only one) request.* Of these three goals, this is the toughest to achieve. Ironically, if this goal is not your only priority, you are more likely to achieve it. That is to say, if you can leave a meeting feeling good about what you've learned and the rapport you've built, you have a higher probability of hearing yes to your request.

The one request you make (and the exact language you use) is important, and we'll discuss this more in later chapters. However, it's important to remember that getting the buyer to say yes may take more than one meeting. This is why learning and rapport are so crucial. They are more easily achievable goals. They are confidence builders. And, most important, they greatly increase the probability that your request will be granted.

Let's move on to the next question, "What do they want?" In many ways, this question is the heart and soul of Square One. You can never be too good at figuring out what's going on in the other person's head.

What Do They Want?

When it comes to ascertaining what the buyer wants in the meeting, you can accept as a given that the buyer's first goal is to disqualify you as quickly as possible. He may not say no out loud at the time that he makes the decision, but that's his primary goal. A no protects the buyer and saves time. The sooner he can feel good about saying no, the better.

For many buyers, when a seller stumbles during the presentation it's an automatic no. It's a safe conclusion that the seller isn't ready. After all, if he can't handle himself in the room, how well is he going to do the actual work? For buyers, it's not worth the risk to find out.

At the same time, buyers are looking to say yes—to the right request, the right person, the right project. It's their dream to have that one breakout meeting. They want to be swept off their professional feet.

Keep Adjusting Your Answer

As you get more and better information about the buyer, your answer to question #2, "What do they want?" will be a work in progress. For example, in Hollywood, buyers are constantly asked "What are you looking for?" Most say something generic, like "good material" or "stories with great characters." There's an attitude of "If I have a bunch of meetings, I'll know what I want when I see it." This is unhelpful, but it's normal in Hollywood and in other industries for buyers to be unaware of exactly what they want.

Thus, you want to keep adjusting your answer as you learn more. It may start as "good material," but then you'll realize that every time the buyer references a movie in the meeting, it's a comedy or action film. You might revise your answer to "comedies and action movies." Eventually, you might research all of the movies the buyer referenced and discover that the comedies tended to have female leads and the action movies were made for less than $40 million. Thus, your revised answer would be "comedies with female leads and action movies that can be made for less than $40 million."

Once you understand what the buyer wants, you can begin adapting your pitch to meet his needs. However, for your pitch to achieve maximum impact, you must consider the buyer's expectations and adjust accordingly.

What Do They Expect?

If you have ever invested in the stock market, you know that expectations are crucial. A company can release great news about increases in earnings, but if the earnings aren't as high as were originally expected, the stock's value will fall. If earnings are higher than expectations, the stock's value will soar. Thus, in the market as well as in meetings, it is crucial to be able to meet expectations—and exceed them.

The first step to being able to exceed the buyer's expectations is being able to understand what those expectations are in the first place. To do this, you have to find out what your competitors are doing. How do they present themselves? What materials do they use? What are their core messages? How are your competitors positioning themselves?

Once you know that, you know what the buyer would expect in a meeting with a competitor. That tells you more about your own position. Your "position" means where you are in the marketplace with respect to your competition. When you are clear about your positioning, the buyer will have an easy time understanding (and wanting) whatever you are offering.

Positioning is an important topic. If you want to know more about positioning, there are some great books, notably *Positioning* and *The 22 Immutable Laws of Marketing* by Al Ries and Jack Trout. However, at a very basic level, you have found a good position when:

You are in a category by yourself.

This is the essence of positioning. When the buyer asks you, "Why should I work with you and not your competition?" you can say, "Because I'm the only one who does _____." Whatever goes in the blank, that's your position.

You Must Exceed Expectations

Steve, a friend of my husband, was the CEO of a relatively new market research firm that was expanding into doing jury research. Steve's company applied traditional market research techniques to help determine which arguments would appeal most to jurors. In one week's time, he had a meeting with the law firm representing the defendant in a civil suit being litigated between two Fortune 500 companies. A lot of money was on the line.

Steve knew that the defense was considering the most elite jury consulting firms in the country. No matter how good his pitch was, no matter how he presented himself, there was no reason they should choose to work with him (having very little experience in the field) as opposed to a more established competitor.

So he started back at Square One. He reviewed his goals for the meeting: to learn, to develop rapport, and to be asked to submit a detailed proposal. Then he made some guesses about their goals for the meeting: to meet him and determine if they might have any use for his company now or down the road, and to gain any possible advantage in their case. Then he addressed their expectations for the meeting—and this was where he made the breakthrough.

What Steve figured out was that one of the buyer's expectations in the meeting was that all of the sellers jockeying for the job would say something like "Here's why you should work with us instead of the competition . . . ," Steve knew he could do this well, as his company is in a category by itself—his is the only company that applies certain market research techniques to jury trials.

But Steve decided not to do what he anticipated everyone else would be doing. He would start his presentation in accordance with the buyer's expectations—he would explain why his company could do everything that the buyer needed and better than anyone else. But then he would explain why the buyer should hire one of the more experienced firms *as well as his own firm.* After all, his methodology was so different from all of his competitors'. Hiring Steve's company wouldn't cost them much and they might learn something they wouldn't have learned from the traditional approach, and for a case this big, even a small advantage might make all the difference.

Do you see how Steve positioned his request in terms of what the buyer wanted and expected? The buyer asked Steve to submit a detailed proposal and eventually hired his team to work on that case and many more thereafter.

Positioning Your Presentation

One of the ways you can communicate your position to the buyer is through the structure of your presentation. This is another opportunity to use what you've learned about the competition. When you know how your competitors structure their presentations, you can design yours differently to highlight your uniqueness.

To continue the previous example, Steve knew that his competitors were primarily lawyers with lots of jury consulting experience. They would show off their impressive track records and then explain their methodology, typically in a ten-to-fifteen-minute PowerPoint presentation. Thus, Steve decided to skip his usual PowerPoint presentation and complete his pitch in seven minutes. He also decided to use several statistics in his presentation that the buyers had probably not heard before.

That's how Steve used his presentation to communicate his positioning. By doing a seven-minute presentation, he exceeds the buyer's expectations and communicates the message "My company delivers answers *faster*." By using statistics the buyer hasn't heard before, he's reinforcing the message "My company uses research techniques to find valuable information. If you work with me, you'll learn things you didn't already know—and that might make all the difference."

Positioning Yourself

In the same way that your presentation must be in line with your position, the way you look must be as well. Buyers make quick judgments based on how you dress. There's no way to avoid that. The trick is to position yourself relative to the expectations of your stereotype.

There, I said it. *Stereotype.* It's a bad word, I know. Obviously, the way you are stereotyped is not who you are. At the same time, I hope you can admit that others will stereotype you. It's so common that we have to factor it into how we position ourselves. My advice is to consider carefully how others are likely to stereotype you and then plan how you're going to play with and against that image.

Our jury consultant Steve knew that his competitors would almost certainly be wearing dark suits in the meeting. Dark suits are standard attire for lawyers and for the courtroom. To dress below that level of formality might communicate to the buyer, "Hey, this guy doesn't get it."

However, Steve isn't a lawyer and his company doesn't use the same methodology that lawyers do. So he decided to wear a jacket without a tie and to take the jacket off in the meeting before giving his presentation.

This may seem like a small thing, but first impressions are so important. It was crucial that Steve wear the jacket to indicate that yes, he does get it. But it was also an important statement for him to skip wearing a tie. That told the buyer to expect something a little different—which Steve then delivered in his presentation.

Holding the Question

One way I've learned to go back to Square One quickly is to practice *holding the question.* This means that, as you go through your day, you hold one question in your mind and every time you encounter someone you ask yourself that question. Suppose you were going to hold the question "What do they want?"

- At the restaurant, you'd ask yourself, "What does the server want?"
- When you give your keys to the valet, you think, "What does the valet want?"
- When you say hello to a co-worker in the morning, you consider, "What does he want?"
- When you're in a meeting and your colleagues are presenting their ideas, ask yourself, "What does this idea—and the way it's being presented—tell me about what this person wants?"

When you do this long enough, Square One gets much easier. You'll see patterns in your own thinking and in the thoughts of others. Every time you walk into a room, you'll know what you want, what the other person wants, and what he or she expects. This is crucial information in determining how to successfully make a request.

CHAPTER 7

Make It Easy on the Other Person

There are ten ways to make it extremely easy for the buyer to say yes. The catch is that you have to go beyond putting in extra time and energy. You must also overcome a psychological obstacle: *You must subordinate yourself to the buyer.*

In other words, you need to remember that the buyer has higher status simply because he or she is the buyer. This seems easy enough to understand, but I've seen a lot of people who say that they understand this and act like they don't. It happens to people who *think* they want to be successful but who really want respect.

Success Versus Respect

People who want respect do not like to subordinate themselves to others. They like to take up a lot of space with their intelligence and capability. They see themselves as the equal of the buyer, or even higher in status. Those of us who are vulnerable to the success/respect trap are often very bright and hardworking. If we offer a bright idea or make a significant effort, we want the respect we deserve. It's understandable. It's just not helpful.

I used to see this all the time in script development meetings with extremely smart writers who had a high-profile assignment. Often, other senior executives would be interested and we'd all meet with the writer together. From a screenwriter's perspective, this is a dream opportunity. However, when one of my colleagues would ask the writer to·make a significant adjustment to the work he'd already done, the writer's face would get red. His jaw would clench. He'd avert his eyes. Eventually, he'd grumble, "Well, let me think about it."

Many of us get upset when we feel we don't get the respect we deserve. However, there's no upside to letting the buyer know you're upset. Of course, it is difficult to respond calmly when the buyer makes a terrible suggestion.

Trust me, I know. Even those of us who don't have a boss above us in the organizational chain of command still answer to the buyers of our company's products or services. Some of those buyers will have horrible ideas and inappropriate expectations. Some buyers will occasionally be obtuse, selfish, insensitive, and disrespectful. This is no different from any other group of people in the world.

One of the crucial dimensions of being a successful professional is being able to work with buyers who may not be as talented, smart, or capable as you are. So don't fall into the success/respect trap. Concede that the buyer, simply by virtue of being the buyer, has higher status. Remember that your job is to make things easy for him. You're lucky if you're smarter—you don't need the buyer to acknowledge that fact. Instead, use your superior abilities to increase your chances of being successful.

Ten Ways to Make It Easy

I. *Work around the buyer's schedule.* Many sellers do not do this as well as they could. Instead of saying, "What's the best time for you to get together?" they say, "I'll be happy to meet with you at a mutually convenient time," or worse, "I've got Wednesday open

from 2 to 4 P.M." The underlying message is clear: *I'm busy, too.*
And you might be busy—but do you want to play games to see
if you have the buyer's respect, or do you want to win his or her
business? Instead, get used to saying things like:

- What would be a good time for you?
- What's convenient for you?
- Would you rather meet at your office or would you prefer
  somewhere nearby?
- What works best with your schedule?

2. *At the beginning of the meeting, explicitly state the purpose of the meeting.*
   Don't assume that the buyer remembers why you're there. He is
   busy, he is distracted, and he may not be as prepared as he
   would like to be.

3. *Make only one request.* Too often, sellers enter a meeting with a list
   of requests. "Will you read this material?" "Will you set a
   meeting with your supervisor?" "Will you buy this project?"
   When you ask for more than one thing, the buyer has to determine which of your requests is of highest priority—and that's
   a lot of work. If you only ask for one thing, the buyer only has
   to make one yes-or-no decision. Less is more.

4. *Have your materials ready.* Buyers hate to watch you shuffle through
   papers, grope for materials, or struggle with technology. They
   feel like you're wasting their time and it makes them wonder if
   you prepared for the meeting in the first place. If you're going
   to use materials for a presentation, make sure the process is
   smooth.

5. *Provide context without being patronizing.* Anything that is essential to
   understanding your project should be said in the room. For example, your pitch may lead off with a reference to something in
   pop culture, sports, business, literature, or history that you expect the buyer to know. He may not know. And he may not
   want to admit that he doesn't know. Therefore, have a brief
   statement ready to provide context. It should start like this:
   "You probably already know this, but . . ."

6. *Utilize summary statements.* Whether the buyer has just come back from taking an emergency phone call or has been distracted for another reason, a summary statement is a helpful way to keep the meeting on track.

7. *Be two steps ahead.* The buyer may not only say yes to your initial request, he may want to take another step. Plan for this contingency. Have materials ready so that you can continue to meet the buyer's needs in the event she wishes to go forward.

8. *Offer to handle the follow-up.* Whatever details need to be handled regarding the outcome of this meeting or in preparation for a subsequent meeting, volunteer to handle them. Each task is an opportunity to demonstrate that you are reliable and capable.

9. *Be willing to send the buyer a written synopsis.* Most people avoid taking notes because they're afraid that the buyer might ask them for a copy—not to mention the extra work involved in taking notes. However, this can be turned to your advantage. If the buyer asks to see your notes, say something like, "My handwritten notes may be confusing, but I'll be happy to type them up and have a summary sent to you soon." It's another chance to demonstrate your capability and can-do attitude.

10. *Arrive early and if possible leave early.* You know the benefits of arriving on time, so I won't belabor that. However, you may not have considered the benefits of getting out ahead of time. Certainly, you should allow the buyer to dictate when the meeting ends. However, it's smart to schedule forty-five minutes for a thirty-minute meeting. That way, when the meeting ends, the buyer feels like she's been given a gift. She may even have some time to act on your request.

The buyer should not have to do research. He should not have to keep track of every detail of your presentation or prioritize multiple requests. The buyer should have to do as little as possible—other than say yes.

CHAPTER 8

The Nature of Confidence

There's no doubt that having confidence is important. We all know that. But how do we develop the kind of rock-solid confidence that will sustain us through a high-stakes meeting?

Some people seem to have an innate confidence. They are charismatic and ebullient. They have an easy smile and a way with people. I won't deny that these naturally confident folks have an edge in the room. However, I'll tell you a secret—often it's the shy, introverted people who are the most capable sellers. Buyers see a lot of slick salespeople every day. A quiet confidence can be refreshing and often indicates that there is an idea of value being presented.

How to Increase Your Confidence

Many authors and experts seem to think that you can increase your confidence by using affirmative willpower. Their advice is essentially an exhortation. "Be confident!" they say. "Look at yourself in the mirror and tell yourself: 'I'm confident! I'm *so* confident! I'm confident because I'm great at what I do, and gosh darn it, people like me!'"

If this works for you, keep doing it, but it does very little for me. It always reminds me of that scene in romantic comedies where the guy is about to go on the big date. He hums while taking a shower, dresses in his best "player" clothes, looks in the mirror, points to himself, and says something like, "You da man. Yeah, baby, I'm talking to you! You da *man!*" Then what happens on the date? Crash and burn.

My experience is that true confidence is the result of only one thing: *creating patterns of success over time.* The question is, how can we define success in a way that allows us to build more success (and more confidence) more quickly?

Define Success in a Realistic Way

If you think you should be hearing yes and you're not, the problem may be your expectations. Creating a pattern of success is all about defining success in a useful way. This means having expectations that are appropriate for who you are today—not who you'd like to be in the future.

When your expectations are too high, you interpret small victories as failures. This inhibits your progress. Remember, confidence is built on a pattern of success. You can build this pattern by acknowledging and celebrating achievements of all shapes and sizes.

I believe that there are two types of success: process-based and results-based. Process-based successes are useful habits—for instance, arriving at the location fifteen minutes early so you can do a last-minute review and still be at the meeting exactly on time. Results-based successes are what we commonly think of as goals—as an example, making the sale. It's about "getting" something.

Victories of either type deserve a reward. Process-based rewards are particularly important because they reinforce behavior. In other words, if you do something and then you get a cookie (literally or figuratively), you're more likely to repeat the behavior. Over time, this increases your chances of having results-based successes.

For example, I believe that you should acknowledge and reward yourself:

- If you do your research about the buyer
- If you create and test your pitch
- If you arrive with time to spare
- If you submit a polished proposal on time
- If you adjust your presentation in the moment
- If you stay calm when the meeting is interrupted
- If you land that first meeting
- If you and the buyer build rapport easily
- If the buyer is so engaged that he asks tough questions
- If you get asked back for another meeting
- If your request is granted
- If you get a referral

You get the point. Create patterns of success by being honest and realistic about what constitutes a victory. The yes is not the only metric that matters. Keep track of all of your progress. Find different ways to give yourself "cookies" and reward yourself for every victory. Your confidence will grow as a result.

Faking It

Let me be clear. In general, I don't like to fake anything. *Anything.*

However, it takes time to increase your confidence, and along the way, there will be times when you feel pretty shaky. This is when it's appropriate to fake it as best you can. Buyers do not want to sit across from a perspiring ball of anxiety or hear you pitch in a quavering voice. So if you feel tense on the inside, there's nothing wrong with pretending to be confident on the outside. But what's the best way to do this?

Instead of exhorting yourself to be confident, I recommend making some specific tactical changes to your presentation style. In general, I believe in a less-is-more approach:

- Talk less.
- Speak in shorter sentences.
- Pause when the buyer is done speaking.
- Breathe deeply.

In other words, let the buyer fill the space and keep the spotlight on her. If you fill less of the space, you have more time to breathe. You use less energy and won't sweat as much. Plus, if the spotlight is shining on the buyer, while she is giving you valuable information you can take a moment to center yourself.

Confucius Says

Here's my ultimate tip on confidence. I got it from a fortune cookie. It said, "If you are willing to die, it is easier to live." Now, this is pretty basic, but there's wisdom in the place where philosophy and sugar come together.

To restate this in everyday terms, if you're detached from the outcome of the meeting, you're more likely to achieve that outcome. This can be hard to do when you want the meeting to go well. It's normal to fantasize about how life might be different if you hear "Yes." How would your career change? What would you do with the money? Whom would you thank in your Nobel/Oscar/Pulitzer acceptance speech?

There's nothing wrong with having desires and fantasies. And there are meetings which are incredibly important. However, I believe that the best way to succeed in any given meeting is to keep your professional life in context. Life is a lot bigger than the games we play to put money in the bank. I find it helps to take a deep breath and remind myself of that sometimes.

When I do, I give myself a cookie.

Part II

■

Titles, Teasers, and Trailers

One of my favorite things to do when I'm working with clients is to help them craft the language they will use to market themselves and their ideas. For whatever reason, I seem to have a knack for developing messages that hook, intrigue, and persuade. That's what this section is about.

Titles, teasers, and trailers are the strategic phrases and responses that you use when you are asked common questions such as:

- "What do you do?"
- "What's your project about?"
- "What do you propose?"

The answers you give to these questions are the packaging that sells your ideas. If the packaging isn't terrific, the buyer is not going to be interested in whatever you've got for sale. Formulating your pitch in the language that buyers want to hear is often the difference that makes the difference.

In the following chapters, we'll go more deeply into how to create great titles, teasers, and trailers. But first, some definitions.

Titles

Can you imagine seeing a movie called *3,000 Dollars*? Can you even identify the genre? Well, that was the original title of *Pretty Woman*. The sum was the fee charged by Julia Roberts' character for her "services." In terms of packaging the movie, that's a big difference, right?

The power of titles can be seen far beyond Hollywood. In the world of business, from the Fortune 500 to small business start-ups, a company's name is the centerpiece of all marketing and advertising efforts. Then there are the names of the company's products or services. These names, these *titles*, are crucially important because of how quickly they hook the buyer.

In the fast-paced world we live in, the quicker we can grasp the essential facts we need, the better. This is why titles and subtitles are important to anything written: books, movies, annual reports, PTA proposals, real-estate advertising, and even Internet dating profiles. You can't overestimate the value of a great title.

Teasers

Teasing is like flirting. In a romantic context, we tend to flirt before we make a serious move. This is an attempt to interest the other person without taking on too much risk. If you flirt with someone and that person flirts back, things can move forward. If you flirt and the other person doesn't respond, you can walk away with no harm done.

In the movie business, this process is known as "teasing." Teasers are short previews of the movie. They are usually ten or thirty seconds long and can be seen in the theater, on TV, and on the Internet. Teasers usually debut before the longer previews. Their primary goal is to intrigue the audience and get them talking. You know, to create buzz.

In the business world, teasers are small bites of communication with a similar goal: *to intrigue the buyer with minimal risk*. Teasers are often used when you are meeting someone for the first time, for example, in networking situations. If someone asks you, "What do you do?" it may not be to your advantage to give him a comprehensive answer. He may just be making conversation.

Instead, when someone asks, "What do you do?" you use a teaser. This is like giving him an invitation to take the conversation further. If he is interested, then as the conversation develops you will probably find a better opportunity to explain more about what you do for a living. I'll show you exactly how this is done in Chapter 11, "Teasers for All Occasions."

Trailers

In the movie industry, the term *trailer* refers to the two-and-a-half-minute advertisement for a coming attraction, commonly known as a "preview." It's called a trailer in Hollywood because, long ago, the ads used to follow the movie, not precede it. Of course, when it became clear that people tended to leave the theater after the movie, the studios began showing the trailers first.

Your trailer is a longer and more comprehensive (yet still efficient) version of your teaser. We'll go into this more in depth in Chapter 12, "Trailers That Work."

To persuade you to see a movie, in general, you need to be hooked by the title, intrigued by the teaser, and persuaded by the trailer. If you aren't interested in any one of these three marketing tools, you give the movie a thumbs-down before even seeing it.

When you walk into the room as a seller, the buyers you meet may feel the same way. If your titles, teasers, and trailers aren't dynamite, they start thinking about what else they can do with their time. In this section, I'll help you develop these three valuable marketing tools.

Before we can start, however, I need to bust a myth that may be getting in your way. That's the subject of the next chapter, "The Myth of the Elevator Pitch."

CHAPTER 9

The Myth of the Elevator Pitch

Networking gurus, marketing moguls, and career coaches extol the virtues of using a prepared elevator speech or pitch. This is a pitch that's brief enough to be used even in a short elevator ride. It is supposed to encapsulate your entire proposition and is designed to be used in any situation. The idea is that if you share your elevator pitch with everyone you meet, the doors of success will open.

Not true.

Prepare to Change Your Mind

Yes, I know that the elevator pitch is a *very* popular concept, promoted by some *very* successful experts. But here's the truth: The elevator pitch is deeply flawed. It's a catchy term but, on further examination, just plain wrong.

In my experience, while some people may use an elevator pitch effectively, most do not. When someone finds out that I work in the business, I frequently get pitched "elevator-style." I was pitched by the receptionist at my dentist's office while I was clutching my jaw in pain (loose filling). I was pitched on a five-minute ride to my hotel by a cab driver. I was pitched at an open house by a real-estate agent. A yoga teacher pitched me once right before class.

The problem is that the term "elevator pitch" is misleading. While it does capture the importance of clear, quick, effective communication, it also encourages us to make three classic mistakes:

- Pitching in the wrong places (e.g., elevators)
- Pitching to the wrong people (e.g., people in elevators)
- Pitching the wrong things (e.g., cookie-cutter concepts)

Never Pitch in an Elevator

You should never pitch an idea when you don't have time to continue the conversation. Why would you pitch someone in an elevator? Or while waiting in line for the bathroom? Would you roll down your window and pitch to the person in the car next to you when you are stopped at a red light?

A moment's access is not an opportunity.

Never Pitch to Someone You Don't Know

Your first interaction with another person sets the stage for the relationship to come. If you jump in too quickly and start pitching yourself or your idea, you are wasting your time.

Why would you pitch someone before you know who she is? When you first meet someone, you don't know enough about her or her needs.

Why would you pitch someone before she knows who you are? She doesn't know enough about you to care about what you're saying in the first place. It's a lose-lose situation.

Someone you don't know is not an opportunity.

Never Pitch Without Customizing

A lot of people are eager to deliver their elevator pitch as soon as they meet someone who might be a buyer or a source of referrals. They've done it so many times, it rolls off the tongue automatically. Unfortunately, when the buyer realizes that you're repeating to him what you've probably said to a dozen other people, he loses interest. He knows you're an amateur. You haven't built rapport with him. You haven't asked him any questions to determine his precise needs. Why should he listen to your cookie-cutter pitch?

Every buyer and every situation is different. Your pitch should reflect those differences.

Deliver a Pitch the Way You Would a First Kiss

When you meet someone whom you want to date, do you try to kiss that person right away? No. You have an initial phone conversation. You get together, have some coffee, and maybe go out to dinner. Then, if things are going well, a first kiss.

You have to feel that it's the right moment. If you want to have the possibility of a relationship, you can't just walk up and plant a big wet one on someone. Yet this is how most sellers pitch: "Hi, I'm Jack." *Smooch.* "Okay, this is my floor—call me!"

The first kiss is a big deal. Your pitch is, too. Much like a first kiss, your presentation needs to be delivered in the right place, at the right time, in the right way.

CHAPTER 10

The Title Creation Word Grid

Over time, you're going to meet buyers in a variety of circumstances. To make the best use of these opportunities, you need to have marketing tools that can be adapted to the specific situation. The first step is to create a dynamite title. In this chapter, I'll show you how.

Qualities of a Great Title

A great title should be SMART:

- S: *short* (the fewer words in the title the better)
- M: *memorable* (something that stands out or has an element of drama)
- A: *accurate* (correctly representing your proposition)
- R: *repeatable* (sounds good when spoken out loud)
- T: *tonally appropriate* (in accordance with the genre of the project)

You already know what short, memorable, accurate, and repeatable mean. But what does it mean for a title to have the right tone?

Tone refers to a feeling that's evoked, a subtle quality or flavor. For example, based only on a movie's title, you can usually tell whether it is a comedy or drama and whether it's for adults or for kids. In other words, the title creates expectations as to the "genre."

If a movie title doesn't hit the right tone, it can mislead the intended audience. For example, the reason the movie *Cinderella Man* starring Russell Crowe was a flop at the box office (though critically well-regarded) was because it was aimed at an adult male audience, and yet "Cinderella" is in the title. I think most sportswriters would describe James Braddock's boxing comeback as a classic Cinderella story. However, purely on the basis of the title alone, *Cinderella Man* could be a story about a guy who goes to a royal ball and leaves a slipper behind. The title was accurate, but it wasn't tonally appropriate.

The same principle applies when you create a title for any project. If the tone is off, you may turn off potential buyers for your project. When you want the intended audience to have the right expectations for what's to come, the subtext is just as important as the text.

SMART describes an extraordinarily high standard that not every title will meet. So, as you go through the process of creating a title, remember that a great title is a work in progress. You may start with only two or three of the ingredients; eventually, you hope to end up with all five. I believe that coming up with the right title is so important that I've developed the following method to help you get there.

Catching Lightning on Paper

Step 1: Brainstorm immediately

Brainstorm titles as soon as you start working on a new project. If your initial inspiration *is* the title, keep brainstorming. Capture all of your related and seemingly unrelated ideas—*all of them*—on paper or in a digital file. It's important. You see, from the moment you get the first lightning bolt of inspiration, that means there's a mental storm in progress. There're probably more useful ideas in there. Write down as much as you can to make sure you record all of the ideas flashing through that noggin of yours. Make the most out of your initial creative impulse.

Step 2: Create an accurate working title

A working title is the title you are using at the moment with the understanding that, eventually, you will come up with a better title. Often people will use the working title that sounds the best. I believe there is a better way.

In my opinion, the best way to use a working title is to be as accurate as possible. Focus on the A in SMART. This allows your conscious mind to focus on the precise nature of what your idea is and digest the essence. Eventually, your unconscious mind will have an easier time supplying a title that has the magic.

Step 3: Gather the storm

Take out a clean sheet of paper and turn it sideways ("landscape" style). Draw vertical lines to create columns for each of the words or concepts in your working title. Those words and concepts are the headers for the columns. Then, using a thesaurus, make a list of words and phrases that are synonyms and close cousins to the headers.

As you build your list, you will discover other concepts that should be headers. Start a new list on the same piece of paper and keep going.

Step 4: Allow your mind to wander

If you don't come up with a great title while building your list, don't give up. Incubation is an important part of the creative process. Let your unconscious mind incubate for as long as it takes (an afternoon, a week, even a month). Stay alert for notions and ideas. Add words and phrases to your list as they bubble up from the depths of your unconscious mind. Eventually, inspiration will come.

Step 5: Conduct research

Whether or not you have a title you really like, at a certain point in the process it's beneficial to solicit feedback from other people. I suggest getting feedback from:

- The smartest and most creative people you know
- Members of your target audience
- People who tend to disagree with you but give honest feedback

Step 6: Be ruthless

A decent title is good. A good title is great. A great title is the fountain of youth, a perfect credit rating, and school being cancelled on account of snow all rolled into one. Don't be afraid to throw out every title you've got so far, even some of your favorites, if they aren't SMART. It's the only way to create a truly great title.

Step 7: Amp up the accuracy

If you go through this process and your unconscious mind doesn't give you what you want, revisit your working title and then repeat the process. Can you make your working title any more accurate? Add a word or two? Cut a word or two? Even a small tweak can result in a massive creative boost.

Case Study: J.J.

As you'll probably recall, J.J.'s starting a company devoted to providing technical support focusing on Macintosh computers. After recording his ideas in Step 1: Brainstorm Immediately, J.J. goes to Step 2: Create an Accurate Working Title. He comes up with:

A Technical Support Service Devoted to Macintosh Computers

After asking himself if that was as accurate as it could be, he expanded the working title:

A Technical Support Service Devoted to Macintosh Computers and Their Users

To J.J., this seemingly small addition creates a world of difference. Why? Because he does more than simply fix computers. He helps his friends *use* their computers as well. This could be a way to distinguish himself from the other technical support companies—by providing not only information and support but also instruction to end users.

Continuing with Step 3: Gather the Storm, J.J. gets out a clean sheet of paper and makes columns for each of the words or concepts in his working title. His headers are: *Technical/Computer, Support/Service, Devoted, Macintosh,* and *User.*

Note: When you're brainstorming, one idea will lead to another and it's important to follow your creativity wherever it takes you. In this case, when J.J. wrote "first aid" it made him think of another header, "Doctor," which he then developed.

J.J.'s Step 3: Gathering the storm

Technical/ Computer	Support/ Service	Devoted	Macintosh	User
digital	help	provide	Apple	person
mainframe	ease	focus	iPod	typist
technology	maintain	care	Mac	client
mechanical	sustain	aid	Steve Jobs	customer
scientific	fortify	first aid	PC	student
analog	console		PowerBook	
Geek Squad	champion	**Doctor**		
home computer	benefit	clinic		
machine	assist	infirmary		

Technical/ Computer	Support/ Service	Devoted	Macintosh	User
	support desk	Doctor		
		health center		
		emergency room		
		urgent care		
		healing		
		TLC		

As J.J. worked, different titles popped into his head. After he had lunch and let his mind wander, he came up with a few more. Here's what he's got so far:

- Console Consolation Clinic
- The Computer Care Unit
- Mac Maintenance
- The Macintosh Healing Center
- J.J.'s Apple Support
- Mac TLC

Now J.J. can go through the rest of the steps. He can send an e-mail to his four-person feedback group, and he can continue to assess which of his titles is the SMARTest. Which of these titles is your favorite? Do any of them hit you on a gut level? Later in the book, we'll find out which title J.J. eventually chose.

I work with a lot of highly creative people and many of them use a method similar to this. Although some have the ability to occasionally pull a great idea from empty space like a rabbit from a hat, they don't rely only on that ability. They rely on a process such as the Title Creation Word Grid because it enhances the abilities they already have. Ultimately, top creative professionals are vigilant about practicing Step 6: Be Ruthless. They know that the difference between "No, thanks" and a six-figure sale can be just a few words.

CHAPTER 11

Teasers for All Occasions

What do you do when you meet someone new and you want to know if she is a potential buyer of your idea, product, or service? Many networking books and experts advise that you should "qualify" the other person within a few minutes and move on if she is not a good fit. As a result, sellers meeting someone new usually move quickly to find out:

- Is this person a potential client for me?
- Which of my products or services might interest them?
- Could this person also be a source of referrals?

The traditional method sellers use to determine if someone is a good fit is to ask for information. While getting information is important, asking directly can be perceived as too aggressive. The reason is that when you're asking for information, you're the one taking control of the conversation. But if you want a yes, it is better for the buyer to feel in control.

Therefore, don't use the traditional method and ask for information. Use one of the many teasers you're about to create and *get feedback from the buyer first.*

Gauge the Buyer's Interest

The teaser method is to say something SMART and assess the other person's response. Intrigue him with a comment, not a question, and then gauge his reaction. Is he interested in talking with you? Does he want to find out more?

Different Types of Teasers

There are many kinds of teasers. Your goal is to have a whole bunch so that, whatever the context, you've got a teaser that's right for that occasion. These are my favorite types of teasers:

- Startling statistics
- Purposely nonspecific phrases
- Long-term benefits

What I'd like to do now is go over a case study so you can see how these three types of teasers work. This will help you find your own teasers and show you how to use them.

Case Study: Fangxiao

Fangxiao, our financial advisor, has lost almost all of her clients because of new laws that restrict trading on behalf of non–U.S. citizens. Now she's attempting to rebuild her practice.

Previously, Fangxiao worked primarily with foreign nationals whose languages she spoke. Now that she can work only in the United States, she needs to appeal to new markets. After examining her client files, she realizes that her favorite clients have been women. She decides to focus her marketing efforts there.

In the course of her research, Fangxiao finds out that the women who seem to need the most help investing are (1) business owners, (2) professionals like herself, (3) parents trying to send kids to college, and (4) divorcées.

After more research and a great deal of thinking, Fangxiao prepares multiple versions of the three types of teasers so that she's ready to market herself in any conversation.

Startling Statistics

Statistics can be great if they come from a reliable source and are simple enough to be understood. A good stat makes you look like an expert and gets the buyer thinking, "I wonder what other valuable things she knows."

In the course of her research, Fangxiao comes across three intriguing statistics:

- Only 44 percent of new small businesses last four years or more. (Office of Advocacy at the U.S. Small Business Administration, 2005 Small Business FAQ)
- Forty-seven percent of all stocks are owned by women. (Peter Hart, NASD, and the Investment Institute, 2004)
- Women represent 60 percent of socially conscious buyers. (*Business Week*, 2000)

Here's how Fangxiao converted one of these statistics into a teaser in preparation for the question "What do you do?": "As you probably know, only 44 percent of small businesses last more than four years. I make sure my clients are in that 44 percent."

How does Fangxiao help her clients to do this? Is she a business consultant, a tax expert, a financial advisor, or a banker? At this point, the other person doesn't know. If she's intrigued, she'll ask. If not, then Fangxiao can still have a great conversation with her because Fangxiao hasn't taken control of the conversation to extract information. She hasn't risked any rapport in order to qualify the potential client.

Fangxiao also knows that even if her potential client doesn't respond to the teaser, she might be thinking about it. She can return to that topic later in the conversation or ask for Fangxiao's card when they wrap things up—but only if they still have rapport. This is why Fangxiao practices the teasing technique. It protects rapport.

Of course, this is a teaser that would work best with a female entrepreneur or possibly an executive. How might Fangxiao use the teaser technique to intrigue a mother who wants to send her kids to college?

Purposely Nonspecific Phrases

For Fangxiao to appeal to women who are not executives or in business themselves but who are taking care of a home and raising a family, she'll have to use a different teaser. Here are some of the nonspecific phrases Fangxiao has come up with that could be effective teasers in response to the question "What do you do?":

- "I'm a personal CFO."
- "I help parents find their quarterly number."
- "I'm like a financial midwife."

If a parent, entrepreneur, or other potential buyer then says, "What's a CFO?" or "What's a quarterly number?" then Fangxiao will answer directly. If the person doesn't ask, Fangxiao can let the conversation take a new course.

Long-Term Benefits

Another type of teaser involves presenting long-term benefits. Long-term benefits are attractive to the buyer, but they exist in the distant future. When you promise a buyer this type of benefit, it implies that you build long-term relationships and are worthy of trust.

Here are the long-term benefits Fangxiao sees of her financial advisory service:

- Retiring early
- Feeling safe in one's golden years
- Minimizing tax liability
- Sending kids to college

It's relatively simple to turn these into teasers that could be used to answer, "What do you do?":

- "I help people who want to retire early."
- "I help people plan for their golden years."
- "I help families reduce the amount they pay in taxes."
- "I help people send their kids to college."

When should Fangxiao use which long-term benefit? It depends on with whom she's talking. If she's hanging out with a dot-com entrepreneur, early retirement might be the right benefit to emphasize. If she's talking to parents of young children, sending them to college might be more appropriate. This is the benefit of using teasers—when you have enough of them, you can find a way to intrigue just about anyone.

How to Tease

- *Before teasing, test.* Try out your stats, purposely nonspecific phrases, and long-term benefits on friends and family. If they seem intrigued, impressed, or surprised, you may have a winner.
- *Be conversational.* A tease needs to be offered with warmth and in a casual way.
- *After teasing, stop talking.* The whole point of teasing someone is to let the buyer make the next move. If he is genuinely curious, you'll be able to tell. If he is mildly curious, you can adjust accordingly. If he changes the topic of conversation or if he doesn't seem interested at all, then no harm done. Let it go and just enjoy the conversation.

In the same way that coming on too strong can ruin your romantic chances, teasing with the wrong tone or with the wrong intentions can prevent the formation of a long-term business relationship. However, if you do it well, teasing is a way to get valuable information about how best to proceed.

Now the question is, *what happens if the buyer is intrigued?*

If the buyer is intrigued by your teaser and wants to know more, you might have a chance to deliver your trailer. While it's still a very brief form of communication, the trailer is the most comprehensive of your three main marketing tools. Creating a dynamite trailer is fun and can serve as the foundation for great teasers and titles as well.

CHAPTER 12

Trailers That Work

I magine that you're sitting in the movie theater. You're part of a captive audience. Before you get to see the movie you've paid for, you watch six trailers. Each of those trailers is usually two and a half minutes long and has been designed by an entire industry of writers, directors, editors, and designers who have worked for months.

Perhaps you enjoy watching trailers; perhaps not. Regardless, ask yourself this: How many of these trailers *work*? How often are you persuaded by the trailer to see the movie? How often do you see a trailer and think, "I need to see that"?

Probably not that often. Most of the time, the trailer occupies your attention but doesn't blow you away. Why is that? Think back on the movie trailers you've seen recently and see if any of the following answers ring true for you:

- They're boring.
- They're confusing.
- They're generic.
- They're not for you.
- They show you all the best parts (so you don't need to see the movie).

Then again, there are those trailers that grab you for two and a half minutes and leave you on the edge of your seat. That's the kind of trailer I want you to have. This way, when the buyer asks you a question that follows up on your teaser, or when you're in the room and the buyer asks you, "So, what's your project about?" or "What's your proposal?" you can deliver a trailer that captivates and persuades.

Overview

When a film editor looks through the raw movie footage, he or she is looking for "trailer moments." These are the scenes and lines of dialogue that stand out. Your process will be much the same. You are looking for catchy phrases, interesting ideas, compelling metaphors, and ways of talking about the benefits you provide that really capture just how great it would be to say yes to you. These are your "trailer moments," which you'll use to prepare a variety of trailers for different situations.

Construct the Five Lists

To find trailer moments, first you need to create a lot of raw material. When I work with clients, I recommend a process called the Five Lists. They are:

1. Potential buyers (separated into categories)
2. Client complaints (the "pain" the client is experiencing)
3. Features of your service or product (the details of what you do)
4. Benefits of those features (what the client gets)
5. Metaphors/comparisons (what you do in other terms)

Case Study: J.J.

J.J. has decided to name his business the Macintosh Healing Center. Using the metaphor of healing (as opposed to computer maintenance) carries a positive connotation and captures the kind of personalized service J.J. provides. It also differentiates him immediately from his competition.

After doing some research, J.J. decides to market himself to individuals and small businesses with fewer than five employees. This way, he can work more one-on-one. And, because people who use Macs are often in creative professions, he'll focus there first.

List 1: Potential Buyers

- Small business owners
- Writers
- Designers
- Artists
- Architects
- Musicians
- College students

You might think that J.J.'s doing pretty well. He has a good list of potential clients and he could move on to List 2: Client Complaints. However, he realizes the importance of making a really comprehensive list. Thus, over time, he adds to this list until it looks like this:

List 1: Potential Buyers (Improved)

- Small business owners
- Writers
- Designers
- Artists
- Architects
- Musicians
- College students

- People who have just bought a new computer
- People who have been given a computer as a gift
- People who have recently switched to Mac from PC
- Experienced computer users
- Computers used by people with different needs (e.g., a family)
- People who are learning new software
- Telecommuters
- Day traders
- Internet-based businesses

List 2: Client Complaints

- Not being able to print
- Computer freezes or crashes
- Scared of viruses
- Want to save money
- Difficulty translating files into different formats
- Trouble networking
- Problems learning software
- Work flow issues

At first, J.J. thinks, "Hey, I know what my clients are going to need." Then he realizes that making the Five Lists is a good way to ensure that he'll be able to handle more situations easily. Thus, he goes through his list of potential clients and brainstorms client complaints for each group. That way, he'll know which concerns are most likely shared by everyone and which are highly specific. This could be useful information when deciding which benefits to emphasize to a particular buyer.

List 2: Client Complaints (Improved)

- General
    - ~ Not being able to print
    - ~ Computer freezes or crashes

- ~ Scared of viruses
- ~ Want to save money
- ~ Difficulty translating files into different formats
- ~ Trouble networking
- ~ Work flow issues
- Small business owners
  - ~ Automating payroll, expenses
  - ~ Going paperless
  - ~ Networking several machines to the same printer
- Writers
  - ~ Conversions between specialty software packages
  - ~ Creating a reliable automatic backup system
- Designers
  - ~ Storing and managing very large files
  - ~ Learning shortcuts to complicated software
- Artists
  - ~ Keeping an organized desktop
  - ~ Managing a database of visual work
- Architects
  - ~ Printing highly detailed blueprints
  - ~ Using 3-D modeling software
- Musicians
  - ~ Networking peripherals
  - ~ Learning how to use audio editing software
- College students
  - ~ Buying a reliable used computer
  - ~ Accessing files from multiple computers around campus
- People who have just bought a new computer
  - ~ Installing software
  - ~ Learning new operating system
- People who have been given a computer as a gift
  - ~ Installing new memory chips
  - ~ Buying the right peripherals

- People who used to use PCs and have recently switched to Mac
  - ~ How to use the Mac control panels
  - ~ Translating PC files to Mac
  - ~ Operating a Windows environment inside a Mac OS shell
- Experienced computer users
  - ~ Networking machines that use different platforms
  - ~ Debugging code
  - ~ Adapting LINUX
- Computers used by people with different needs (e.g., a family)
  - ~ Setting up different user profiles
  - ~ Parental controls
  - ~ Hard-drive partitioning for game users
- People with a new job who are learning new software
  - ~ Learning new things is frustrating
  - ~ Time pressure and the expectation to learn quickly
  - ~ Lack of tech support at the office
  - ~ Previous files in great disarray
  - ~ Overwhelmed by e-mail
  - ~ Syncing with PDA
- Telecommuters
  - ~ Learning time management software
  - ~ Utilizing alerts and alarms to meet deadlines
- Traders
  - ~ Utilizing multiple screens
  - ~ Keeping connection speed as fast as possible
- Internet-based businesses (e.g., eBay-based sellers)
  - ~ Database management
  - ~ Work flow solutions to get from order form to address label

Use the Client's Words

If you can, add to List 2: Client Complaints the words of the client. For example:

- "I just can't get it to work."
- "I know there's a way to do it, I just don't know how."
- "I think it's broken, but I can't tell."
- "I hate to read directions."
- "This used to work just fine, but suddenly it's not."
- "I have no idea what's going on."
- "I'm just not good with machines."
- "The instructions don't make sense to me."

List 3: Features

J.J.'s features can be divided into two groups. The first includes the specific services he provides, and the second includes the attributes he brings to his work.

- Specific services
  - ~ Virus protection
  - ~ Networking different machines
  - ~ Software training
  - ~ Technical support
  - ~ Backup automation
  - ~ Purchasing hardware
  - ~ Repairing damaged machines
  - ~ Translating files
  - ~ Customizing the user interface
  - ~ Database management
- Personal attributes
  - ~ Will travel to your location

~ Easy to work with
~ Speaks in layperson's terms
~ Available until 10 P.M. on weeknights

List 4: Benefits

The most important part of this process is identifying what your clients really need and capturing your ability to meet that need in words they understand. These are the *benefits*.

Of all J.J.'s clients' complaints, the hottest complaint is computer freezes and crashes. This is the complaint most frequently shared and it's also the one that has caused the most suffering to his clients.

The features that address this issue are virus protection, file repair, and most especially, creating an automatic backup system. However, J.J. knows that clients understand the services he provides in terms of the benefits, not the features.

Thus, J.J. decides to focus on identifying all the possible benefits that a client could get from an automated backup system. Some of the benefits are:

* You won't lose your work.
* You can stop worrying about how often you save your work.
* You'll have more time to get things done.
* You'll extend the life of your main hard drive.

Then J.J. goes back through all of the features on his list and, for each feature, makes a list of possible benefits. His lists are getting pretty big. However, this kind of work is what pays dividends down the road.

List 5: Metaphors

The goal of this list is to find the metaphors, similes, and descriptive phrases that capture the essence of what you do. Take some time to be creative with this list. Keep track of every idea, even if you think you'll never use it. Here are some questions to get you started:

1. What are some shorthand ways of describing what you do?
2. Are there any famous books, films, or TV shows about people in your profession?
3. Are there any celebrities associated with your industry?
4. If you had to describe what you do to an eight-year-old, what would you say?
5. What is the opposite of what you do? What don't you do?

Once J.J. came up with the benefits that would be most attractive to any possible client, he went through the above questions and answered them in as many ways as he could. About 20 percent of what he came up with turned out to be useful. That's a pretty good success rate. Here's some of what J.J. developed:

- "I'm a computer doctor. I'm always on call. I'll diagnose your problem quickly and I'll prescribe the solution. I also do annual checkups to keep everything running smoothly and catch problems before they happen."
- "I'm like a general contractor for technology. I'll get the right products, handle their installation, make sure everything fits together, and ensure that they keep working for a long time."
- "I fix left-brain problems for right-brain people. I understand how artists and creative people interact with their computers; I help them work with their machines to do their work better."

Basic Trailer Structure

The next step is to look through your lists and highlight words and phrases that you like. Then, you're going to put the pieces together to form some potential trailers. You can start by using the following basic trailer structures:

- "I'm a _____ [professional designation]. I help _____ [client group] who want to _____ [benefit]."
- "I work with _____ [client group] who want to _____ [benefit] and _____ [benefit]."
- "I'm like a _____ [descriptive phrase]. I specialize in helping _____ [client group] to _____ [benefit]."

Putting It All Together

It's great to have a group of trailers to work with because you never know which trailer will be most appropriate to the situation you're in. This is also why making all of these long lists is so important. The more comprehensively you've prepared, the better you'll be able to improvise on the spot.

Here are some of the trailers J.J. can use to answer the question "What do you do?":

- "I do tech support and coaching exclusively for Mac users. Once I understand how someone uses her machine, I can help her configure the computer to make it easier to use."
- "I work with creative people to help them get the most out of their Macs. Mostly, I show artists the shortcuts they need and help them to optimize their software so they can forget about the computer and just focus on doing their work."
- "I own my own business, called the Macintosh Healing Center. I work with business owners to make sure that files are easy to find and never get lost or erased."
- "I'm like a chief technical officer for businesses that use Macs. I help them get the most out of their existing machines and incorporate new technology in a seamless way."

Notice how each of these trailers would be more suitable to different markets. The first trailer is applicable to any individual Mac user;

the second trailer is oriented to people in the creative professions; and the third and fourth trailers are devoted to connecting with the needs of small business owners. While the third trailer would appeal more to an entrepreneur or freelancer with only one computer, the fourth trailer is aimed at small business owners who have several employees who use Macs.

Try It Out Loud

You might notice that the trailers use really simple language. This is because, while a trailer can be written in an e-mail or letter, it is most often used verbally. You may love the way a phrase reads on the page, but it can sound awkward and stilted when you say it out loud. On the other hand, a phrase that doesn't seem particularly engaging to you on paper may just be the right combination of spoken words to intrigue a potential buyer.

Despite the hard work involved, the benefits of having great trailers for yourself or your ideas cannot be overestimated. This way, no matter whom you're talking to, you've always got a great answer to the question "So, what do you do?"

CHAPTER 13

The Four Questions

One of the techniques I teach my clients is how to answer the Four Questions. Your answers to these four questions can have a tremendous impact on your professional life. Why are these questions so important? It's because—drumroll, please—*you are very likely to be asked these questions:*

The Question	With a Good Answer, You Will:
1. *What's your name?*	Be remembered more easily.
2. *Where are you from?*	Launch into a great conversation.
3. *What do you do?*	Intrigue the other person.
4. *What's that like?*	Tailor your message to the person's specific needs.

You want to be prepared with a variety of strategic answers to these questions. This way, you can smoothly transition in and out of professional and personal topics, build rapport, and engage the buyer more effectively.

What's Your Name?

The fact is that our name is incredibly important in representing who we are. It's our most personal "title." Most of the time, the name we use is the one we were given. Thus, great care is exercised in choosing a baby's name—parents know it will last a long time. Some parents discuss the issue for months, some hire consultants to help, some pray for inspiration. Of course, some procrastinate and, when contractions start, go to the library for a baby name book on the way to the hospital. Hi, Mom!

I believe that the name you should use is the one that puts your best foot forward and makes it easy for the buyer to remember you. If you're blessed with a catchy name that's easy to remember and pronounce, good for you. If not, you have some options.

First, let me say that I know plenty of people who are purists about their names. Even if their name may be hard for a buyer to remember or pronounce, that's how they introduce themselves. If that's how you feel about it, that's fine. I would never advise you to utilize a name that makes you feel uncomfortable.

However, I'll also point out that most of us have several names. We have childhood names and nicknames. Friends may call us by one name and grandparents by another. Some women take their husband's name but keep their maiden name for business. So you may have a little more flexibility in this area than you might have thought initially.

Regardless of what name you were given when you were born, you can make use of all the following techniques to make sure that when you tell someone your name, you're remembered:

- *Use a nickname.* There is a rich tradition of this in Hollywood, as with Bernie Mac and Chevy Chase. Introducing yourself by your nickname can be a great way to break the ice socially, though it works best with nicknames that are not too outlandish or campy.

Your college friends may call you "Ace" or "Speedball," but that doesn't create a professional image (unless you're a drummer in a heavy metal band).

- *Use an abbreviation.* I know a doctor from Bombay whose name is Dr. Ravindranath. In India, that might be easy to remember since it's more common. It's not so easy for some of his patients in Los Angeles. When he first meets a patient, he says, "I'm Dr. Ravindranath, but you can call me Dr. R." Those who can remember his full name use it. Those who don't have an alternative that they can use without embarrassment.

- *Use a "sounds like."* If your name is unusual but rhymes with a more common word, you can use that word as a mnemonic device: "I'm Vandy. That's like *candy* with a *V*."

- *Use your middle name.* This is common practice in Hollywood. For example, Tom Cruise is actually Thomas Cruise Mapother IV.

- *Use a hook.* A hook is an interesting fact or detail that is memorable. For example, if I know someone's a golfer, I might introduce myself by saying, "Hi, I'm Stephanie Palmer, like Arnold Palmer but no relation."

- *If necessary, choose another name.* Granted, this is done more often in Hollywood (Carmen Electra, Elvis Costello, Larry King) than elsewhere. However, people take new names for all sorts of reasons. You may have grown up as Richard Wanker and you've had enough.

I'm not saying that you should Anglicize or artificially punch up your name. Just acknowledge that how you introduce yourself is important, and that if people have trouble with your name, you have options.

Where Are You From?

Often, a movie will begin with what is known as a "flavor scene." This scene gives us the sense of where the story takes place or where the hero comes from. We may experience a flavor of small town, big city, East Coast, West Coast, conservative, liberal, or another world. It can be fast, but a particular image or scene sets a tone and creates expectations.

Let's see how Liz, our salesperson and executive, applies this concept in networking situations.

Case Study: Liz

Liz is looking to get promoted to an executive position at Tall People Furniture. Part of her promotion will depend on her ability to bring in new business, and that means being able to connect with people quickly in any situation.

Liz was born in Tennessee, was raised in New York, and went to college in Boston. She moved to Los Angeles several years ago. When she is asked "Where are you from?" depending on the circumstance, she can truthfully say any of the following:

- "I was born in Tennessee."
- "I was raised in New York."
- "I've lived in a few different places, but for a long time I've called Los Angeles home."

Each of these places carries with it a different connotation and sets a different tone. Thus, Liz can choose to use one response or another depending on what she feels will help her connect to the other person. Here are some other ways she could improve her answer to the question "Where are you from?":

- *Add geographical context.* Were you born or raised in a major city or did you grow up near one? Near an unusual landmark? For example, Liz could say, "I was raised in New York, just down the street from the New York Public Library." Or she could say, "I was born in Memphis, just outside of Graceland."

- *Add cultural context.* Is your hometown or home state famous for anything? If Liz was talking to a football fan, she might say, "I'm from Tennessee, home of the Titans."
- *Add an interesting detail.* Liz might say, "I was raised in New York in a house my grandfather built from the ground up."

When you tell people where you are from, they often use that information to make certain conclusions about who you are and what they can expect from you. Therefore, be judicious about the information you give them and make sure that however you represent yourself, you're prepared to follow up on that thread of conversation.

"What Do You Do?" or "What's Your Project About?"

In the last chapter, we covered how to create teasers and trailers to answer "What do you do?" The trailer creation technique can also be used to answer the other versions of this question, such as "What's your project about?" or "What's your idea?"

As you know, the first step is to use a teaser to gauge the other person's interest. Once you know that he's intrigued, use the trailer that you think has the most potential for a business fit. Then, just like when teasing, stop talking and assess the response. Don't push forward into a more "business-y" conversation unless the other person is on board. Remember, you want to protect the rapport you have developed. You can cool off a conversation quickly if you're talking business and the other person isn't interested.

Case Study: Elliot

Elliot's our artist. While he freelances as a journalist for the elite geek magazine *Prime Numbers,* he spends his free time writing screenplays and has begun to think of himself as a screenwriter. But Elliot doesn't tell people that he's a screenwriter.

In Hollywood, if you meet someone socially and that person works in the business, it can be a real turnoff to mention at the beginning of the conversation that you are a screenwriter. The other person may start anticipating that you will ask her to read your script or introduce you to people. Rather than risk being solicited, she'll take the first opportunity to get away.

Now, I have great respect for writers. Writing is really, really hard and often goes unappreciated. It's especially hard to feel like a writer when you're not being paid for your work. This is why it's so important for writers to believe that, yes, they are writers.

Just don't tell other people until you've gotten to know them well.

Being a Seller Can Be a Turnoff for Buyers

What happens in Hollywood to aspiring screenwriters also happens to sellers in other industries. Many insurance agents or real-estate agents have the same problem—as soon as they tell someone what they do, the other person tends to think, "Ugh. I have to get away from this guy before he asks me whether I own my home."

Buyers are wary of meeting sellers in social situations.

Thus, when you meet someone, develop the relationship and build rapport. Don't talk business unless the other person takes the conversation in that direction. It's not a deal breaker if you're a seller—but it can be if you *lead* with that information.

To continue our case study, instead of telling people he's a screenwriter, Elliot chooses to focus on his day job, writing for *Prime Numbers*. Thus, he answers the question "What do you do?" in one of the following ways:

- "I'm an investigative journalist. I focus on the intersection of art and technology."
- "I write articles for *Prime Numbers* magazine for people who love technology."
- "I help people who love gadgets figure out what will work best for their style."
- "I help geeks find new gadgets."

If Elliot senses that he has an opportunity with someone in the movie business, he might say, "My day job is as a writer for *Prime Numbers* magazine, but I'm also developing a couple of films for people who love adventure." That's what I call a trailer with a teaser chaser. It gives the listener the option to ask about *Prime Numbers* or about his film work.

What's That Like?

If you've delivered your answer to the previous question and the other person is interested, you'll probably be asked a follow-up. This is the fourth question. Often this fourth question is "What's that like?" but sometimes you'll get "How long have you been doing that?" or "How does that work?" If you get this opportunity, that's a good sign. It means your answer to "What do you do?" intrigued the other person enough for her to pursue the topic.

The way to answer is simple: Emphasize the benefits most likely to interest the listener. You may have language from one of your other trailers. You may have a teaser that applies. Go for it. The answer to the fourth question can be whatever you want it to be.

There are other questions you can anticipate. If you walk into a party with a cast on your hand, you can reliably assume that someone will ask, "What happened?" Perhaps you slipped on the ice or fractured your ulna playing rock-paper-scissors. Regardless, with some thought you can create an answer that has rapport-building potential. My point is this: Anytime you can predict that you'll be asked a particular question, it is to your great advantage to take the time and spend the energy to develop a strong, effective answer.

Additional Resources

In this section, I've covered the techniques for creating communication that is effective in high-stakes meetings. However, for those of you who want to learn more about how language is used to persuade in other mediums, I recommend the following books:

- *Made to Stick,* by Chip Heath and Dan Heath
- *The Copywriter's Handbook,* by Robert W. Bly

Your answers to the four questions and your titles, teasers, and trailers are some of the most important tools in your marketing toolbox. Reading books like the ones above will broaden your perspective about how these tools can be used.

Once you have prepared these strategic pieces of communication, it's time to get out into the field and *use* them. That's what the next section is all about.

Part III

■

Getting in the Room

A crucial component of being good in a room is getting into the right rooms in the first place. In Hollywood, as in other industries, getting in the room with the right buyers for you and your ideas depends a great deal on whom you know—and who knows you. In other words, *networking.*

Here's my feeling about networking: Ugh. I dislike going to networking events. I find them boring, full of people who don't get it, often expensive, and rarely productive.

If only there was another way to meet people that was more effective and less painful. . . .

That's the subject of this section. I'm going to describe a way to meet people that is interesting, enjoyable, and, best of all, gets results. To start, let me explain the difference between my approach and traditional networking.

The Quantity-Based Approach

Traditional networking books recommend that you divide the people in your Rolodex into three groups, A, B, and C. Group A is for really useful people, Group B is made up of less useful people, and Group C is for people who aren't that useful.

Dividing people into groups with generic labels like A, B, and C is kind of depressing, I think. Does anyone wants to be on anyone else's C-list? Probably not.

These categories are the result of what I call the quantity-based approach of traditional networking. The idea is that if you meet enough people, if you accumulate enough names, you will eventually find quality people who are a good fit. On the surface, this seems to make sense. You need to maintain a large pipeline of new people because, statistically, only a few of them will be right for your business.

If you are focused on quantity, your goal is to attend networking events full of potential clients, meet as many of them as you can, quickly determine their usefulness, and then follow up with everyone after the event. As these relationships develop (or not), you sort them into A, B, and C categories.

It's basically a bulk-mail strategy. Send out a lot of letters and see what comes back. After all, even though most of us throw out our bulk mail, some people don't. Bulk mail works. Of course, bulk mail has the advantage of being expandable. You can print and mail as many letters as you'd like.

You and I, however, are not expandable. We cannot be duplicated, folded, stuffed, stamped, and shipped by a machine. The bulk mail approach doesn't work so well in establishing genuine relationships because *we only have so much time.*

I know networking experts who say that you and I should be networking all the time. Respectfully, I disagree. I don't want to go to networking events every night of the week and I'll bet you don't either. Most people I know have no interest in making networking a lifestyle.

We only have so much time. Therefore, instead of spending small amounts of time with lots of people, I suggest spending more time with fewer people who you choose more carefully. In other words, upgrade from bulk mail to a handwritten letter with a first-class stamp.

In the next chapters, I'll describe a new approach to networking that focuses on quality, not quantity. The first step is to avoid being caught by the number one sales trap. That's what is covered in the next chapter, "Stop Networking Now."

CHAPTER 14

Stop Networking Now

S eriously. Stop networking. Why? There are better ways to meet people.

If you use a traditional method of networking and it works really well, that's cool, though you should know you're in a very small minority. In fact, I think most people who use traditional networking techniques successfully do so *in spite of* those techniques, not because of them.

My goal with the next few chapters is to introduce you to a better way of developing new relationships. In order to do that, I need to explain why the traditional methods of doing this aren't so effective. Then we can talk about new ways of doing things that can increase your chances of success in the future.

Events to Avoid

A networking event is any event where people gather specifically to form business relationships. Often, networking events are marketed specifically to people who want to find new clients and grow their busi-

nesses. If your primary goal in going to an event is to network, here are
some types of events that promise a lot and deliver very little:

- Country club mixers
- Annual professional conferences
- Award dinners
- Chamber of Commerce events
- Anything with the word *networking* in the title, such as Power Net-
  working Breakfast

There are many specific circumstances where it is appropriate to attend these events, and I'll discuss them later in this chapter. However,
most of the time, if you go to one of these events intending to meet
clients, you will fall prey to the number one sales trap.

The Number One Sales Trap: Talking Business Too Soon

Of all the mistakes that sellers make, talking business too soon is the
most common, the most serious, and the easiest to fix.

Remember, business is personal. The best way to get a short-term
yes and create a long-term business relationship is by starting out with
and emphasizing personal connections. Networking events, however,
attract people with a "business first" mind-set. They are "business
first" environments. Thus, they are poor places to kick off a great relationship with a valuable client.

For example, it is common at a networking event for the host to remind participants how important it is to meet a lot of people. Following this advice will help you get a lot of business cards, but it is a lame
way to meet clients and generate long-term business.

If you meet someone in a business context (like at a traditional networking event), making a request at any point in the future seems cal-
culating. If you've met someone in a personal context, when it becomes

appropriate to ask for something down the road, the foundation that supports your request is the genuine rapport you've already created. Ultimately, this makes additional requests much more likely to succeed. Rapport also earns you the benefit of the doubt (in case you make a mistake) and greases the rails of any future negotiation.

A Classic Blunder

In my second year as an executive at MGM, I had already decided that I wanted to leave my job. It was a prestigious executive position, but I was miserable. I spent my time saying no to people and was embroiled in the social warfare of studio politics twelve hours a day. While I wasn't sure what I was going to do after I left, I knew that I cared about artists and creating quality work. There just wasn't enough of that side of the business in my work.

I took business classes and workshops. I read books on entrepreneurship, small business development, and marketing. Over and over, I was told of the benefits of networking. So I decided to leverage my current position and develop one quality relationship with a highly placed executive at each of the major production companies.

I was confident in my ability to do this. After all, I had high-stakes meetings all the time, and I was contacting only people with whom I was likely to be in business in the future. So I looked through *The Hollywood Creative Directory*, found the executives who were at my level or above, then called and invited them to lunch. Everyone accepted.

Amidst my previously scheduled meetings regarding current projects, I found the time to have two of these networking lunches per week. As there were forty or so executives, this effort took about five months to complete. When I was done, I felt so proud of myself. I put their contact information in Outlook and made a plan to follow up.

Over time, this effort resulted in . . . zero personal relationships. Zero friends. Zero business.

Busy people meet each other and develop lifelong personal and business relationships all the time. However, this rarely happens at networking events or in business-first environments. The meetings I had with the other high-level executives, despite being held under the best possible circumstances, were quite obviously business first. When I started making the phone calls to follow up, I had already lost them at "hello."

When to Go to Traditional Networking Events

You may be wondering, "Is it ever appropriate to attend a traditional networking event?"

Sure. A traditional networking event is worth it if you want to:

- Practice your rapport-building skills
- Research a particular market
- Refine your teasers and trailers
- Earn brownie points with a client by showing your support
- Be "seen" to raise your profile in the community
- Develop a relationship with the speaker or the organizer
- Learn more about the subject of the conference
- Enjoy the community of people who are in your industry

So there are a lot of reasons to go to traditional networking events. Just not for networking.

Still, what if you are at a traditional networking event and have the rare opportunity to meet a great potential client? Should you walk up and introduce yourself? Absolutely not.

To understand why, we need to talk about the only networking principle that means anything. Once you read the next chapter and understand this core principle, your networking skills will increase almost immediately.

CHAPTER 15

The Only Networking Principle
That Means Anything

The only networking principle that means anything is: *Control your introduction.*

The most crucial aspect of networking is how you and the other person connect for the first time. This is why (to answer the question from the previous chapter) you shouldn't walk up to a big potential client at a traditional networking event and introduce yourself. The person you'd like to meet is approached all the time. Even if your confidence is high and you feel great, even if you've done your research and have a great trailer ready to go, without a referral you're just another schmo trying to get business. That's not the way to kick off a valuable long-term relationship.

As you probably know, the best way to meet someone is through a referral. A referral, whether it's a letter of recommendation or a casual compliment about you at a party, communicates an incredible amount of valuable information to the buyer. You've already been vetted by someone the buyer knows and trusts. A referral says that you are established, are accessible, and can be held accountable for your work.

This makes the buyer much more likely to consider doing business with you. In fact, most successful people are so inundated with requests that they won't even consider anyone who doesn't come to them through the proper channels.

Here are the criteria buyers use in evaluating a referral:

1. How close they are to the referrer
2. Their opinion of the referrer's ability to assess your work
3. What the referrer specifically says about you

How to Ask for an Introduction

In general, people who are close to a high-level buyer are asked for referrals a lot. They tend to say no. Their job is to protect their friend the buyer—unless you can make it clear that you have something the referrer wants. This something is *the chance to do the buyer a favor.*

To the extent you can prove that you have something of real value to offer the buyer, this favor will be clear. Therefore, when you meet with someone who could refer you, you must know precisely what you are offering. You must have your teasers and trailers ready to go. You must make it easy for her. In short, you must prepare just as comprehensively as you would if you were meeting with the buyer.

What do you do if you can't get a referral? First, stop your traditional networking efforts. Then, take the time you would spend at the Springfield Chamber of Commerce Holiday Networking Lunch and use that time more effectively. You can learn how by reading the next chapter.

CHAPTER 16

The Best Networking Events

R ecently there was a public meeting held at my local city hall so that homeowners could discuss some of the zoning laws that pertained to home ownership. You know who showed up? Very few homeowners and tons of real-estate agents. The parking lot at city hall was practically a Mercedes-Benz showroom.

There's an understandable logic to this. Real-estate agents are thinking, "Where can I meet lots of people who may want to sell their home?" If they find an event populated by their target market, they go there to network. This is a traditional strategy.

In my opinion, what the agents should be thinking is, "How can I meet people who may want to sell their home *and who will trust me enough to want to work with me?*" Let's face it: If you're going to sell your home, which real-estate agent do you prefer—the one you met through a friend you trust, or the one you met at a zoning meeting?

Put Your Enthusiasm First

Traditional strategy evaluates a networking event based entirely on *who* is there. However, a great deal of the networking potential of an event depends on *why* you are going. If you go to an event primarily because you want to grow your business, everywhere you go will be a business-first environment—and that's a trap. However, if you go primarily because of genuine enthusiasm, then you're in the game.

If you put your enthusiasm first when deciding how to spend your time, the people you meet are more likely to share your enthusiasm. You will immediately have something in common. This makes rapport-building easier and long-term business relationships possible.

Do What You Like to Do

The best way to network is to do what you enjoy. Here are a few things that my friends and clients find interesting and which have led to valuable personal and business connections.

- Small dinner parties
    - ~ Double dates
    - ~ Potluck dinners
    - ~ TV events, such as the Oscars, the Super Bowl
- Activities for exercise
    - ~ Basketball league
    - ~ Salsa dance classes
    - ~ Running group
    - ~ Spinning
    - ~ Yoga classes
- "What the hells"
    - ~ International Rock-Paper-Scissors Tournament
    - ~ Skydiving
    - ~ Improv comedy class
    - ~ Cooking seminar
- Starting a club
    - ~ Book club

- ~ Movie club
- ~ Parents' group
- ~ Poker or bridge night
- ~ Knitting group
- ~ Wine tasting
- • Organizing an event
  - ~ Hiking or biking trip
  - ~ Afternoon barbeque
  - ~ Weekend retreat

I have a friend who is a successful insurance agent and loves classical music. All he does to market himself is the following: Once a month he hires a string quartet to play a concert in his house, followed by coffee and dessert. He invites his friends and tells them that they are welcome to bring another couple who would enjoy the concert. He never talks business at these events, and many of the same people come every month. From a traditional networking perspective, he's not doing very well. He doesn't see a lot of different people. He doesn't talk business. However, he has common ground with everyone there and it's easy to build rapport quickly with new people. After each event, he gets several new referrals.

If all you did was host small dinner parties, you would be a networking star. You can't do much better than breaking bread with friends and friends of friends.

The +1 Technique

The best networks are built one person at a time.

Developing the quality relationships that lead to long-term business takes effort over time. Your effort will go further if, when you meet someone interesting, you can focus on growing that relationship. Meeting someone who is a good fit is rare. Take the time to make it count.

For example, if you had the choice, what would you prefer: meeting ten people for six minutes each, four people for fifteen minutes each, two people for thirty minutes each, or one person and having the kind of conversation that's exciting enough to last a full hour?

Certainly, it would be great to have two half-hour conversations. But an hourlong conversation means you've got fantastic rapport. That's a person you probably want to spend time with and be in business with. You can bet the other person feels the same way about you.

CHAPTER 17

Discover More Good People to Know

Who are Good People to Know?

"Good People to Know" is the first of my networking categories. While Good People to Know (GPTK) is the biggest category, it's not a simple replacement for the C-list. The C-list, for most people, is the record of everyone they've ever met. It's where business cards go to die.

Conversely, if a person makes it onto your Good People to Know list, he is, as you might expect, a good person for you to know. In your GPTK, you would like to find:

- Clients and potential clients
- Current friends and new friends
- Talented, competent, and interesting people of any sort
- Anyone you genuinely like, no matter why you like them

Stay in Touch

If someone is a good person to know, it's worth maintaining contact with him. This is no small thing because, let's face it, you're busy. You can only make so many phone calls and send so many e-mails. Even if certain people only get a holiday card, that takes time. How many of those do you really want to write?

Don't get me wrong, I enjoy sending and receiving holiday cards. But in Hollywood, the holiday card phenomenon has become impersonal because people have holiday lists of thousands of people. This is how a lot of people do their holiday cards and, in general, manage their network. It's the quantity approach.

And what happens when you get a basic holiday card with a pre-printed name or just a signature (or an assistant's signature)? I doubt that you save it in your picture album or scrapbook. But you might keep a handwritten card that was chosen just for you.

Thus, when it comes to staying in touch, I recommend being selective. This ensures that your communications are more likely to build rapport and have impact.

Set the Bar High

Some people like to brag about the number of people in their network. However, in business as in other areas, it's not the size of your network, it's how you use it.

The first way to use it is to *protect it.* Keep your standards high when it comes to whom you consider a Good Person to Know. Be careful about with whom you spend time.

If you go to a conference, don't save every business card you receive and enter the data for each one. This is an exercise in collecting. It's being a relationship pack rat.

My advice is to value efficiency more than acquisition. If you've got no intention of getting in touch with someone you've met, when you get back home or to your hotel room, throw the business card away. That's not offensive, it's just common sense.

Keep the cards only from people with whom you intend to follow up. Then use the time you would have spent entering everyone else's information to write dynamite follow-up e-mails to develop your relationship with those few people. If someone is a Good Person to Know, she is worth the time and attention.

Three Kinds of Diversity

Many of us have people in our network who are very similar to us. Birds of a feather do tend to flock together. At the same time, homogeneity in a network is a serious weakness.

We all have areas of knowledge and skill sets in which we are weak and those in which we are strong. People who are like us tend to have similar aptitudes. They also tend to have similar interests, experiences, and opinions. If your network is full of people like you, you've got redundancies in your strong areas and gaps in your weak ones. Not good.

Diversity in your relationships means new ideas, fresh perspective, and partners who have complementary knowledge and skills. This is why you will probably need to discover Good People to Know. It takes a little more work to find and develop a relationship with someone who is very different from you. However, it's worth it. Here's what you're looking for:

- *Professional diversity.* This kind of diversity is commonly touted in traditional networking books, and is quite right. You would like to know a great doctor, lawyer, real-estate agent, broker, therapist, plumber, politician, contractor, computer support person . . . You get the idea.

- *Demographic diversity.* You've probably also figured out that it's valuable to know people who are demographically diverse. Do you know good people of different races, ages, and geographical backgrounds? How about people who live in entirely different countries?

- *Personality diversity.* This may be the most important kind of diversity. Make sure to include people in your network who have personalities different from yours. Do you know people who are extroverts, finishers, researchers, introverts, or out-of-the-box thinkers?

There are many personality types, of course. There are good resources online and in the bookstore if you want to know more. Regardless, the essence of personality diversity is to figure out who you are and look for complementary qualities in other people.

Finally, stay alert for the most valuable of all of the personality types: the *person who tends to disagree with you.* Assuming you have good rapport, it's a tremendous advantage to know someone who will comprehensively critique your plans and ideas. Being confronted with counterarguments forces you to clarify the merits of what you propose. If you can convince the person who disagrees with you, you're probably on the right track. If you can't, at least you've got a good grasp of both sides of the argument and you've minimized your blind spots. A warm relationship with someone who genuinely disagrees with you is incredibly valuable.

The people who may be more valuable to you than Good People to Know are your Very Important People—your VIPs. In the next chapter, we'll talk about how to cultivate these important relationships.

Cultivate Your VIPs

"VIPs" is the second of my new networking categories. These are the people who are most likely to be powerful allies for you in growing your business. Is this category a lot like the traditional networking A-list? Yes. Your VIPs are those few people who can really make an enormous difference and who deserve special attention.

However, there's an important difference between the VIP list and the A-list: most people want their A-list to contain as many "stars" as possible. I'm not referring to Hollywood celebrities. I mean the successful, respected, and high-profile people in your industry.

A star is anyone who is well-known and influential in his or her field. It might seem logical that you'd want these powerful people in your network. However, I don't think that stars are good candidates for your list of Very Important People.

Don't Be a Starf*cker

In Hollywood, some people love to get close to stars. They hang up the phone on their loyal friends when a celebrity friend calls. Whenever possible, they try to "upgrade" their social circle so that they spend more and more time with the "right" people. Starf*ckers seek to achieve status and success by virtue of their association with successful, high-status people, and will kiss a lot of butt to make it happen.

However, pursuing the people who are commonly known to be stars is rarely a good strategy. Stars are naturally suspicious of those they do not know extremely well. Even if you are referred to them—and they tend to meet people only through referrals—they will assume that you want something from them because, in all likelihood, you do. The reason that starf*cking does not work is that no matter how nice a star is to you, he probably does not trust you and therefore will not put himself out on your behalf. A star can be a VIP for you only if you got in on the ground floor.

By comparison, the people who belong in your VIP category have two characteristics:

- They are mentors, clients, or potential clients.
- They like, respect, and *trust* you.

Don't waste your valuable time making friends with stars. Cultivate the people who can make the most impact on your business—and that means being selective in a different way.

Choose Wisely

VIPs are busy. Their time is precious. You're not going to get much time with them, so cultivating a relationship with a VIP requires extensive preparation to make the most of the time you get. Because you have only so much time for writing e-mails, talking on the phone, and having meetings, you can have only so many VIPs. I recommend a maximum of twenty VIPs on anyone's list.

Find the "Hidden Producers"

If you look at the producers' credits of a big movie, you'll see some names you recognize and some you don't. The big-name producers are the "stars" and everyone in Hollywood competes for their attention—for instance, Brian Grazer, Paula Wagner, and Jerry Bruckheimer.

These producers are inundated with requests. Everyone wants them to read their material, produce their project, or hire their cousin's son as a production assistant. Layers of assistants protect them. They are virtually impossible to reach and are unlikely to make good VIPs for you unless you knew them before they made it big.

The "hidden producers" stand in the shadows of the marquee producers but are often intimately connected with the production. These are the associate producers, co-producers, and other varieties of producer who are usually on their way to becoming a marquee producer. More often than not, few people are seeking their attention.

If you cultivate a relationship with hidden producers in your industry, you are much more likely to be able to add value to their lives. They are more likely to appreciate your attention, they will have more time and energy available to build a relationship, and the chance that you will actually be able to do something substantive for them is much higher. This is the kind of person who belongs on your VIP list.

How to Cultivate a VIP Relationship

VIPs require extra TLC in the same way that patrons of five-star res-
taurants expect exceptional service. Once you have been successfully
introduced to a VIP, or if you are reinvigorating a neglected relationship, then the real work begins.

To facilitate VIP relationships, I recommend:

- Read everything that they have written.
- Read everything that has been written about them.
- Read everything that they recommend you should read.
- Check their Web site regularly.
- Sign up for their newsletter.
- Stay in touch regularly by phone and e-mail.
- If you meet with them over a meal, always pick up the tab.
- Don't ask for anything until you've built a really solid con-
  nection.

This last point is really important. In the initial stages of your relationship, never ask a VIP for a favor. Don't make any requests. Don't
ask for a referral. Eventually, the person will see the value you bring to
the table and she will make the first move toward talking business. If
she doesn't, then she's still a good person to know, but she's not a VIP
for you.

If you do give a VIP a gift, make it personal. Give her something
that could come only from you. It may reflect something the two of
you have discussed, or it may be a private joke. It must be something
that requires some thought and has a personal feel.

For example, one of my VIPs travels a lot working for Habitat for
Humanity. He's a down-to-earth guy but has a thing for gourmet coffee. Everywhere he travels he takes a bag of his favorite coffee and a
glass French press. He never complained about it, but I suspected that

it was a pain because he would have to pack it carefully and, if it breaks, he's screwed. So I got him a plastic one that's virtually inde-structible.

That might sound easy, but it took several months for me to get to know him and figure out just what would be the perfect gift. As with any relationship, cultivating a VIP takes time. Be patient.

CHAPTER 19

Nurture Your Inner Circle

T he "Inner Circle" is the third (and last) of my new networking categories. There is really no category from traditional networking that's similar. I define your Inner Circle as the family members and close friends who love you for who you are. These people can be some of the most powerful professional allies you will ever have.

Strengthen Your Foundation

I was watching poker on TV recently and the announcer asked one of the famous players what the most important ingredient is to being a great poker player. His reply? He said that you've got to have a strong family life. You've got to know that you can take risks at work, potentially fail, and still come home to love and support. Without that, you might telegraph your feelings at the poker table and crack under pressure.

If the people you keep closest to you do not fundamentally see, respect, appreciate, and love you for who you are, you may find yourself unconsciously seeking personal attention in professional situations. This may cloud your judgment and affect your behavior.

Who Should Be in Your Inner Circle?

The standards I'm about to describe are pretty high. Feel free to change them in any way you like. Still, you may find that someone very close to you is not in your Inner Circle for one reason or another. That's okay. You can still respect and love them. But let's be honest with ourselves. The people you want in your Inner Circle are those who will back you up all the way.

- *They know and like the real you.* We all have relationships with people where we have to pretend—even just a little—that we like them more than we do, or that we enjoy spending time with them when at times we don't. These relationships can be valuable. But no matter how important they are to your business, if you can't be 100 percent yourself with them, they are not in your Inner Circle.
- *The feeling is mutual.* In order for someone to be in your Inner Circle, you've got to be in that person's Inner Circle as well.
- *You are not in competition with each other.* Your Inner Circle should be composed of people who have nothing to gain from your failure or from watching you struggle, but instead are fans who applaud your success.
- *You enjoy them personally.* You look forward to being with them. So much so, in fact, that when they call you actually pick up the phone.
- *You trust them to keep your confidences.* Anyone who can't keep a secret should not be in your Inner Circle.
- *They can be depended on in an emergency.* People in your Inner Circle are there for you no matter what, especially in a crisis.

How to Build Your Inner Circle

- *Take care of the people who are in your Inner Circle.* Never take them for granted.
- *Gently nudge other people out to make space.* You can't welcome new members of your Inner Circle if it's filled with people who don't really belong there. Remember, you've only got so much time. Nurture the people who really nurture you in return.
- *Show up in the world as your authentic self.* When you present a façade to the world, your true self does not come through. You may have lots of friends, but these people do not know you because you don't let them see who you really are.

With a strong Inner Circle, when you finally get a great opportunity, you will not be seeking attention. You will be able to focus all of your energy on the task at hand—selling yourself and your ideas.

Part IV

■

Inside the Room

Remember the "hot and cold" game you played as a kid, where you'd come into the room and there was some object you had to find, and when you got closer people would say, "Getting warmer . . ." and when you got farther away, they'd say, "Getting colder . . ."?

Whether you're meeting the buyer in her office, at a restaurant, or on the ski slopes, being "inside the room" is a lot like that game. Only this time, you know what you're looking for—a yes—and you don't have your second-grade classmates helping you out. You've got to take the (figurative) temperature of the room yourself.

This is the first law of being in the room: *Always be aware of the temperature.*

The temperature of the room depends on many things: the mood of the people already present, the atmosphere/condition of the actual space, and the first impression you make when you walk in the door. From then on, you need to maintain constant awareness of what warms the room (and what cools it off) to be able to adjust your tactics during each of the five stages of the meeting.

What? You didn't know that every successful meeting goes through five stages?

Don't worry, most people don't. But you'll be one of the few people who understands basic meeting structure after you read the next chapter, "The Five Stages of a Meeting."

CHAPTER 20

The Five Stages of a Meeting

When I had several pitch meetings a day, I began to see that every meeting followed certain predictable patterns. I became curious. I got interested. Then I got obsessed.

I became a meeting anthropologist. I observed the habits of the indigenous people before, during, and after the meeting. I immersed myself in their culture to try to understand their behavior. I had matzo ball soup at Nate and Al's. I shopped at Fred Segal. I attached radio transmitters to alpha males and females so I could follow them through the dense Hollywood jungle.

All right, I didn't do that. But after three thousand meetings, I identified the following five stages, which were present in every successful meeting:

1. Deal breakers
2. Rapport
3. Information gathering
4. The pitch
5. Closing

While there are some exceptions, these stages occur in this order pretty much every time. Therefore, if possible, you want to follow this pattern in every meeting. Also, for each of the five stages, there's a goal as well as a trap (or multiple traps). Avoid the traps, achieve the goal, and you get to move on to the next stage.

Deal Breakers (Chapter 22)

Trap: Not getting it
Goal: To avoid the immediate no

This first stage starts when you walk through the door and usually ends soon thereafter. It's about your first impression and initial choices in the room. Deal breakers show the buyer that you don't get it. It can be as obvious as wearing inappropriate clothes or as subtle as taking the wrong chair.

Have you ever felt like you were told no before you really got started? Have you ever felt like you didn't even get a chance? If so, there is a strong likelihood that one of your ingrained habits or an aspect of your first impression is breaking the deal.

Rapport (Chapter 23)

Trap: Talking business too soon
Goal: To connect in a personal way

Once the buyer has decided that you're not an automatic no, then you can get to know each other. This is the small-talk phase, which, if you're prepared, may turn into a deeper conversation about your common perspectives and interests.

This stage is also where most sellers blow it. They want to get right down to business and so they skip the most important part of the meeting. Remember, your personal connection with the buyer is the chief determinant of whether or not you will succeed. Thus, you want to warm up the room and build rapport before moving forward.

Information Gathering (Chapters 24 and 25)

Trap: Pitching before you have sufficient and accurate information
Goal: To ask great questions and to listen with 100 percent outward focus

In the third stage, you're making sure that you and the buyer are on the same page. A lot of things can happen between the time the buyer agrees to have the meeting and the actual meeting. Even if you've got a really good idea of what the buyer wants, you need to test your assumptions and assess the reality of the current situation.

The way to do this is by asking thoughtful questions and listening intensely. That way, when you get to the pitch, you'll be able to customize it with any new information you've learned.

The Pitch (Chapters 26 and 27)

Traps: Various—boring the buyer, presenting poorly, missing the target
Goal: To make a natural presentation that hooks the buyer and maintains his interest

This is where you actually deliver your presentation. There are two parts: the actual pitch and the Q&A. In the pitch, you use the combination of teasers and trailers that you believe will best capture the attention of the buyer. Then, if the buyer is genuinely interested, you are likely to be asked a number of difficult questions. Extended Q&A is a good sign—it indicates that the buyer is seriously considering your proposal.

Closing (Chapters 28 and 29)

Traps: Various—being too aggressive, impatient, or unpolished
Goal: To get a commitment, exit smoothly, and leave a great last impression

Once the buyer is out of questions, it will probably be clear if she is interested in going forward. At this time, you are in the final stage and it's time to close out the meeting. Ask for what you want and transition out of the room on a good note.

Moving from Stage to Stage (Chapters 30 and 31)

There are no hard-and-fast rules about how to navigate through these five stages. Sometimes you'll jump from one stage to another and then back again. You may spend more time in one stage than you expect. However, here are some general guidelines to help you figure out when to transition.

- Try not to move forward until you have fulfilled the goal of the stage you are in. This means that if you're in a casual meeting, you may want to spend as much time as possible building rapport in Stage 2 because you've only just met.
- Sometimes a meeting will end before you've been through all five stages. That's okay. If you've taken up most of the time getting to know each other, don't rush to pitch. Instead, shift gears and schedule another meeting to continue the conversation.
- When you believe that you're ready to move on from one stage to the next, give the buyer the opportunity to lead the transition. For example, if you've gathered enough information in Stage 3 and you're ready to move on to Stage 4, don't just roll into the pitch. If possible, let the buyer prompt you.

Of course, if you walk into the room and the buyer wants you to get right to the pitch, you can't say, "Hang on, I've got two more stages to get through." It's not ideal, but satisfying the buyer's needs is paramount. If she wants the pitch, you'd better get to it. However, because you understand the five stages of the meeting and the importance of establishing a warm personal connection, you'll be looking for every opportunity to segue back into rapport building and information gathering.

A lot of your ability to navigate the five stages depends on the way in which you prepare for the meeting in the first place. That's the subject of the next chapter.

CHAPTER 21

Before You Go into the Room

How many times have you packed your bags for a vacation, gotten on the plane, arrived at your destination, unpacked, and found that you had forgotten something important?

We've all done it. On a vacation, it's an inconvenience. In a business situation, it's a potential disaster. The best solution I have found is to get my list of everything I need out of my head and onto a piece of paper. Here's my official Good in a Room Pre-Meeting Checklist:

The Pre-Meeting Checklist

Two Days Before

- ❑ Research rapport-building topics
- ❑ Create specific information-gathering questions
- ❑ Prepare buyer portrait

Buyer portrait. When preparing for a meeting, you will collect a lot of research on the buyers you intend to meet. You should know as much as possible about them, including their past projects, anything they've published, the position they occupy in the company, and more. Instead of trusting your memory, I recommend preparing a brief summary for yourself of the relevant details. If and when you meet with these buyers again, their "portrait" can be adjusted without you having to redo your research.

One Day Before
- ❏ Confirm the meeting
- ❏ Gather materials, visual aids, presentation notes, technology
- ❏ Print out a map
- ❏ Update PDA with buyer's contact information
- ❏ Charge PDA and cell phone

The Night Before
- ❏ Lay out clothes
- ❏ Check Internet for new developments regarding buyer
- ❏ Choose waiting room material

Waiting room material. The material you bring to the waiting room is not just to help you wait. It is to provide a potential conversation starter, make the right impression, and, most importantly, put you into the right frame of mind for the performance to come.

The Day Of
Make sure you have the following:
- ❏ Cell phone
- ❏ Pens
- ❏ Notebook
- ❏ Computer, power cord, Internet cable
- ❏ PDA
- ❏ Eye drops
- ❏ Breath mints
- ❏ Digital audio recorder
- ❏ Visual aids
- ❏ Business cards
- ❏ Makeup/grooming kit for the car
- ❏ Meeting review sheet

Meeting review sheet. The buyer portrait, questions to connect with the buyer and build rapport, and information-gathering questions can all be written down on one piece of paper or entered into your PDA. This gives you something to review while you're waiting. It's also a great way to keep track of the meetings you're having, especially if you've got more than one meeting scheduled per day.

What to Wear

I suggest working within the following general guidelines. Wear something that:

- You have worn before
- Makes you look good
- Doesn't show sweat
- Is comfortable enough to be worn all day
- Matches the buyer's level of formality
- Is in line with your positioning

If you forget to use the checklist or simply don't have time, don't panic. You'll probably be fine. However, in any high-stakes situation where you may be competing with other sellers, the little things matter. The Pre-Meeting Checklist is a way to make sure that when you walk through the door, your game is as tight as possible.

It's also a good way to prevent the costly mistakes known as deal breakers.

CHAPTER 22

Avoid Deal Breakers

M any sellers break the deal within a couple of minutes of walking into the room. They do or say something that shows that they don't get it, and right at that moment, the switch in the buyer's mind flips to no.

However, even though most deals are broken early on, it's possible to break the deal during any of the five stages. That's what's in this chapter—all of the mistakes I've seen over the years.

Although you may already avoid most of these, you may find one or two to be a wake-up call. So be honest with yourself. Is it possible that you sabotage yourself and break the deal in any of the following ways?

Tactical No-No's

- *Sitting in the wrong seat.* Obviously, if you're in the buyer's office, you wouldn't sit behind the desk. But frequently, meetings are held in conference rooms or other places where the buyer's chair isn't immediately apparent. Thus, always let the buyer sit down first. Ask them, "Where would like me to sit?"

- *Not including everyone in the room.* When I was having a meeting with a seller and one of the male junior execs was present, the seller would often address his pitch to him. The seller might glance at me from time to time. Eventually he would ask the junior exec, "Well, what do you think?" My colleague would turn to me and say, "Well, Stephanie, what do you think?" Even if you know who the senior person is, don't just pitch to him or her. If other people are in the room with you, assume there's a reason for them to be there.

- *Assuming they know who you are.* The buyer may have forgotten why she ever made the appointment with you in the first place. Have a casual summary ready that includes your name, your company, and the purpose of the meeting.

- *Addressing the buyer too informally.* Some people try to create instant friendships by calling the buyer by a first name or even a nickname. This is a risk not worth taking. Instead of forcing intimacy, err on the side of formality. Let the buyer suggest moving to a first-name basis.

- *Starting before the buyer is ready.* Let the buyer finish phone calls, get papers arranged, and otherwise get herself together before you start your presentation. Use your waiting room materials if necessary.

Emotional Violations

- *Anxiety.* For many buyers, if you seem anxious, that's an immediate deal breaker. After all, if you lack confidence, they can't introduce you to their colleagues or their boss and say, "I vouch for this person." So if you walk into the room and you're sweating, that's strike one. If you shake the buyer's hand and your hand is wet and clammy with nervousness, that's strike two. If your throat is so dry that your voice cracks when you start to talk, you're out.

- *Obsequiousness.* A little flattery goes a long way. Any more than a little flattery, however, goes a very short way. If you are too complimentary, if you are too overawed, if your nose gets too brown, you are showing weakness. To the buyer, it seems like you're afraid that what you're selling really isn't good enough.
- *Spinelessness.* If you agree to unreasonable requests from the buyer, you are out of the running. You don't win points for being a pushover. For example, if you agree to wait a few minutes, let someone else into the meeting, or cut five pages from your proposal, you're a professional. If you agree to reschedule five times, give your presentation to an intern instead of the buyer, or simply accept all of their notes without question, game over.
- *Frustration.* Getting upset over small details during the meeting is an amateur move. If you get asked a tough question and you groan or make excuses, you're not the right person for the job. If you can't handle yourself professionally in the room, how can the buyer expect you to handle even higher-pressure situations?
- *Impatience.* Don't drum your fingers or check the time repeatedly. In the room, you're on the buyer's schedule. Don't give the impression you'd rather be somewhere else.

Pitching Transgressions

- *Using jargon that is not known to the buyer.* You want the buyer to understand every word you say. If you use a word, phrase, or acronym with which he is not familiar, he may not want to ask you what it means. Now you're pitching a buyer who may be confused and feeling stupid. You're out.
- *Phoning it in.* How do you know if you're phoning it in? If you haven't customized your trailer, you are. Buyers can tell if your pitch is something you've presented the same way countless times before. Little tweaks make a big difference.

- *Talking too fast.* Some people naturally talk fast. However, it's not smart to talk faster than the buyer can process the information. Plus, talking fast often means that you're nervous—and you know how buyers feel about anxiety.

Classic Mistakes

- *Starting with an apology.* Don't say something like "I'm not very good at selling," "I'm pretty inexperienced," or anything else that reflects negatively on you. Buyers only want to do business with players, not wannabes.
- *Making a big deal about where you went to college.* If you and the buyer went to the same school, that may be a rapport-building topic. Otherwise, you can mention the school you attended once, casually. Over-emphasizing your educational pedigree makes you look like a tool.
- *Talking business too soon.* If you haven't established good rapport, the buyer is probably not listening to your proposition—he's still gauging what he thinks of you.
- *Mentioning money too early.* Often buyers want to know what something will cost. However, until they are convinced that you are trustworthy and that your products or services are exactly what they need, any discussion of cost can break the deal. You want to postpone it until you have met these criteria. If you are pressed to make an estimate (and you may be), acknowledge the buyer's interest and segue back into information gathering. "I understand that you want to know how much this will cost. I need to find out some more information first because I want my estimate to be accurate. Can you tell me more about _____?"

Major Blunders

- *Sexism.* Female executives should be looked in the eye, if you get my drift.

- *Desperation.* Just like when you're on a date, overt signs of desperation are a turnoff. I once met with a writer who came in to pitch, and though he handled himself well, I just wasn't interested in his ideas. Unfortunately, he thought this was his big chance and he wouldn't leave my office until he pitched me something I liked. Eventually I was holding my office door open, looking at my watch, and tapping my foot, while this writer just kept pitching and pitching: "Wait, I've got a comedy about the Khmer Rouge from Pol Pot's point of view. . . ." Game over.

- *Too much information.* Some people feel comfortable talking with people they've just met about medical conditions, financial situations, or romantic escapades. I met with one writer who blurted out in midpitch, "I haven't had sex in twelve years." Yikes! In general, if you wouldn't want to see it on the front page of the local paper, don't share it in the room.

- *Profound anxiety.* One time I heard a pitch from a guy who was sweating so profusely, when he stood up my couch had a writer-shaped sweat stain. I felt bad for him, but if I have to reupholster my couch after the meeting, that's a no.

- *Weirdness.* One of the most memorable pitches I ever heard was from a brother-sister writing team. They handled themselves well in the room for the first few minutes as we got to know each other, but when they started pitching their romantic comedy, I got more and more uncomfortable. At one point, they looked lovingly into each other's eyes and leaned in for a tender, heartfelt almost-kiss that signified the end of the first act. I ended the meeting before they pitched the climax of the story.

Of course, I'm not really worried that you are going to sweat through a couch or kiss your sister. I am concerned that you may be committing some of the more subtle deal breakers without knowing it. After all, it's not as though buyers will be taking you aside after the meeting to give you criticism and feedback like, "Hey, just so you know, you talk too fast." However, if you can avoid the deal breakers I've described, you will almost certainly be able to advance to the next stage of the meeting.

CHAPTER 23

Dumb Is the New Smart

Congratulations. You've passed the first-impression deal breakers and now you and the buyer (or the group of people to whom you're presenting) are settling in to get to know each other in Stage 2, rapport building. To build rapport, you know that it's important to be likeable, stay in sync, and keep the spotlight on the buyer. You've done your research and prepared some questions that are likely to lead to common ground. If you've gotten this far, you're pretty smart.

But don't be too smart. If you attempt to demonstrate that you're more intelligent than the buyer, there's a good chance you will not get through this stage successfully. It may seem counterintuitive, but superior knowledge and ability can be your worst enemy when your goal is to build rapport. Then again, if you use your brain correctly, it can be your best friend.

Here's an example to show you what I mean. The Brothers Grimm are the nineteenth-century German professors who first collected and published *Grimm's Fairy Tales*, including "Hansel and Gretel," "Rumpelstiltskin," "Rapunzel," "The Golden Goose," and "Snow White."

When Ehren Kruger (the writer of *Arlington Road* and *The Ring*) wrote a script titled *The Brothers Grimm*, a fantasy adventure about how the brothers might have battled powerful evil forces described in their stories, I believed it could be a great movie. The script was just fantastic. Unfortunately, there were some serious production issues, and the completed film didn't live up to the potential of the script.

The point of the story is that when we were putting the project together, in pitch after pitch, I discovered that many of the agents and producers crucial to getting the stars and financing the project did not know who the Brothers Grimm were. They'd never heard of *Grimm's Fairy Tales.* I'd say, "So, you've probably heard of the Brothers Grimm . . ." and they'd say, "Um . . . sure."

That's no way to start pitching an idea. We adapted by preparing a casual summary about who the brothers were: "As you probably know, the Brothers Grimm are the nineteenth-century German professors who first collected and published 'Hansel and Gretel,' 'Rumpelstiltskin,' 'Rapunzel,' 'The Golden Goose,' and 'Snow White.'" When we told the buyers in this way, we didn't make them feel stupid for not knowing. It was a small adjustment, but it made all the difference in building support for the project.

Success Versus Intelligence

Whether you've got some information the buyer doesn't have or whether you're simply a superior intellect, be careful of the success/intelligence trap. This trap catches people who like to be seen as smart. They like it so much that they prefer to demonstrate their knowledge rather than actually be successful.

Flexing your intellect has two negative consequences. First, you may be perceived as emotionally needy. Taking the spotlight with your ideas is a way of trying to win the appreciation and respect of the other person. Second, depending on what you say, you may make the buyer feel awkward if she can't follow you. That's threatening and can break the deal entirely.

However, let's suppose you've cured yourself of the need to show how smart you are in the meeting. You can restrain yourself from flexing your mind in front of the buyer. If you're smart, you may still have a listening problem.

Why Smart People Are Bad Listeners

We all think at a rate far faster than we can talk. Some research puts the average speed of talking at 100–200 words per minute and thinking at 250–750 words per minute. The smarter you are, the more likely it is that you're mentally multitasking while the other person is talking.

Now, you might be thinking, "I'm fully capable of listening while thinking about something else. I can also pat my head and rub my stomach at the same time. It's not so hard."

What you may not realize is that the buyer knows she doesn't have 100 percent of your attention. She may not say anything; she may not even be conscious that she knows. However, at some level, she knows. That's not good.

Most of what takes place in a conversation is nonverbal. We are communicating through our posture, gesticulations, vocal intonation, and eye movements. These nonverbal communications take mere microseconds and are out of our conscious control—they can't be turned off. This means that if we are mentally multitasking underneath, at some level this is apparent to other people.

Others see when your eyes wander for a split second (indicating that you're thinking about something else). They can tell when you lean back just a little (indicating boredom). They know when you don't react to their punch line (indicating a lack of interest). Ultimately, even if they don't say anything about it, they just don't like you as much as they could (indicating an increased likelihood that you'll hear a no).

If your mind tends to wander, you have to work harder to be interested, keep your concentration, and maintain 100 percent outward focus. If you can, you will build rapport better, gather information more effectively, and perform to your fullest potential in the room.

Let the Buyer Be Slightly Higher-Status

Even if you think you are smarter and more capable, more charming and entertaining, when you are building rapport you need to let the buyer be the alpha—just not by too much. If you're too far "beneath" the buyer, you're not worth his time. But if you're perceived to be "above" him at all, you may be seen as a threat.

This isn't about being fake or pretending to be someone you're not. I'm suggesting that you allow the buyer to take up slightly more space, have more of the spotlight, and otherwise be the center of your attention.

Five Ways to Get Smart

1. Don't show off. Instead, help the buyer to show off.
2. Instead of saying, "I know . . . ," ask the buyer, "What do you think?"
3. If you're trading jokes, let the buyer have the last laugh—even if you've got a topper.
4. Don't assume that the buyer knows anything. Always provide context.
5. Learn to concentrate *all* of your attention on the buyer.

If you're blessed enough to be smart and talented, use your intellect and devote yourself to building rapport. Become a fantastic listener. If you listen to buyers with all of your attention, they will enjoy being with you and you'll get through Stage 2 with flying colors.

CHAPTER 24

100 Percent Outward Focus

istening is a crucial component of building rapport in Stage 2 and the main way that you gather information in Stage 3. Gather more and better information than your competition and you will have the edge. It's just that simple.

You Are About to Make Ten Million Dollars

Imagine that your closest friend comes to see you at two o'clock in the morning. His face is flushed and he's breathing quickly. "I've only got five minutes—my ride's waiting for me outside," he says.

You've never seen your friend like this before. You know something's up, but what? He continues, "You may not believe this, but it's entirely true. You're the only person I can tell." He looks around to make sure the two of you are alone.

"I just saw a map to buried treasure. It's legit and I don't have time to explain how I know that. What I can tell you is this: If you follow the clues I'm about to describe, there is a good chance you will find $10 million in unmarked, untraceable $20 bills."

He describes the map and the clues. Midway through his frenzied description, you realize that you should be writing this down, or better yet, tape-recording. Unfortunately, looking for your digital audio recorder would take up valuable time that you don't have. If you miss one detail, all may be lost. You focus your brain at full power so you don't miss a single detail.

Your friend finishes describing the map, embraces you quickly, and leaves. You sit there a moment, stunned. Then you rush after him and shout, "Hey—why aren't you going after the treasure?" But he's already gone . . .

Here's the point: When you listen to someone describe a treasure map, you are listening with your whole body. You want the verbal content, nonverbal content, and every last scrap of information. You're listening with 100 percent outward focus.

This is how you want to be listening in a meeting. Because, after all, you are a treasure hunter in search of the precious yes. To find it, you're going to need to absorb and make the most of every clue the buyer gives you.

How Most People Listen

Most of us are used to listening with about 50 percent outward focus. With the other 50 percent of our attention, we're thinking about how we look, organizing our to-do lists in our head for the coming day, planning our next witty response, or checking out other people in the room. Dividing our attention like this can result in many different kinds of mistakes.

- *Making excuses.* "I'm bad with names." "I'm a little ADD." "I didn't hear what you said." "I have a terrible memory."
- *Pretending to be interested.* We smile and nod. We murmur vague encouragements such as "Mm-hmm," "Oh, yes," "Absolutely," or

"Fascinating." Guess what? The buyer knows our mind is elsewhere.

- *Changing the subject unnecessarily.* We don't want to be caught not listening, so when we realize we don't know how to continue the conversation, we change the subject: "So . . . have any vacation plans this year?"

Listening takes practice and consistent effort over time to get good. The reason most of us listen at half power is because our listening muscles are out of shape. They need to be stretched and exercised. The first step in improving our listening muscles is to focus our attention on the most valuable elements in any conversation. Specifically, you want to be listening for clues to the treasure.

What You Are Listening For

Clues come in two varieties: nonverbal and verbal. Let's start with the nonverbal.

I think of nonverbal communication as being like conversational traffic signals. Specifically, the buyer's body language tells you whether you should be slowing down or moving ahead, and the way the buyer emphasizes his communication dictates where you're supposed to turn.

Body Language

Entire books have been written about body language, but here's a primer. There are four basic signals, each of which is giving you the green, yellow, or possibly red light. If you can spot these signals and react to them correctly, it will be easier to stay in sync with the other person.

- *"Tell me more."* This is often manifested with an open body posture, wider eyes, nodding, and leaning forward. Go—you've got the green light.
- *"That concerns me."* This is reflected by closed body posture, wrinkling the brow, narrowing the eyes, pursing the lips, and sighing or groaning. Slow down—you're getting the yellow light.
- *"Let's move on."* If you notice the buyer looking away, checking her watch, or otherwise diverting her attention from you, that's the red light. In all likelihood, it's because the spotlight is on you and not on her. Stop what you're doing and shift tactics. A good technique is to ask a question and turn the spotlight back on the buyer.
- *"I'm about to speak."* Most of us are used to being interrupted, so when we feel the other person take in a breath or get ready to say something, we plow ahead faster and more vigorously. Instead, if you hear the buyer take a breath, yield. Pause, make eye contact, and say, "Please, go ahead."

Emphasis

Many buyers are not sure about what they want. However, they will emphasize certain words and ideas. On your treasure map, these clues are like road signs that tell you where to turn. Following the emphasis will lead you to the topics that are worth focusing on.

Here are ways that people emphasize certain ideas:

- They say them with an emotional inflection.
- They repeat them.
- They mention them first.
- They speak more loudly when expressing them.
- They highlight them with a gesture.

For example, if you are in a conversation with a buyer and the buyer says, "A, **B**, C, and D," other things being equal, you want to pick up on topic B and take the conversation in that direction. If A, C, or D is important, you'll circle back to it naturally at a later point.

Three Pieces of Magic

When it comes to verbal communication, ideally you would remember every single word the buyer says. But unless you have a photographic memory (or your glasses are CIA-issue), you're going to have to make choices. You can only remember so much.

"Three Pieces of Magic" is a term I've developed to help my clients listen for the words and phrases that most accurately represent what the buyer wants. Specifically, you are listening for the following three magical pieces of communication:

1. A simple goal statement
2. A simple positioning statement
3. Hot words

Case Study: J.J.

Our tech support guru, J.J., is having a meeting with an architect who uses a Mac. After passing through Stages 1 and 2, J.J. asks her a series of information-gathering questions. In response, she lists a wide variety of issues that they've had in the company and how challenging it has been to find a reliable tech-support person. She uses lots of adjectives to describe her vision of what she wants and specifies a number of different issues he could address.

At the same time that the client is describing her needs, J.J. is having his own vision about what he might do for her and what that might look like. J.J. knows that he will not get the job and be able to do it well unless his vision matches her vision accurately.

If you remember your high school geometry, the number 3 is very important. In studying sequences, three numbers make a pattern. Three points also determine a plane. Similarly, a vision is defined by Three Pieces of Magic:

1. *A simple goal statement.* While the buyer can list a number of different goals, it is essential to understand the highest priority among these goals and, if possible, to be able to capture it in one sentence.

   In J.J.'s conversation with the client, she listed all sorts of objectives, including having a computer that doesn't crash, ensuring a secure network, standardizing the versions of software that the architects and support staff use, making all the outgoing e-mails look consistent, and improving the security of client records. J.J. asked two additional questions: "What is the ultimate goal of this project for you?" and "Of all of the goals you have listed, which one is most important to you?" Her answer: She wanted to stop worrying about losing her work if the system crashed.

2. *A simple positioning statement.* One of the goals you have as a seller is to get the buyer to tell you her position in the marketplace. In this case, the client sees herself as providing innovative design solutions by working exceptionally closely with her clients. This may not be so unique, but it is the client's position. Thus, if possible, it would be great to tweak her technology in ways that make relating to clients easier.

3. *Hot words.* Hot words are adjectives and phrases that the buyer uses to describe what they want. For example, J.J.'s potential client said that she wanted to have a reliable backup system, programs that worked efficiently, and security for all of their files. She said a lot of other things, too. What J.J. did was choose the few words that he felt most accurately described what she wanted: *reliable, efficient,* and *secure.*

Once J.J. felt he had a clear understanding of what his client wanted, he used the Three Pieces of Magic technique. After she had finished describing her needs, J.J. presented a quick summary to her to demonstrate that he understood what she wanted.

He said, "Let me make sure that we're on the same page. When you work with clients to create innovative design solutions, you collect a lot of information about them, some of which is personal. You want to have a reliable computer network that makes sure you can find the files you need efficiently and also keeps those files secure, so even if there's a lightning storm, you don't lose anything. Is that right?"

Do you think she hired J.J.? Well, sure she did. How could she not want to work with a guy who asked such great questions and demonstrated that he knew how to listen?

CHAPTER 25

How to Ask Great Questions

G reat questions allow you to build rapport faster and gather information far more effectively. They also begin to demonstrate the value of your product, service, or idea before you get to the pitch. Questions are the seller's most frequently used tools. Without great questions, a seller is like a carpenter without a hammer, saw, or screwdriver.

The question is, what is a great question? In my experience, the only way to tell is by the answers you're getting. If the buyer is opening up and really sharing her concerns with you, then you're asking great questions. If you're not getting helpful responses, it's time to adjust.

My belief is that every sales situation is different. I don't think you should limit yourself to one system of asking questions or another. Do what the most successful sellers do—mix and match techniques from every system to create your own approach.

Thus, in this chapter I've put together fifteen principles of asking questions to give you the same opportunity. Think of it like a conceptual buffet. You can decide which techniques will work best for you in your unique situation.

Are you ready to get started?

Principle 1: Use an Indirect Approach

You may have heard the old fable about a quarrel that the sun had with the wind about who was more powerful. They saw a man wearing a jacket walking from town to town, and the sun and wind bet on who could get him to remove his jacket. The wind blew and blew, making the air colder and colder, and the man pulled his jacket around himself more tightly. Then the sun shone brightly upon the man and made him warm . . . so he took off his jacket.

If your style of asking questions is too direct, you're like the wind— your questions may cause the buyer to tighten up. Therefore, don't try to *get* information. Create a climate of warmth and personal connection that allows the buyer to *give* you information. In other words, use your listening skills, build rapport, and develop the relationship. With good rapport, your few, well-chosen questions are more likely to elicit the information you want.

Principle 2: Keep It Simple

The best questions are short and uncomplicated. Complex questions imply (I) that you don't know your material well enough to be able to express yourself in clear language and (2) that you may be grandstanding in order to show off how smart you are.

When it comes to questions, less is more.

Principle 3: Maintain Neutrality

The tone of your voice should be conversational and the content of your questions unbiased. If you ask with bias, it's as if you're telling the buyer that you already know what he thinks, or worse, that you know what he ought to think.

Of course, if you've prepared sufficiently, you may have a pretty good idea of what's going on in the buyer's mind. However, your assumptions are not factual knowledge. Ask your questions with genuine curiosity. You might be surprised.

Principle 4: Favor Open Questions

Most of us need to learn to ask more open questions. These are the questions that we learned in grade school: who, what, when, where, and how. Open questions are useful when you want information:

- "What would be an ideal outcome?"
- "Who's involved?"
- "What are the main issues?"
- "How would you like to proceed?"
- "What's your near-term strategy?"
- "How do you envision this process working?"

Open questions *open* the conversation. In general, it's important to favor questions of this type because they encourage the buyer to give you information.

Principle 5: Make the Correct Diagnosis

Sometimes buyers aren't exactly clear on their own priorities. I think we've all felt this way at one time or another—sometimes *everything* feels like the top priority. However, you aren't likely to get the yes unless your pitch solves the buyer's highest-priority need.

To help you figure out what that is, try using some questions that help the buyer to figure out his priorities:

- "If you could, what's one thing you would change about _____?"
- "What's something that has surprised you about _____?"
- "What's your biggest obstacle to getting _____ done?"
- "What has to happen first in order for you to _____?"

Principle 6: Access Thoughts, Feelings, and Experiences

You can use open questions to invite the buyer to reveal thoughts, feelings, and personal history.

- "What are your thoughts on _____?"
- "How do you feel about _____?"
- "What's been your experience with _____?"

Questions about thoughts, feelings, and experiences have a way of taking the conversation in a more personal direction and can be used to build rapport with a buyer as well as gather information. However, no matter how interested you are, resist the temptation to ask the buyer *why* he thinks or feels a certain way.

Principle 7: Don't Ask Why

"Why" tends to be seen as oppositional and puts the buyer on the defensive. Instead, try:

- "What's your thinking on _____?"
- "How did you come up with the idea to _____?"

If you need to ask a question that begins with "Why," pay very close attention to your tone. Then see how the buyer responds. If she gets defensive at all, make sure to warm the room back up before your next substantive question.

Principle 8: Summarize, Then Use a Closed Question to Confirm

Closed questions begin with a verb, such as *do, are, would, could, should, can, is,* or *will.* These questions usually elicit a yes-or-no answer and are often used to confirm something important.

For example, suppose a buyer (in response to one of your open questions) tells you about his goals for the coming year. He says, "We need A, B, and especially C before the end of the year." You might want to make sure that *C* is the buyer's top objective, so you would summarize and confirm like this: "So, in this first phase you need C before the end of the year. *Is this your number one priority?*"

When you hear a crucial detail, make sure you and the buyer are on the same page by using a closed question.

Principle 9: Get Specific

You want the buyer to give you details so that you can share the vision the buyer has in his or her head. Plus, if you're interested in the details, it shows that you understand that getting the details right is important. Try asking questions like these:

- "Can you give me an example of _____?"
- "What would _____ look like?"
- "How do you envision _____ working?"

Principle 10: Consider Implications

Buyers are often aware of their immediate problems but haven't fully considered the longer-term consequences. These consequences are the "implications." As the seller, you have spoken to many different buyers; you've seen certain patterns recur. Thus, you may be more familiar with the implications of certain issues.

In his book *SPIN Selling*, Neil Rackham says that implication questions tend to work best with decision makers. He speculates that this may be because "a decision-maker is a person whose success depends on seeing beyond the immediate problem to the underlying effects and consequences."

Once you know the buyer's desired outcomes and the issues that she's facing, you can use the basic formula for an implication question: *What effect does _____ [the problem or issue] have on _____ [some aspect of the buyer's desired outcome]?*

- "How does hiring and training new employees affect your existing staff?"
- "What happens on the line when your technicians find a substandard component?"
- "When you change the delivery method, what happens to customer satisfaction?"

Warning: Implication questions focus the buyer's attention on what's wrong. If the room isn't warm enough, an implication question can make the buyer feel threatened. This is why these questions are risky. Even if you build the value of what you are selling in the buyer's mind, if it damages rapport it's not worth it.

Principle 11: Be Patient

You may not get the right answer the first time. Sometimes it's because the buyer doesn't understand his own needs very well. It can be frustrating, but remember—if you help a buyer to clarify what he wants and why, that makes you valuable. Try questions like these:

- "I'm not sure I understand. Could you explain it another way?"
- "Could you talk a little more about the aspect of _____?"
- "Just so I'm clear, could you tell me about _____ in another way?"

Principle 12: Emphasize the Positive

To gather information and build rapport at the same time, ask the buyer something that maintains a positive slant to the conversation. A little flattery goes a long way. You can, for example, reference the buyer's success, vast experience, or recent victories:

- "What are you doing that's really working?"
- "If you were in _____ [another high-profile person]'s position, how would you handle _____?"
- "What do you think are the key ingredients to your recent success?"
- "What is it about _____ that's interesting to you?"
- "What was your favorite part of _____?"
- "What was the highlight of _____?"

Principle 13: Be on the Same Team

Buyers tend to like people who are team players. If appropriate, you can give your questions a more inclusive feel:

- "How might *we* approach _____?"
- "Can *you help me* understand _____?"
- "What would you think if *we* focused on _____?"

Principle 14: Assess the Value of Solutions

A value assessment question is really the inverse of an implication question. The implication question makes the buyer think, "What will happen if I say no?" The value assessment question gets the buyer thinking, "What will I get if I say yes?"

The general formula for a value assessment question is: *"What effects would _____ [possible benefit] have on _____ [buyer's needs]?"*

- "How would _____ be helpful to you?"
- "When you finish _____, what happens next?"
- "If you had the ability to _____, how would your business adapt?"
- "When you can _____, who else in the company will benefit?"

Value assessment questions are important for two reasons. First, you've got the buyer imagining a positive outcome to saying yes to you. Second, and more important, you can ascertain to what extent your solution will benefit the buyer. This information is crucial in shaping your pitch in the next stage of the meeting.

Principle 15: Avoid the World's Most Dangerous Question

The world's most dangerous question is, "Am I right?" Versions include:

- "Could the reason be _____?"
- "Are you aware that _____?"
- "Isn't it true that _____?"

Often, these questions are sly ways of introducing your own ideas to the buyer long before it's appropriate. It's a way of trying to get the buyer to say, "Wow! You're brilliant!"

When you do this, you're no longer focused on gathering information about what the buyer wants. Now you're gathering information about whether or not the buyer likes your ideas. It's a dangerous course of action that can break the deal.

You see, when you introduce a new idea to the buyer in this way, you're probably in a lose-lose situation. If your idea is bad (or the buyer doesn't like it), your value decreases. If your idea is good and the buyer acknowledges this, now the conversational dynamic is reversed— now *you're* the one giving the *buyer* information. This is a dangerous place to be.

It is desirable to know more than the buyer. It is not desirable to showcase that knowledge. To prove your worth, avoid asking questions like "Am I right?" Instead, use questions that help you understand the buyer's needs. This keeps the focus on the buyer and sets you up to succeed in Stage 4 of the meeting: the pitch.

CHAPTER 26

Show, Don't Tell

You've gotten into the room, made it past the deal breakers, built rapport, and gathered information. Now it's time, finally, to get in there and actually pitch. It's Stage 4 of the meeting, and there's really only one thing you need to know.

The first secret to making a compelling pitch is . . . *show, don't tell*.

"Show, don't tell" is one of the most common comments movie executives give to screenwriters. It means that the writer is using too much exposition instead of conveying the information through action. While most writers find it easier to explain what's happening in a scene, explanations aren't visual. They aren't as engaging or satisfying to the audience.

The problem is that telling is so easy and showing is so hard. This is why our soap operas, other TV shows, and movies are often filled with expositional lines of dialogue: "I have to go, I've only got ten minutes to stop the terrorists before they detonate a nuclear bomb downtown—but I want you to know that I love you even though you were planning to kill me before you knew I was a double agent."

Consider what happens when you see a truly great scene that shows and doesn't tell. A classic example is a scene Frank Capra improvised when a writer gave him twenty pages of dialogue depicting a marriage on the rocks. Capra said, "Here's what we'll do. We show the husband and the wife in an elevator. The husband has his hat on. Elevator stops. A pretty girl gets into the elevator. The husband takes his hat off for the pretty girl."

In this chapter, I'm going to share a number of techniques you can use to help you "show, don't tell" more effectively. Additionally, you'll see how the four characters (J.J., Elliot, Liz, and Fangxiao) use each of these techniques to improve the way they pitch.

Telling Without Showing: Common Mistakes

Here are some of the ways people tend to blow it right off the bat when they get to Stage 4:

- *Giving your own opinion of your work.* If you say "I've got a really great idea for you," the buyer's thinking, "Who thinks your idea is great? You? Amazing. You love your own idea. I'm floored."
- *Telling the buyer what her opinion should be.* "You're going to love this." Now the buyer's thinking, "Really? I'm glad you can read my mind. That's lucky for me because I'm unable to form my own opinions. Would you mind telling me what I'd like to order for lunch?"
- *Using jargon that's accurate but which the buyer doesn't understand.* "I recommend a central VAX server running LINUX with twenty X-terminals." This gets the buyer thinking, "Well, that might be the right solution, but if I can't understand it, how am I going to explain to my colleagues how I spent the money?"
- *Using a weak opening move.* "This is a story, based on my life, that covers loss, sadness, anger, and isolation." Okay, great. But what's

the idea? Whom is it for? What's the hook? If you can't start your pitch with a great first sentence, the buyer isn't listening to the second sentence.

Put the Relevant Details Up Front

It's crucial that the buyer sees a vision of what she gets if she says yes. This vision needs to appear in the buyer's mind as soon as possible.

This is why the guy selling the magic knives spends most of his time demonstrating their chopping power. He doesn't need to tell very much when he takes a paring knife and makes spaghetti out of a leather shoe. But what if you don't have a tangible product? What if you're selling an idea or a service? How can you demonstrate that what you have works?

Here's how: start with the relevant aspects of your idea or service that *immediately* build a vision of what you are selling in the buyer's imagination.

Case Study: Elliot

In anticipation of getting a studio meeting, Elliot is preparing how to pitch his screenplay. But he's struggling with how to start.

What details define his project? For many beginning writers who are pitching a screenplay, what defines their work is why *they* started writing the story—it's about what *they* find interesting. Here's how Elliot starts out pitching his movie, *The Last All-Nighter:*

"First of all, I think anyone who ever went to summer camp will love this movie because they'll remember how much growing up happens over the summer. This movie is set at a camp in Wisconsin that was formerly the territory of the Hopi Indian tribe. The Hopis weren't one of the bloodthirsty Indian tribes like the Apache and they had an evolved vision quest ritual where boys of a certain age would go off on an adventure prescribed by their elders and return with a vision or a trophy. Based on that, the elders would give the boy a new name.[1] Of course, in modern days, there really is no equivalent for kids. This is why I found it so fascinating[2] that kids from the suburbs end up going to these Indian-themed summer camps."

What's this movie really about? It's hard to tell. For the buyer to have a clue, he'll need to know more relevant details upfront. For a story, those details (at a minimum) are genre, protagonist, antagonist, and nature of the central conflict.

Let's look at how Elliot puts these relevant details up front in his revised pitch:

"*The Last All-Nighter*[3] is a thriller[4] about two teen rivals[5] who join forces to solve a murder. It's the last week of August, and during the annual Camp Appaloosa treasure hunt, Joe (the brainy athlete) and Aaron (the rugged outdoorsman) discover the dead body of the camp director where the treasure should be.[6] Someone's altered the hunt—but who, and why?"

Isn't that better? If Elliot's done his homework and is pitching to a studio executive looking to buy teen-themed adventure material, this meeting has a chance to actually go somewhere.

UNDER THE SURFACE

[1] *Because the buyer probably doesn't think this is a movie about Hopi Indians, when he hears this idea of a "new name" he thinks that it's central to the story. It's not, of course, but doesn't it seem a fair assumption?*

[2] *This is more about the author than the story. Remember, the buyer doesn't care about the seller's opinions.*

[3] *Relevant detail: title.*

[4] *Relevant detail: genre.*

[5] *Relevant detail: heroes.*

[6] *Relevant detail: the hook.*

Case Study: Liz

Our sales executive, Liz, works at Tall People Furniture. Her boss, George, has announced that he is planning to promote one of the salespeople to a managerial position. Liz wants to be considered, but she knows that she's got an uphill battle. From going back to Square One, she's figured out that while George wants to increase his sales, he's expecting to promote the person he likes the best—probably the guy with the most seniority. This is because, from George's perspective, all of the salespeople have (pretty much) the same capabilities, and if someone's going to get promoted, it might as well be the person with whom he'll have the easiest working relationship.

Plus, no matter whom he promotes, George knows he'll be rocking the boat. Promoting the most senior guy means the boat gets rocked the least. So Liz has figured out George's likely decision—now she has to position herself accordingly.

Liz decides to position herself as a marketing expert with a practical plan to meet the company's needs. In the meeting, she'll have to accomplish three things:

- Showcase her marketing expertise
- Demonstrate her leadership ability
- Build rapport with George

In short, she has to make George see that promoting her is worth rocking the boat a little more. To do this, she wants to show him that she can help him achieve his goals, run the sales team, and that she'll be fun to work with on a daily basis. When the time comes to pitch, she's going to have to blow him away.

Here's the first draft of her pitch:

"First of all, you've built a great company and I would just love to be the sales manager.[1] I think I could do a great job. As you know, I've been one of the top producers here,[2] and because I'm the only girl and a lot shorter than the other guys on the sales team, I use a lot of techniques that the other guys don't use. If I were in a position to train them, their own performance would increase[3] and that's good for everyone.[4] Also, I've got a degree in marketing from Boston University. Here's my marketing plan. If you'll look on page three . . ."[5]

However, Liz knows the importance of getting to the relevant details as quickly as possible. She reworks the pitch until it looks like this:

"George, you've told me that you want this company to expand,[6] and with this plan, I think I can help you grow net sales by 20 percent in one year.[7] When I was getting my degree in marketing at Boston University my team[8] used the following strategy to help a company with a business model similar to ours[9] increase sales with minimal[10] advertising. Here's what we did. . . ."

UNDER THE SURFACE

[1] George knows that she wants to be the sales manager. That's what the meeting is about. In this situation, this isn't a context statement—it's telling the buyer something he already knows.

[2] Also something the buyer already knows. This is typical, however, for people who want to be promoted—they focus on how they're doing their existing job well instead of showing the buyer how they could do the NEXT job well.

[3] There is a sound idea in here but this isn't the place for it. This should be prepared as an answer for a question in Q&A.

[4] This is a judgment on the future. George doesn't need Liz telling him her opinions on what will be good for him down the road.

[5] She finally gets to the meat of her pitch and she has him looking at the material—instead of at her.

[6] Demonstrating that she's listened to him and heard his chief concern.

[7] This is the central and most relevant detail. Therefore, it goes first.

[8] Excellent—Liz is letting him know that she can lead a team.

[9] Use of "ours" is great. She's building this idea of being on the same team.

[10] The use of the word "minimal" here is great because Liz knows that George is wondering what this 20 percent increase is going to cost—but if it's minimal, it might not be so bad.

Now, you might be wondering, why doesn't Liz just show him the marketing plan she's made right at the beginning? Liz wants George paying attention to her, not reading along. As well, Liz has very cleverly planned for a surprise at the end—she's going to give George the proposal as she leaves. If she's supersmart, she'll try to finish the meeting with five or ten minutes to spare, so George has time to look over the proposal when she's done.

Tell a Great Story

Another effective way to "show, don't tell" is to tell a great story. You might be thinking that this is really something just for the Hollywood crowd. Not so. Every pitch can be adapted to tell a story.

First, you've got to know the story you're telling. The basic story line is, "How the buyer gets from point A *past the obstacle* to point B."

The rules of storytelling for a story in this format are much the same as they are for writers when pitching a movie:

- Pitch from the point of view of only one person.
- Use no more than three characters, max.
- Have a beginning, a middle, and an end.
- Use descriptive language throughout.

Case Study: J.J.

J.J. is the entrepreneur who is looking for new clients for his computer tech support business. He has a meeting with an architectural firm that has had some trouble with their computers.

When J.J. gets in the room with Annie, the architect, she already knows a lot about his business. She's seen his flyer and they've spoken briefly, so she knows he can do some of the specific things she wants. She also knows that she can hire him for a few hours and see how it goes. Because there's not much money on the line, hiring J.J. is a relatively low-risk proposition. Thus, the success of the meeting will largely depend on whether or not she likes him.

Still, J.J. is much more likely to get the job if he can show and not tell. One of the ways he can do this is by pitching the benefits of his services with a story.

> "Okay, Annie, I understand that the last time your[1] computer crashed you couldn't get your presentation ready in time for your meeting.[2] It's the worst, I know. That kind of crash[3] makes you sweat, makes your heart race—it's no fun. When you call me,[4] the first thing I'll do is help you get the files you need off your computer and onto another one so you can finish your work. Then, by the time you've returned from your meeting, your computer will be back online and ready to go. Eventually, my goal is to make sure that your computer won't have those debilitating crashes at all anymore."[5]

The benefit of using smart storytelling techniques in your pitch is that you're more effectively building a vision in the buyer's mind of what the future could be like if she says yes. The only thing better than telling a great story is having the pictures to go along with it.

Use the Magic Pencil

Researchers have studied this phenomenon and you've likely experienced it yourself. There is a dynamic shift when the seller picks up a pencil, pen, or marker and starts drawing his or her ideas on paper, the whiteboard, or the overhead projector. Even if the buyer's eyes were starting to glaze over, the act of creating holds his attention.

UNDER THE SURFACE

[1] Using the buyer's point of view.
[2] Point A.
[3] Obstacle.
[4] Two characters—Annie and J.J.
[5] Point B.

Case Study: Fangxiao

Fangxiao is the financial advisor who wants to grow her client list. She knows that the clients she would like to work with are approached often and the competition for their business is intense. She decides to focus on improving the way she communicates and work on making complex financial terms more understandable.

Fangxiao has learned that many of her prospective clients start to look a bit confused when she uses the term "asset allocation." She could tell them, "Asset allocation is a diversification strategy where we plan to invest in different types of instruments sourced in different economic sectors. Different asset classes offer non-correlated returns and protect against uncertainty."

That would be a mistake. Much better would be to use the magic pencil. So instead of boring her potential client, Fangxiao picks up a pad of paper and a pencil and begins.

"Imagine if you lived in a house with a big kitchen window." She draws a big square on the page—the window.

"Your next-door neighbors have young boys who are constantly hitting baseballs through your window." She draws a big X through the window.

"You're getting tired of paying for the expensive window to get fixed, so you decide to replace it with a window that has four panes." She draws another big square and then horizontal and vertical lines through it, creating four panes.

"Now, if your kitchen window gets broken again . . ." She draws an X through one of the small squares.

". . . you'll only have to replace one of the small panes, instead of the whole window." Then she redraws the unbroken four-pane window. "And that's basically the idea behind asset allocation. Instead of putting all of your assets into one area, which could be exposed if something happens, we want to divide your assets into smaller sections, which will provide you greater protection."

Do you see how this works? The magic of drawing is so powerful, you might consider putting away your PowerPoint presentation. (Gasp! Did I just say that?)

Why You Should Avoid PowerPoint

Unless a PowerPoint presentation is truly necessary, I recommend that you avoid it. First of all, many buyers are already tired—the last thing you want to do when you start pitching them your valuable idea is to dim the lights. Second, when you do begin to pitch, you want the buyer to be focused on you. After all, *you* are one of the major selling points of your proposal. Finally, you want to be able to see the buyer's nonverbal communication as you pitch. This is crucially important because it allows you to adapt what you're saying on the fly—for instance, to explain a little more if you see the buyer getting confused or shift gears if you see him getting bored.

Finally, think about this—what do *you* do when you're sitting through someone else's ten- or twenty-minute PowerPoint presentation? Do you anticipate each new slide with bated breath? Do you eagerly take notes? Or do you check your e-mail and text messages on your PDA? Do you let your mind wander to your to-do list? Do you try to remember one or two salient details so you can ask one decent question when the lights go back on?

This is what most people are doing. Sorry, PowerPoint. *Software is no substitute for genuine communication.* Thus, if you are considering a typical PowerPoint presentation, ask yourself these questions:

- Are you going to read what's on the slides out loud? If so, don't use the slide. We can all read, thanks very much.

- Could this slide be better as a handout or a video? Can you do without it entirely? The fewer slides you use, the better.
- Can you draw what's on the slides instead of simply displaying a graphic? If so, grab a marker and start drawing on a whiteboard or flip chart.

If you must do a PowerPoint presentation (and there are situations where it's required), my suggestion is to spend only a fraction of the time allotted using PowerPoint. Spend the rest of the time presenting in other ways and answering questions.

You should be the presentation. Let PowerPoint sing backup.

And the Good in a Room "Best Pitch" Award Goes To . . .

I found this pitch in an issue of *Fast Company*. I'll summarize it here, though you can find the full article online.

Microsoft was looking for a new design team for the Xbox 360. They requested proposals from three top design firms. The pitch that won the job was from Michael Jager of JDK Design. Here's how he applied the principle of "show, don't tell" to win the account.

First, he slashed an X in a piece of paper with a razor and poked his head through. "X [the Xbox 360] today is all *aaargh*," he said. He compared it to the Incredible Hulk in terms of raw power. Then he reversed the paper and showed how Xbox could become an opening, "an invitation into an experience." He compared this to Bruce Lee, who had "a quiet power that is lurking, something still incredibly dangerous but with more of an elegance and grace." Jager's pitch involved a piece of paper and the beautifully simple trailer of "less Hulk, more Bruce Lee." Microsoft bought it and the rest is history.

Now it's time to get to the second secret of the pitch. It's just as important as showing and not telling, and it's the subject of the next chapter.

CHAPTER 27

Why You Should Love Q&A

The second secret to making a compelling pitch is to embrace Q&A. Buyers *love* Q&A. You see, even if your presentation is excellent, you've had a lot of time to prepare, memorize, and practice. You might just be someone who can give a solid presentation. But if you handle Q&A well, that shows that you're more than just a good speaker.

Buyers want to surprise you and see how you respond. They want to point out potential problems and weaknesses and see how you address those concerns. In general, the buyer doesn't really trust that you're the real deal until they've had a chance to put you to the test. That test is Q&A.

Therefore, one of the key principles of winning over any audience is to think of your pitch in two parts: Intrigue them with your presentation, then convince them with your answers to their questions.

The Preemptive Answers Trap

Many sellers want to avoid Q&A. They would rather do a twenty-minute presentation that answers everything in advance so that there's no need for questions at the end. This is foolish.

First, when you try to preemptively answer the buyer's questions, you're essentially telling the buyer that you know what's going on in her mind. No one likes to hear that. Next, you're trying to retain control of the conversation. An extended pitch prevents the natural give-and-take characteristic of successful meetings. Worse, it indicates that you may be scared of answering the buyer's questions.

How to Prepare for Q&A

Try to anticipate the questions the buyer will ask and create answers that highlight the benefits of working with you. You need to prepare answers for questions that are asked all the time, questions you've been asked before, and questions that have the potential to push your buttons.

Questions That Are Asked All the Time

- "What inspired this idea?"
- "How long have you been working on it?"
- "Where are you in the process?"
- "What else can you tell me?"
- "What else do you have?"
- "How much would this cost?"
- "Why you and not a competitor?"
- "Why now and not later?"
- "Why shouldn't I do this?"

Questions You've Been Asked Before

So often, people think of the pitch as being their presentation only. They see Q&A as an opportunity to clarify the few things that they may have forgotten to mention. However, Q&A is actually the second half of your pitch.

Every time you have a meeting, you may be asked questions that you've never been asked before. Your goal is to develop great answers for these questions so that the next time you're asked, you don't have to scramble to come up with something.

The buyer is looking to surprise you and get you off your script. Sometimes, that will happen—but it should never happen with the same question twice. If you stumble over a question in a meeting on Monday, that's fine. But if you get the same question on Tuesday, you should have a response in your back pocket, ready to go.

Questions That Push Your Buttons

Too often, sellers attempt to gloss over or conceal the weaker parts of their ideas. Then when the buyer starts asking questions and homing in on the sensitive spots, sellers get defensive. This is where it's easy to break rapport and lose the deal entirely.

Instead, take a ruthless inventory of where your proposal is weak. Ask yourself what you don't want to be asked. Then carefully prepare answers for these questions.

Case Study: Fangxiao

Fangxiao, our financial advisor, is about to get asked some tough questions. By anticipating them instead of reacting defensively, she's able to come up with persuasive answers.

Buyer: *Why should I hire you when I could do my own investing online for a lot less money?*

Fangxiao: That's a good question. It all depends on how much work you want to do. Think of your portfolio as a garden. It takes time to decide what to plant, to do the planting, to water and weed at the right times . . . So it all depends on how much of the work you want to do. My goal with my clients is to reduce their workload as much as possible.

Buyer: *The market is in a downturn. Don't you think I should wait to invest until later?*

Fangxiao: Actually, I think there are some great undervalued stocks right now. This is an excellent time to get involved, provided you make good choices.

Buyer: *Do you own all of the stocks you're recommending to me?*

Fangxaio: Sometimes I do own what I recommend. If I do, I'll always disclose that to you. But your needs may be different from mine. My strategy is to help you create the portfolio that's right for you and your family.

Case Study: J.J.

J.J., our computer support person who's opened his own company, the Macintosh Healing Center, anticipates that clients will be weighing working with him versus hiring a more established vendor. He's anticipated three questions that address this.

Buyer: *Why shouldn't I use an Apple-approved vendor like _____?*

J.J.: You absolutely can. While they are very successful and have thousands of clients, I maintain a much smaller list of clients, which enables me to give each person more attention. This way, I'm easily accessible and more familiar with your particular machine and your needs.

Buyer: *How many clients have you had so far?*

J.J.: Over the years, more than a hundred. While I've just started doing tech support full time, I started in college and have been fixing computers part time for the last eight years.

Buyer: *What happens if you work on my computer and I'm not happy with the results?*

J.J.: I haven't encountered that before, but I offer a money-back guarantee for all of my services. If you aren't happy with the service you receive or if I'm not able to fix your machine, you won't have to pay.

How Not to Answer Questions

Unfortunately, many sellers interpret a buyer's questions as criticism or disrespect. It's almost as if they assume that if the pitch is clear enough, that should be it. They expect the buyer to say, "This sounds fantastic. Where do I sign?"

The fact is, you want the buyer to have questions. If you've finished your pitch and you were only asked a couple of questions before the meeting ended, you can be pretty sure that you're getting a no. A few questions is not Q&A. It's just a way of being polite.

If you are asked a series of difficult, repetitive, and possibly even annoying questions, you can be sure that you are really in Q&A. Getting to this point is a victory. Relish it, but not for long—otherwise you might make one of the following mistakes:

- *Getting defensive.* If a buyer is attempting to poke holes in your pitch, it probably means he is interested. Sure, it could also be to prove that he is smarter than you are or to see whether you can "handle it." Regardless, it's never to your advantage to get upset. Even if the buyer turns the heat up, keep your cool.
- *Saying no.* If you can help it, avoid saying no. Instead try "I'll get back to you on that" or "Let me find out about that."
- *Saying "Remember before when I said _____?"* There's no need to point out anything that the buyer has forgotten or remembered incorrectly. Instead, tell him again in a new way as if it were the first time.
- *Interrupting the buyer.* If the buyer is saying something that's incorrect (and which needs to be corrected), wait until he is done. Then, repeat what he's said and gently correct it. When you let the buyer know you've really heard him, he won't mind it so much when you correct him. This keeps the conversation on track.

How to Say "I Don't Know"

Admitting that you don't know something is perfectly reasonable. It isn't a sign of weakness; it means you are a professional who will stick to the facts. The key is to emphasize that you will get back to the buyer. By making yourself accountable for providing the buyer with an answer, you soften the fact that you don't know while giving yourself a chance to prove your competency.

When you honestly don't know (or when you need to avoid giving an answer right then), say something like:

- "I don't know that offhand, but I'll find out and get back to you shortly."
- "That's a very important question. Let me think about it and I'll get back to you soon."
- "I know this is important to you. Let me check with _____ to confirm and I'll send you the details this afternoon."

You know you've reached the end of the Q&A phase when the buyer stops asking questions or you sense an energetic shift in the room. Often, the buyer will pause and then say something like, "Okay, so where do we go from here?" This is your cue to move to Stage 5, closing.

CHAPTER 28

The Closing Sequence

Okay—the finish line is in sight! This fifth and final stage of the meeting, "Closing," can be very exciting. It can also be confusing, and even experienced salespeople make costly mistakes when they close incorrectly. In this chapter I'll talk about what closing is and the best way to close the deal.

What Is Closing?

"Closing" is a term that comes from the jargon of professional salespeople. It refers to the end of a transaction, completion of a negotiation, or the confirmation of agreement. It also refers to the special tactics often used by the seller in this final stage.

I know that some of you are thinking that if you've pitched well and if the buyer wants what you've got, they'll just ask to do business with you. It's rare, but it does happen. Most of the time, however, you will have to close in some way. Because if you aren't able to close with proficiency, you're at a serious disadvantage.

Why Closing Is Important

Closing gives you information you just can't get any other way. By closing, you ask the decision maker to actually make a decision. This moment of making a decision is the point at which the buyer is feeling the most risk. You want to know—you *need* to know—if the buyer is prepared to take that risk. If so, great. If not, you have a chance to discover the buyer's objections.

The other reason you need to be able to close is to protect your time and energy. It takes a lot of time to find the right buyer and prepare for a high-stakes meeting, and it takes a lot of energy to concentrate and perform in the room. The buyer doesn't have to do much—except decide. If you don't ever ask the buyer to make a decision, you won't know who is ready to take the risks and receive the rewards of working with you, and who can't (or doesn't want to) make a decision.

Why Closing Is Dangerous

One of the foundations of rapport is the idea that you, the seller, are there to meet the needs of the buyer. You are at their service. However, when you close you are applying subtle pressure to the buyer. You are asking them to take action. This creates a dynamic where the buyer is there for you. That's dangerous because if they are even a little uncomfortable with how you close, you may not get the yes and you almost certainly won't get a referral.

Therefore, the golden rule of closing is: *Closing must preserve rapport.* Preserving rapport is the most important thing. When you close, the rapport you have with the buyer provides a necessary psychological cushion. Plus, you're more likely to have your request granted and you're much more likely to get referrals.

The Best Closing Technique

You might be selling pretzels or pendants, stocks or real estate. You might be pitching a cost-cutting plan to your boss or asking for a raise. Perhaps you're looking to finance a small business or a creative endeavor. Regardless, the best way to close the deal and preserve rapport is to be straightforward and direct: *Ask for what you want.*

Let's imagine that you're taking a meeting and everything has gone well. You've made it past the deal breakers of the first ninety seconds, built rapport, asked good questions, delivered a great pitch, and handled the Q&A. As the buyer's questions wind down, the moment of truth has arrived. It's time for you to close the deal.

What should you say? Use what's known by professional salespeople as "the direct close" and ask for the buyer's approval. This is not only the simplest way to close, in my experience it's also the most effective. Variations of the direct close include:

- Would you like to sign up?
- Will you finance this project?
- Does this arrangement work for you?
- Would you like to move forward?

How to Ask

When you use the direct close, follow these rules:

- *Ask for one thing only:* Part of making it easy on the buyer is building your meeting around one request that you know they can grant.
- *State your request simply and directly:* Anything complicated implies that you lack clarity about what you want. Use as few words as necessary.

- *Maintain a warm, conversational tone:* If you sound the least bit impatient, aggressive, or condescending, the room can cool off quickly and you can lose the opportunity.
- *Make it as easy as possible for the buyer to complete the transaction:* In other words, have the documents and a pen and whatever else you need ready. If they say yes, it does not demonstrate competence to root around in your briefcase for the contract.

When to Ask

You may know what to say and how to ask—but if you don't ask at the right time, you can break the deal. If you ask too soon, you seem overeager and impatient. If you wait too long to ask, you look like an amateur. Timing is important.

Suppose you're eating in a sit-down restaurant and you're finishing your meal. The server would like you to order coffee and dessert—but when should he or she approach you? If the server comes to your table and says, "Can I get you anything else?" and you're still chewing, you might feel rushed and slightly uncomfortable. But if the server waits too long, you could lose interest and be ready to leave.

Ultimately, the question of whether you stay for coffee and dessert is mostly about whether or not you want to stay. The server's role is small—but there is a role to be played. Simply, the server's role is to maintain rapport with you so that you continue to feel comfortable at the table. Therefore, the question of "when should the seller close?" is a lot like asking "when has the buyer finished eating?"

What to Do If the Buyer Says No

The buyer may say some version of no, including:

- "This is not what I was expecting."
- "I need to think about it."
- "I don't think this solves the real problem."
- "I'm not sure this will work for us."

If this happens, keep your head. Remember that you're not in control of the buyer's decision, but you are in control of whether or not you build rapport and learn. Thus, return to Stage 3, Information Gathering. Gently inquire as to why the buyer doesn't want to move forward. Try saying something like:

- Could you explain your thinking on this?
- What would work for you?
- What's not working for you?

You may learn that you and the buyer are not a good fit. That's okay. You'll be able to improve for next time and you've proven to the buyer that you can handle yourself in the room. You may end up working with this buyer down the road or with someone else the buyer knows. If you've maintained rapport, even a meeting that ends without a yes can be a win.

Of course, as you gather new information, you might have an answer to the buyer's sticking point. If you are able to handle the objection, offer a solution. Then, stop and gauge the buyer's response. If the buyer doesn't show obvious signs of interest (like perking up or asking more questions), the meeting is likely to end relatively soon. However, if the buyer does appear interested, then when the right moment comes you should close again. Just be careful that you don't fall into the final three traps.

The Final Three Traps

It's just as possible to break the deal in the final stage as it is in the first stage. Beware of the three final traps:

- *Closing over and over:* It's crucially important that you don't use your closing technique to grind the buyer down or bully him or her into making a decision. That will break rapport and is therefore a costly mistake. Persistent closing almost ensures that you will not get referrals. No one wants to send a friend or a family member to you if you use high-pressure tactics.
- *Closing without confidence:* If the moment comes for you to close and you hesitate or trip over your tongue, that indicates that you may still be a little green. An easy antidote is practice. Work with a partner at home, record yourself with an audio or video recorder, and actually practice the close of the meeting. You may not feel confident on the inside, but with a little practice you can seem confident on the outside.
- *Showing disappointment:* When you close and the buyer says some form of yes, you can play it cool, but you're allowed to show your appreciation. It's okay for the buyer to see that you're satisfied. If the buyer says some form of no, however, don't reveal your disappointment. When you seem disappointed or frustrated, the buyer realizes that you're only there for the sale, not for the relationship. This breaks rapport.

Even if rapport is your highest priority, sometimes you want the sale so badly that when you hear no, it's hard to take. This is why closing technique is so important. With good technique, no won't throw you off your game. You'll keep your expression neutral and segue naturally into gathering more information.

Additional Resources

Closing is the bridge between sales and negotiation. While there are many guides to closing for salespeople written by salespeople, you may find some new ideas in books written by professional negotiators. Here are some of my favorites:

- *Start With No*, by Jim Camp.
- *Secrets of Power Negotiating*, by Roger Dawson.
- *The Only Negotiating Guide You'll Ever Need*, by Peter B. Stark and Jane Flaherty.

Whatever industry you are in, you can strengthen and refine your closing skills by reading these books and experimenting with the techniques that feel right for you.

Once you've closed, there's one more step. It's time to make a smooth, graceful exit.

CHAPTER 29

How to Get Out of the Room

O kay, I'm sure you know that your last impression is just as important as your first impression. So let's skip the part where I explain to you that it's *really, really* important and get to the nuts and bolts of how you get out of the room and bring Stage 5 to a successful conclusion.

Echo the Cue

At the moment the buyer decides that the meeting is over, he will often give you a subtle cue. This cue is usually nonverbal. You've probably seen many different variations on what I'm about to describe. In essence: *Let the buyer give you the cue, then echo it back.*

Look for when the buyer:

- Closes a notebook or a folder
- Shifts physical position in preparation to get out of the chair
- Places hands flat on the tops of the thighs

- Pauses just a little longer than usual
- Checks the time

When the buyer begins getting ready to end the meeting, your job is to notice this and begin preparing for the end of the meeting as well (casually gathering your things, etc.). When you respond to the buyer's nonverbals with your own, you show that the two of you are in sync. Then your exit will go more smoothly.

In their excitement, however, some sellers miss these cues. Some sellers haven't finished some aspect of their presentation and choose to ignore these cues. Either is a serious mistake. You know you've taken a wrong turn in Stage 5 if you get one of these signals:

- *The smile and nod*—when the buyer's answers get short, nodding becomes more frequent, and she says things like "Okay . . . Yep . . . Uh-huh . . . Sure thing . . ."
- *The multiple time check*—quickly looking at the clock, then checking her watch, glancing at her computer screen, opening her cell phone . . .
- *Loss of attention*—looking out the window, looking at the door, fiddling with items on her desk . . .

These are cues you do not want to see. It means you aren't paying attention to the buyer's needs. You aren't sensing the temperature of the room as it cools. You don't get it.

A Little More Rapport

Once you and the buyer have tacitly agreed that the meeting is to end, one of two things will usually happen: either the meeting will proceed directly to the finish line or you'll engage in a little rapport building.

If you do start talking about something personal, this is not the time to relax in your chair. Continue finalizing your preparation to leave the room. That way, you can talk for as long as the buyer remains interested and be ready to make a quick exit as soon as you get the signal.

When You Get the Signal, Wrap It Up

When the buyer pauses and says, "Okay . . . ," "Well . . . ," or "All right . . . ," you know it's time to go. At that point, you want to wrap things up. A good wrap-up statement involves a summary of the next steps and the follow-up, as in these examples:

- "I'm going to do A, B, and C, and I'll give you an update after the weekend."
- "I'll check in next week. I'm looking forward to getting your feedback."
- "I'll get everything ready before our meeting next Thursday."

Sweeten the Last Step

The last thing you say to the buyer should be positive:

- "This has been a pleasure. Thanks so much for your time."
- "I would love to work on this with you. I'll be in touch soon."

Usually, this last step happens in concert with some form of physical contact. In general, the rule of etiquette in the United States is that all parties shake hands after a business meeting. If you know the buyer personally, you may end up in some combination of a hug, handshake with a half hug (aka "the bump"), and cheek kiss.

In general, let the buyer lead. However, if you feel unsure, you can always extend your hand preemptively to encourage the handshake. For women, this is usually a good rule.

Finally, turn smoothly, pick up your things, and walk out the door.

Congratulations—you've made it out of the room. But you're not done yet. . . .

CHAPTER 30

After You Leave the Room

One day, while I was at MGM, my assistant told me the following story: He was in the elevator at MGM and a guy got in, talking on his cell phone. Apparently this guy was a writer who was so incensed with my boss's comments on his rewrite, he felt he needed to call his agent immediately and talk strategy. I asked my assistant to poke his head into my boss's office and give him a quick summary of what had been said.

At the time, MGM was in negotiations with this writer's agency on a few different projects. This writer had inadvertently revealed a key piece of the agency's strategy, which greatly enhanced MGM's negotiating position. Ultimately, it probably ended up costing this writer some money and possibly a rewrite job.

The moral of the story is this: *At the time you walk out the door, the meeting is not over.* Don't pump your fist in triumph or hang your head in despair. Don't use your phone. Don't talk to anyone about what has just happened. Do not do anything that would reveal your thoughts or feelings about what has transpired until you're well out of sight.

Collect Your Thoughts

During the meeting, you may have improvised some brilliant new language. You may have been asked a question that threw you off balance. You may have made observations that would help you prepare for your next meeting. The time to collect these thoughts is ASAP. When the experience is fresh in your mind, you may find yourself in a heightened creative state.

To maximize how quickly you can download your thoughts, I recommend carrying a digital audio recorder. Ideally, you would use a post-meeting checklist like the one I give to my clients:

- Date, time, and location.
- Who was in the meeting?
- What personal details did you learn about them?
- What did you do well?
- What do you wish you had done better?
- When did they laugh?
- When were they most interested?
- When did they seem bored?
- What didn't go as planned?
- What questions were you asked?
- What are the next steps?

Hesitate to Act

A meeting can be a heady experience. You may be full of adrenaline. You may feel compelled to take action immediately. However, it is a good idea to avoid making decisions in such an emotional state. Even if you are in a time-sensitive situation, you would be well served by taking fifteen minutes to collect your thoughts and refocus.

If you feel you must take action quickly, this is a good time to check in with one of your advisors. Make sure you are on the right track and not making a rash decision.

Reward Yourself

Studies show that successful people give themselves a treat to reinforce good behavior. Even if the meeting didn't go exactly as planned, even if there is a lot you'd like to change for the next time, the fact that you had the meeting is a success. Reward yourself.

Later, transcribe the musings on your digital recorder before you forget, and create your next action plan. Take a few minutes so you don't lose the valuable insights you recorded. You want to extract as much learning as possible from each meeting. That way, when you go into your next meeting, you're as prepared as you can possibly be.

CHAPTER 31

Before You Go into the Next Room

I t was a Thursday night and I was at a movie premiere. Before the picture started, I had a brief conversation with a screenwriter who is known for being good in a room. He mentioned that he had a romantic comedy idea and asked me if I would be interested in hearing it. I said, "Sure, but not right now. Why don't you come to the office on Monday and you can tell me more about it?"

It's a good bet that this guy went home and started thinking about exactly how he would pitch me on Monday. After all, given his track record and my interest in working with him, if he had a genuinely good idea and if he pitched it well, that meeting on Monday could translate into six months' worth of work. So over the weekend, he was probably doing his research, polishing his presentation, and practicing answers for my likely questions.

Unfortunately for him, the following events occurred over the weekend:

- A romantic comedy on our development slate moved forward when a star was attached.
- My boss announced that he was getting divorced.

Logically, neither of these things should have mattered to his pitch, but as you know, they do. Personally, I believe that if the script is really good, we should buy it—at the very least, we should consider it carefully. But if we've got something similar in development and my boss is down on love, there are two reasons I won't be able to convince him to purchase a new romantic comedy script.

Anyway, Monday afternoon, this writer came in for his appointment. We chatted for a bit and then he started pitching his romantic comedy. . . .

Actually, he didn't do that. He was too smart to fall into that trap. He knew that something might have changed between Thursday and Monday.

What he did was start fresh. He went back through the information-gathering process. I told him about the romantic comedy that was on the fast track and he switched gears. Then he pitched an adventure story that he'd come prepared with just in case. This is the move of a total professional. Ultimately, we had a great meeting that day, and while I didn't buy his script, I did hire him to consult on another project I had in development.

Assume That Something Has Changed

Suppose you've had a couple of meetings with a buyer and you have a pretty precise idea of what he wants. You have prepared a proposal that addresses all of his needs. You meet again today and you're ready to hear him say yes. Watch out—something has probably changed.

Expect it. If you do not expect it, you'll find yourself complaining to your colleagues, "We had agreed to do _____, but then when I came back to get his final approval, he had changed his mind!" Yes, of course, he had. The surprise is when buyers don't change their minds.

Risk Helps Buyers Clarify
Their Objectives

Though it can be annoying, you should welcome it when a buyer changes his mind. It's confirmation that the buyer is actually interested. It means that he has been really thinking about it, working out the details, and getting feedback from other people.

He's preparing to put up the cash and risk his reputation. This causes him to get even more specific about what he wants and how he wants it. He may be considering scenarios that are completely different from what you talked about in the meeting. He may be reevaluating an aspect of his strategy entirely. He is developing a vision of what he wants—and there's a good chance that this vision involves you.

Get a Recap

Instead of picking up where you left off in your last meeting, start fresh. Gather information to clarify where the buyer stands. Ask him to recap what you last talked about. Try saying something like:

- "Just to make sure we're on the same page, can you recap for me what you'd like to accomplish?"
- "I know we've covered a lot of this before, but sometimes things can change quickly. Would you mind giving me a summary of where we are at this point?"

You see, you have a vision of the project and the buyer has a vision of the project. One of your goals in every meeting is to make sure that your vision and his vision are in sync. This is why you must continue to gather information throughout the process. You want to make sure that you and the buyer are always on the same page.

Part V

▪

Mini-Meetings

et's define a *meeting* as an event where you and the buyer have agreed to meet face-to-face. All the communications before, between, and after are *mini-meetings*. Mini-meetings include e-mails, phone calls, and casual in-person conversations that help to:

- Introduce ourselves and build rapport
- Get past the "gatekeepers"
- Schedule meetings with buyers
- Exchange information and advice
- Finalize relevant details
- Maintain relationships
- Persuade others to get on board with our ideas

In my experience, a lot of the work is done in the mini-meetings. This makes them just as important as meetings. Even a conversation at the water cooler or a brief e-mail can tip the scales in favor of yes over no.

Are Mini-Meetings
Different from Meetings?

On the surface, yes. Mini-meetings are shorter, less formal, and often happen via e-mail or on the phone. Underneath, however, mini-meetings have the same basic structure as formal meetings. Whether you're writing an e-mail, making a phone call, chatting in the hallway, or having a formal in-person meeting, the same principles of being good in a room apply.

Four Types of Mini-Meetings

The chapters in this section are devoted to the four most important mini-meeting situations:

- Making requests
- Keeping in touch
- Following up
- Saying no

To explore these types of mini-meetings, I'm going to reveal some of the behind-the-scenes communications of our four characters. I've adapted these examples from real-life situations because I want them to be as useful as possible.

These mini-meetings will actually take us back in time. You've already seen the pitches used by J.J., Fangxiao, Elliot, and Liz in the previous section, "Inside the Room." Now it's time to rewind and look at the mini-meetings used by our characters to find new clients, get referrals, schedule meetings, and get into the room in the first place.

CHAPTER 32

How to Make Requests

Put yourself in the buyer's shoes for a moment. You walk into your office and sit down at your desk. Your assistant comes in with your coffee, just the way you like it. You take a deep breath, and then . . .

You check your phone messages and wake up your computer. You've got seventy-five voice mails and two hundred non-spam e-mails. There's also the basket of unopened mail that you didn't get to yesterday.

After doing an initial scan, you have a list of fifty non-emergency requests for your time and attention. Which ones will you tackle first? Which ones will you defer until later in the week? Which requests do you deny or simply just delete? In other words, which mini-meetings were effective and which were not?

When I was at MGM, where the phone never stopped ringing and the e-mail never stopped coming, I was very aware of which mini-meetings got my attention and which ones didn't. I noticed which requests climbed to the top of my priority stack and which ones fell to the bottom. Eventually, I realized what successful mini-meetings had in common. Here are some ways to improve your communication on the phone and via e-mail.

How to Be Good on the Phone

Phone meetings are pretty much like traditional meetings, with three exceptions:

- *You have to avoid additional deal breakers.* Deal breakers for phone meetings include having a connection with poor sound quality, talking to someone else while you're on the call, and taking your call waiting. Basically, anything that interrupts the conversation from your end of the call is a deal breaker. Make important calls from a landline if at all possible. If you must use a mobile phone, find a quiet place with great reception where you won't be disturbed.
- *You get far less nonverbal feedback from the other person.* Because you can't see the buyer's facial expressions and body position, you have to concentrate more than ever on tone of voice, speech patterns, and content of the conversation. Maintaining 100 percent outward focus is crucial when you're on the phone.
- *It's a lot easier to distract yourself.* It's okay for a buyer to file papers or check e-mail while on the phone with you. It's not okay for you to do anything else while you're on the phone with the buyer. Remember, it's a treasure hunt. One nuance, one clue is all it takes to make an important discovery about what the buyer really wants or to find an area of common ground.

Finally, I highly recommend using a phone headset so your hands can be free to take notes on paper or computer. This is especially important because you want to be able to record the specific language your buyer uses. Then, merely by glancing at your notes, you can incorporate the buyer's hot words and phrases into your communication.

How to Write Good E-mail

When you're using e-mail to make a request, there's no instantaneous feedback like there is in a face-to-face situation. You don't get to see the buyer's immediate reactions. You can't improvise and adapt. However, you do have the ability to precisely control the tone and content of your communication.

Here's how to turn that control to your advantage:

- *Avoid the additional deal breakers.* E-mail deal breakers are basically those that involve poor spelling, bad grammar, and inexact communication. In other words, the basic rules of writing that we learned in high school English still apply.
- *Keep it short.* If you make a request via e-mail, the overall e-mail needs to be brief (though never curt). You want to take up as little of the buyer's time as possible. If the e-mail is too long, you're unlikely to get a positive response.
- *Sandwich the request between slices of rapport.* Even in a business e-mail, it's important to start with something personal, segue into the request, and end on a warm or personal note. You'll see examples of this in the case study below.

Finally, keep your e-mail signature restrained. Whenever you use an e-mail signature, it should contain your relevant contact information in an unobtrusive way. I know a lot of people who have lengthy e-mail signatures that contain logos, branding phrases, mission statements, and quotes of the day. It's tacky and unprofessional. Instead, just make sure that your e-mail signature makes it easy for the buyer to find your contact information. After that, less is more.

Case Study: J.J.

The Macintosh Healing Center is open for business, but very few people know about it. The question is, how should our technical support entrepreneur, J.J., get the word out?

Instead of placing ads in local papers and using more conventional advertising methods, J.J. decides to focus on getting referrals from his existing network. Initially, he'll send e-mails to people in his Rolodex who are Good People to Know, Very Important People (VIPs), and members of his Inner Circle.

He opts to contact them via e-mail because that way, if any of them know someone else who might need his services, they can just forward the e-mail. It will take some time (and maybe a few drafts) to get the letter just right, but J.J. knows that this will make it easier for the other person to agree to his request.

J.J.'s "Good People to Know" Marketing E-mail, First Draft

Dear Friend[1] of the Macintosh Healing Center,

My business[2] isn't doing as well as I'd like[3] and I'm looking for additional people who I could help. Since I fixed your computer before and you know me, I wanted to ask if you could recommend anyone else that might need their computers fixed. If you do, please let me know[4] or if someone tells you that they are having computer problems, I would really appreciate a recommendation.[5]

Thanks,
J.J.

UNDER THE SURFACE

[1] *Too generic—deal breaker. E-mails should be sent to a specific person.*

[2] *Lead with their needs, not yours.*

[3] *Don't open with an apology or a statement of weakness.*

[4] *No—instead, make it easy on the other person. Offer to contact them.*

[5] *Ending the e-mail with the request is, in general, the right technique. However, it would benefit from a little more warmth at the end.*

Now, J.J.'s smart enough not to send this until he gets some feedback. So he sends it to a friend of his who's in direct mail advertising. The friend gives J.J. some good notes and recommends that the letter should be more like a traditional sales letter.

J.J.'s "Good People to Know" Marketing E-mail, Second Draft

Hi![1]

Has your computer been acting up? Don't you hate it when your computer craps out[2] on you at the worst possible moment? Well, look no further, because your all-purpose computer solution[3] is here!

If you know someone who could use some help with their Macintosh, please recommend me!

Thanks,
J.J.

J.J. gets some more feedback and decides he doesn't like the "sales-y" tone. After all, his communication should be SMART, and the T is for "tonally appropriate." Even if his sales-y letter worked and he gets a response, his further communication will be very different. He's not the kind of guy who speaks in exclamation points.

While he wants to get new clients, J.J. knows that he must control his introduction—and the first moment of his introduction could be this e-mail. So he needs to write something that sounds like who he really is and has a tone that captures how he provides service.

J.J. decides to rewrite his e-mail again and tailor each letter to a specific person. While this will take a long time, he provides personal service, and so a personal e-mail is a better way of communicating. He

UNDER THE SURFACE

[1] Exclamation points can seem amateurish or overly aggressive.
[2] Unprofessional language.
[3] Too general. Specificity is credibility.

starts with an e-mail to one of his former teaching assistants from college, a journalist named Elliot.

J.J.'s "Good People to Know" Marketing E-mail, Third Draft

Hi Elliot,[1]

I hope your writing at *Prime Numbers* is going well. I read your last article on the future of video games and enjoyed it a great deal.[2]

You've heard me talk about it for the last two years, but the time is finally here. My tech-support company, the Macintosh Healing Center, is open for business.

Here's how it works:[3] If you or someone you know is having any computer issues, all you have to do is call or e-mail me. I'll fix what's not working, give you the few tips you need, and optimize your software so you can forget about the computer and focus on doing your work.[4]

Check out my Web site for more info: www.macintoshhealing center.com[5]

Thanks for all your help.[6]

Sincerely,
J.J.

---

[1] *Using the buyer's name gets you past Stage 1 of the meeting.*

[2] *Always start with something warm and personal. This is like building rapport in Stage 2 of the meeting.*

[3] *"Here's how it works" is a great way to foreshadow the pitch.*

[4] *J.J. uses the trailer that relates to artists because Elliot is a writer.*

[5] *Ending the body of the e-mail with this call to action is great. Asking people to go to a Web site is a small request that's likely to be granted.*

[6] *Just like in the meeting, this is how to get out of the room gracefully—end on a warm note.*

P.S. I'm offering a 15 percent discount on all my services for students and alums of Michigan. Go Blue![1]

Macintosh Healing Center
(310) 555-1200
www.macintoshhealingcenter.com

As J.J. starts going through his list and adapting each e-mail to the particular person, he realizes that the most important people he needs to contact are his VIPs. He also knows that these people will require even more time and energy to get their e-mails just right. VIP e-mails need to be full of warmth, exceedingly clear, and as short as possible.

For his first VIP e-mail he writes to one of his family friends who is a successful musician.

The VIP E-mail

Dear Tim,

Congratulations on the success of your latest album.[2] It's been quite a while since our chat at my dad's birthday barbeque. I wanted to share some good news. I have started my own business doing technical support for Macintosh users with a unique approach.[3]

My business is called the Macintosh Healing Center and, like a physician who is focused on making sure the whole body is

---

UNDER THE SURFACE

[1] This is an effective surprise saved for the end. It's not the discount, it's the way J.J.'s showing how he's still a part of his collegiate community. This one sentence builds rapport, captures J.J.'s enthusiasm, and suggests others to whom Elliot might forward the e-mail.

[2] This first sentence is a good start. It shows that J.J. is keeping up with Tim's career.

[3] It's subtle, but this paragraph is a little clunky. The first sentence doesn't smoothly transition to the second sentence, nor does the second sentence to the third.

healthy, I provide emergency services as well as long-term preventive care for Mac computers.

I can create automatic backup systems, improve Internet security, and optimize software so that your computer runs smoothly and has the capabilities you need for as long as you own it.

I offer a free initial checkup where I will come to your office[1] and evaluate the health of your computer.[2] Would this be something you would be interested in? No worries if it isn't, but if I can help you or your staff, that would be great.

Please feel free to call me at (310) 555-1200 if you have any questions. I'll call you on Monday and see if you'd like to schedule a time at your convenience.[3]

Give my best to Leanne.[4]

Sincerely,
J.J.[5]

J.J. gets some feedback on his letter from trusted friends and decides that he wants to make it shorter and polish it to complete perfection. Communicating with VIPs requires attention to detail because their time is in so much demand.

UNDER THE SURFACE

[1] Notice he says, "to your office" and not "to your home or office." It's a small thing, but he doesn't want to break rapport by appearing to be inviting himself over to Tim's house.

[2] It's hard to refuse an offer like this. However, it will take a lot of J.J.'s time. Thus, he will probably only make this offer to his VIP's.

[3] This seems a little pushy, though the intention is clearly to make things easier for Tim.

[4] Ending on a warm note is great.

[5] Overall, this e-mail is a little too long.

The VIP E-mail, Second Draft

Dear Tim,

Congratulations on the success of your latest album. Both my father and I have listened to it and enjoyed it a great deal.[1]

I'm writing to share some good news: my tech support company, the Macintosh Healing Center, is open for business. I provide emergency services for your favorite Mac as well as long-term preventive care.

I can create automatic backup systems, improve Internet security, and optimize software so that your computer runs smoothly and has the capabilities you need for as long as you own it.

I offer a free initial checkup where I'll come to your office and evaluate the health of your Mac. Would this be something you're interested in? No worries if it isn't, but if I can help you or your staff,[2] that would be great.

Give my best to Leanne. I look forward to seeing you both soon.[3]

Sincerely,
J.J.
Macintosh Healing Center
(310) 555-1200
www.macintoshhealingcenter.com[4]

UNDER THE SURFACE

[1] *Previously, it seemed that J.J. might have just read in the newspaper that the album was selling well. Now it's clear that he's listened to it. It's a big difference because it communicates a stronger level of respect.*

[2] *Mentioning Tim's staff is great. It gives Tim a way to say yes without being personally involved—he can ask one of his assistants to handle it.*

[3] *This extra sentence maintains the warmth. It wasn't needed in the longer e-mail, but is needed in this shorter version.*

[4] *Great to have the e-mail signature here. Simple and direct.*

Now J.J. can construct an e-mail for his Inner Circle. He can be pretty certain that his Inner Circle will pass along whatever he writes, so he needs to make sure that whatever he sends is easily forwardable.

The Inner Circle E-mail

Hi Mom,

I have written a short blurb about my business. Would you be willing to send this to some of your friends with a brief note from you?[1]

The best clients for me are individuals or small companies of less than five people who use Mac computers.[2] As you know, I do emergency fixes, tech support, and long-term preventative care.[3] Let me know if you have any questions.

I really appreciate your help.[4]
Here's the blurb:

The Macintosh Healing Center
Emergency Medicine and Preventive Care for
Your Favorite Computer

If you have a Macintosh computer and you need some technical support, perhaps I can help. I have six years of tech-support

---

UNDER THE SURFACE

[1] Putting the request right up front is fine here. After all, Mom is Inner Circle. But there would be nothing wrong with some rapport-building beforehand.

[2] This is making it easier on his mother. He's asked her for what he needs—for her to forward the blurb. He's told her precisely to whom she should send the blurb. Then he gives her the blurb.

[3] Crucial—he still has to pitch his Mom. She's the buyer. She needs to understand why she should forward the e-mail. This paragraph is what lets her know that she's giving value to her friends by forwarding J.J.'s blurb.

[4] A note of warmth here helps, even with Mom.

experience and focus exclusively on Macintosh computers and peripherals.

I can help you:

- Prevent your computer from freezing or crashing
- Optimize your software and sync your devices
- Increase your machine's performance in cost-effective ways
- Automate a backup system
- Solve many other technology challenges[1]

I look forward to helping solve your computer issues quickly.

J.J.
Macintosh Healing Center
(310) 555-1200
www.macintoshhealingcenter.com

P.S. I provide a money-back guarantee on all services.

After writing this blurb, J.J. realizes that it would also make a good flyer. It's the kind of thing he could post in an area frequented by young professionals (one of his target markets).

J.J.'s Coffee Shop Flyer

Did you know that Macintosh tech support is available in this neighborhood? Even at the Coffee Fix?[2]

---

[1] *Be careful when you use bullets in an e-mail. If there're too many, the reader's eyes glaze over. Five or fewer would work here.*

[2] *Personalizing the flyer in this way lets the reader know that J.J. is "in," that he didn't just post a thousand of these all over the place. This helps J.J. get through Stage 1.*

The Macintosh Healing Center
Emergency Medicine and Preventive Care for
Your Favorite Computer

J.J. Jones has been doing tech support for six years and can help you keep your Mac running smoothly and at peak performance.

- Prevent your computer from freezing or crashing
- Optimize your software and sync your devices
- Automate a backup system
- Solve many other technology challenges

Call (310) 555-1200 or check out www.macintoshhealing center.com.[1]

Even though J.J. has written this coffee shop flyer and posted it, he's not going to focus his time and energy on getting a flyer into every coffee shop in LA. It's not that it's a bad idea. It's just that J.J. expects greater results from his e-mails to his Good People to Know, VIPs, and Inner Circle, so he's going to focus his efforts there.

While J.J.'s writing another e-mail tailored to a specific person, he receives an e-mail response from Elliot:

J.J.,

I don't need help right now, but I have an idea for you. Call me.

UNDER THE SURFACE

[1] _Notice that there's no P.S. here offering a money-back guarantee on all services. This is because, in the previous example, the letter is going to members of his Mom's network. J.J. needs to be extra careful to maintain rapport with those people. With the coffee shop ad, J.J. needs to make sure that if someone gets in touch with him, they really need his services and aren't just trying to take advantage. Thus, by not extending the guarantee, he makes it more likely that the people who respond to his ad are a good fit._

Elliot
310.876.5432
elliot@primenumbers.com
www.primenumbersmagazine.com

At this moment, Elliot's e-mail is J.J.'s highest priority. Thus he starts immediately to prepare for his mini-meeting with Elliot. He takes a half hour, goes back to Square One, reviews his notes on Elliot, and prepares rapport-building and information-gathering questions.

J.J.'s Phone Call with Elliot

E: Hello.

J: Hi, Elliot. This is J.J.

E: Hey, J.J.

J: Thanks so much for writing me back.

E: Sure thing. So, I've got an idea for you.

J: Great—by the way, how's it going with your script?[1]

E: I'm just about finished. Thanks.

J: Have you figured out what your next project is going to be yet?[2]

E: Yeah, actually, I have this idea for a sci-fi project. It's a thriller about what would happen if the Earth's magnetic poles reversed.

J: That sounds very cool. . . .

Now J.J. can talk with Elliot regarding this new project and continue building rapport until Elliot comes back to business.

E: . . . So, I've got this idea for you.[3]

J: Great, what is it?

UNDER THE SURFACE

[1] *Even though Elliot goes right to business, J.J. takes him back to Stage 2, rapport.*

[2] *A prepared question. J.J.'s looking for common ground.*

[3] *Buyer gives the signal to move to start talking about business.*

E: Well, my writer's group has a message board and I thought I could post a notice about your business since most of the people in the group are Mac users.

J: Wow, that would be great. Would it help[1] if I sent you a draft of a flyer and you could edit it however you'd like?[2]

E: Yeah, that's fine. Once I get it I'll post it.

J: Great. I'll e-mail it to you shortly. Thanks for thinking of me.[3]

E: Happy to help. Talk to you later.

J: Sure thing. Bye.

E: Bye.

J.J. adapts his coffee shop blurb for this new opportunity. Personalizing communication is essential to getting the buyer's attention and holding it for those first few seconds.

J.J.'s Ad for Elliot's Writer's Group

If you use a Macintosh Computer:[4]

I'm not a writer,[5] but I know how important it is to make sure your computer is running smoothly at all times, that it's easy to print, and that you never lose any of your work.[6]

I offer 24/7 computer tech support with an emphasis on preventative care. I'll help you automate a backup system, optimize your software, and keep your machine up-to-date so it won't freeze or crash when you need it most.

UNDER THE SURFACE

[1] J.J. makes it easy on the other person.

[2] Good technique—J.J. understands that if Elliot posts something, it reflects on him. Therefore, J.J. asks Elliot if he'd like to edit the e-mail.

[3] A little warmth at the end.

[4] Notice the change in headline. This may be a more effective headline than leading with the name of his business. The only way to find out is to try different headlines and see what creates results.

[5] This gets him past deal breakers—he's personalizing the message.

[6] Leading right away with the benefits that speak directly to writers.

If you'd like some technical support, I'll come to your location
at your convenience.

J.J. Jones
Macintosh Healing Center
310-555-1200
www.macintoshhealingcenter.com

Later that week, J.J. gets a call.

J: Thanks for calling the Macintosh Healing Center. This is J.J.

A: Hi, J.J., my name is Annie and I heard about your company from
   my son.

J: Do I know your son?

A: I'm not sure, but he got your information from someone in his
   writer's group.

J: Oh, yes, one of my friends, Elliot, is in the same group.

A: Mmm. I think my son has mentioned him.

J: Is your son a screenwriter?

A: Yes, well, he's trying at least.

J: Are you a writer as well?

A: No, no. I'm an architect. That's the purpose of my call. Do
   you know how to set up a network and install memory . . . stuff
   like that?

J: Yes, I do. What's your situation?

A: Well, my business is expanding. I've got ten computers at the office, all Macs, and if any one of them breaks down, it's not
   going to be pretty. But right now I'm just interviewing different
   people. How much do you charge?

J: It's important that I understand the full scope of the issue before
   I give you an estimate.[1] I'd be happy to come to your office

---

UNDER THE SURFACE

[1] *J.J. doesn't want to talk business too soon. He knows he needs to build rapport,
and that will be hard to do on the phone. Therefore, as she seems like a great lead,
he decides to give her the VIP treatment and offer her a free consult.*

and do a free checkup on the machine that is most important to you.[1]

A: Well, sure. That would be good. When are you available?

J: I have some time this week and next. When would be the most convenient time for you?[2]

A: Tomorrow at 3:00 P.M. would work for me.

J: That works for me, too. I'm looking forward to meeting you.

They make the arrangements and J.J. asks for the correct spelling of Annie's name and if they have a company Web site. He takes out his Pre-Meeting Checklist and starts doing his research, designing questions, and creating a buyer portrait.

How to Say Thank You

At the end of the day, J.J. wants to send a note to Elliot to thank him for posting the note and to let him know that he got some business out of it. There are many benefits to writing a thank-you note and it's hard to go wrong. Almost everyone appreciates it when you take the time to thank them because it's a rarity.

Hi Elliot,

I just wanted to send you a quick note to thank you for posting the note on your writer's group message board.[3] A new client[4]

UNDER THE SURFACE

[1] This is so important! He knows she has several machines, but he makes sure to let her know that he'll only be evaluating the machine that's most important to her. This way the expectations are clear. He can use his time efficiently and still have the chance to impress her with his skills.

[2] J.J. could say, "I'm totally free this week and next," but it's better to say, "I have some time. . . ." It's just like dating: better to be partially available than totally available.

[3] Be specific about why you are thanking them.

[4] J.J. doesn't say who the new client is. Keeping confidentiality, even if you're not contractually obligated, is a good practice.

called me today who was referred by someone in your group.[1]
If I can help you in any way in the future, please don't hesitate
to ask.[2]

Best,
J.J.[3]
Macintosh Healing Center
310-555-1200
www.macintoshhealingcenter.com

Conclusion

In this chapter, we've covered some of the basic ideas involved in making requests in mini-meetings and saying thank you once these requests bear fruit. Now, you might think that we're done. After all, this whole book is about getting the yes, right?

What you need to remember is that J.J. doesn't even have a new client yet—he's only got a meeting. To get clients, he'll need lots of meetings. How do you get lots of meetings? To find out, let's go to the next chapter, "How to Keep in Touch."

UNDER THE SURFACE

　[1] *Explain the positive result that was a consequence of their action.*

　[2] *Offering to be of assistance in return is one way to end on a warm note.*

　[3] *Thank-you notes (via e-mail) should be short and sweet. In a written letter, they can be longer.*

CHAPTER 33

How to Keep in Touch

One of the most important uses of the mini-meeting is *keeping in touch*. As I recommend in Part III: "Getting in the Room," use the "first-class stamp" approach to keeping in touch. It takes more time, but the possibilities you will generate will be of a much higher quality.

A small piece of communication, be it an e-mail or handwritten letter, is a gift of your time and energy. Done correctly, keeping in touch says to the other person, "You're important to me and I'm thinking about you." Done incorrectly, it says, "Hey, have you thought about sending some business my way?"

The Myth of "In Order to Get, You Have to Give"

When it comes to networking, many experts promote the idea that in order to get, you have to give. There's a certain sense in that. After all, if you want someone to buy from you or work with you, it's logical to provide them with value first. This proves your worth.

However, if you think about it, the notion that you have to give in order to get is a subtle way of talking business too soon. Think about it like this—when you're building rapport in Stage 2 of an actual meeting, you can have one of two perspectives:

1. "I want to build rapport with you so that you'll buy what I'm selling."
2. "I want to connect with you as a person whether you buy what I'm selling or not."

The first perspective is the "give to get" philosophy. You're giving of your time, interest, and attention so you can get the buyer to say yes. The second perspective is you give of yourself because *rapport is worth more in the long-term.*

It's not always easy to get to know a buyer as a person when there is something you want from them. Then again, no one said success would be easy. Paradoxically, the better you are at connecting with buyers regardless of whether you get anything from them, the more sales you're likely to make immediately and down the road.

Don't fall into the trap of talking business too soon. Instead, focus on rapport and the personal connection with the buyer, not as a means to an end but as an end in itself.

Guidelines for Keeping in Touch

Most of us tend to keep in touch via written communication because it's more efficient. Keeping in touch by phone can seem a little too intimate for a business relationship. However, if you do call someone just to say hello, you can also use the rules for e-mail below.

When you send someone a piece of written communication designed to keep in touch:

1. Open with a personal reference.
2. Don't mention business.

3. Don't make any requests.

4. Touch on something personal.

5. Use a conversational, warm tone throughout.

6. Include a trace of praise for the buyer.

7. Include a trace of humor if possible.

8. Keep it short.

Finally, remember that even a quick e-mail can take time to get the tone just right. There's nothing wrong with drafting and redrafting something to make sure that what you've written says exactly what you want it to say.

Case Study: Fangxiao

To breathe some new life into her business, Fangxiao decides that she's going to spend an entire day keeping in touch with her Good People to Know and VIPs.

Fangxiao knows that she could do this exclusively through e-mail. However, she wants her communication to be as memorable as possible. Therefore, she'll write out each letter by hand. Then, she'll send it in an attractive envelope that she also addresses by hand. Fangxiao knows that these small personal touches make a big difference.

> Dear Pei-Yi,
>
> I wanted to send you a note to tell you how much I have enjoyed working with you over the past three years. I know you'll have a great time at NYU graduate school.[1]
>
> While I'll miss our lunch conversations and your funny stories, I just wanted to tell you that I'm really proud of you for following your dreams. You're a great example and I look forward to hearing about your experiences when you return to

UNDER THE SURFACE

[1] *Notice the absence of anything remotely like, "If you run into anyone out there who needs a financial advisor. . . ."*

town. Please keep in touch and know that if I can ever help you, please don't hesitate to ask.[1]

Warmest regards,

Fangxiao[2]

Dear Teddy,

I saw this article about wind sprints in *Runner's World* and I thought of you. I hope you enjoy it and I'll see you on Sunday.[3]

Best,[4]

Fangxiao

Dear Leslie,

Thanks so much for the contribution of the Il Pastaio gift certificate for the school auction. Your generosity is much appreciated and I know the football boosters will put your donation to good use. Thanks so much for being such a great supporter of the football team and our community.[5]

Best,

Fangxiao

Dear William,

I wanted to send you a quick note to tell you how much I

UNDER THE SURFACE

[1] *Now that Pei-Yi's in school, Fangxiao can tailor her "keep in touch" communication schedule to Pei-Yi's school calendar. This way, her next e-mail won't arrive when Pei-Yi's in the middle of finals.*

[2] *Notice the absence of the business signature. No talking business.*

[3] *This mini-meeting is great because it gives Fangxiao a chance to build rapport with Teddy on the specific topic of wind sprints. But if Teddy doesn't read the attached article, that's okay, too.*

[4] *In today's business world, signing off with "Best" (which is short for "Best regards") is a universally accepted way of closing a letter.*

[5] *If Fangxiao knew Leslie more personally, she'd made this e-mail more personal. However, this is a good mini-meeting because saying "Thank you" builds rapport. In this case, it lays the foundation for the next time Fangxiao and Leslie meet in person.*

enjoyed your article in the Sunday *Post* about baby boomers.[1] It was a compelling story and was very well researched, and I learned so much from your perspective. I forwarded it to my sisters and they both wrote back to say how much it affected them.[2]

Many thanks,[3]
Fangxiao

Dear Jane,

It's been a while since we've seen each other, but I saw this card and thought of you and your newest grandchild. I'd love to grab a cup of coffee with you when you are free. Give my best to Ginny and Jim, too.[4]

Fondly,
Fangxiao

Dear Mr. and Mrs. Baker,

It was great to see you at the game on Saturday. After we left, I remembered that one of the books that I found really helpful when Lizzie went away to college for the first time was called *Letting Go*. The college transition can be so exciting for

UNDER THE SURFACE

[1] Be specific when you give a compliment.

[2] Showing the results makes this compliment stand out.

[3] What's important about this note is why Fangxiao is writing it—it's actually because William wrote a great article, Fangxiao's sisters enjoyed it, and especially because Fangxiao likes William personally. William may not be a client for Fangxiao and he may not be a good source of referrals. She keeps in touch because the rapport is worth more in and of itself. Of course, these personal connections do tend to result in new business—just not in a predictable way.

[4] This e-mail is the first of a two-part series. Fangxiao is also going to keep in touch with Ginny and Jim—but she'll wait a month. By then, Jane may have written back, Fangxiao may have already met with Jane, or Jane may have mentioned her to Ginny and Jim. This creates better rapport-building possibilities for further communication. For example, Fangxiao may be able to open her e-mail to Ginny with, "I was just talking with Jane the other day. . . ." or "Jane wrote to me recently to tell me about. . . ." It's a small detail, but it makes a difference.

the students, but a major adjustment for their parents! I've en-
closed a copy and hope you enjoy it. I look forward to seeing
you again soon.

Best,

Fangxiao[1]

Dear Jerry,

Congratulations on your recent promotion to branch manager! You have moved up so quickly—it's pretty impressive.[2]

Best,

Fangxiao

Dear Mr. Lee,

I wanted to send you a note to let you know how much I
enjoyed working with you over the last six years. Your dili-
gence and attention to detail is remarkable. Even though I'm
not able to continue managing your accounts, I wanted to
check in with you and make sure things are still working out
well with our Beijing office. As one of my best clients, I wanted
to make sure you are receiving the highest level of service.[3] If
there is anything I can do, please let me know.

Sincerely,

Fangxiao

It takes time to compose the right message and write an actual letter
that takes a stamp. Buyers know that. So when they receive a handwritten letter from you, they know they're important to you.

UNDER THE SURFACE

[1] *This e-mail is a bit risky, because there's an implied request: "Read this book."
If the Bakers don't read (or don't like) the book, they may feel awkward around
Fangxiao the next time they see her. However, if they like it, it could be a huge rap-
port builder. The risk is worth it.*

[2] *This e-mail is warm and complimentary, but it is a bit short. Fangxiao should
have redrafted it until she had it right.*

[3] *This is an example of what to write when you want to keep the tone more formal and professional. Even so, Fangxiao does her best to maintain the warmth of
the letter.*

Of course, if all you can manage is e-mail, that's fine. Just take the time to make your e-mail as flawless as possible. That will differentiate it from most of the communication the buyer receives. Though if you can manage one handwritten letter once in a while, the e-mails you send will be read much more carefully.

Now it's time to talk about the most neglected aspect of mini-meetings, and one of the most important: how to follow up.

CHAPTER 34

How to Follow Up

f you had a meeting, sent materials, shared a meal, or had any sort of meaningful interaction with a buyer, the ball is in your court. It's your job to follow up. If you handle the post-meeting interactions well, it will be easier for you to address the buyer's notes and answer his or her questions.

Be Explicit with the Buyer About How You Will Follow Up

Sometimes sellers don't follow up with buyers when they think that the buyers are going to handle the follow-up. Usually, this mistake happens when sellers misinterpret something the buyer says. Thus, here are some examples of commonly used buyer-ese:

- "I'll take care of _____ and get back to you."
- "I'll look at your materials."
- "Let's get together sometime."

These mean:

- "Maybe I'll take care of _____ and maybe I'll get back to you."
- "Unless something of a higher priority comes up, I'll look at your materials."
- "Let's get together sometime, though I am booked for the next two years."

You get the idea. Buyers are busy and they can easily lose track. I know, you're busy, too—but as the seller, you can't afford to lose track. Buyers can. There are plenty of sellers waiting.

Still, keep an eye on the bright side. You've had a meeting. That means that for a little while, you're in the buyer's memory and quite possibly on her high-priority list. Following up is how you convert that meeting into concrete results.

Three Types of Following Up

In general terms, a follow-up is any communication that happens subsequent to the meeting and prior to the buyer doing whatever it is she's verbally agreed to do. Following up tends to take three forms:

- *Direct.* This is where the main focus of your e-mail or phone call is when you say, "So, have you had a chance to _____?"
- *Indirect.* Communication where you don't mention the _____, but you keep in touch in a way that reminds the buyer that _____ is on their list of things to do. Indirect follow-ups include saying thank you, sharing new information and asking for help or advice.
- *Combination.* This is both direct and indirect. You use an indirect format but at some point directly refer to your request in the actual meeting.

Whatever form your follow-up communication takes, your goal is to gracefully remind the buyer that your project is worth her time. You are not reminding her of her verbal commitment. Don't say, "Hey, remember when you said you would do _____? What's up?" All you need to do when following up is to remind the buyer politely that your request exists.

Why People Don't Follow Up

Many people have a meeting and then wait by the phone, hoping it will ring. Usually this is because the seller thinks, "I don't want to bother the buyer. I don't want to pester him or seem desperate." The real reason, however, is just plain ol' fear: Sellers don't want to hear the buyer say no, or—worse—have the buyer not even return their e-mails or calls.

Let me address these two issues. First, if you follow up correctly, you're not a bother. You're not nagging or pestering and you don't seem desperate. You're actually being helpful. You're reminding the buyer (in a respectful way) that there's a high-priority item that would benefit from his attention.

As for being afraid of hearing no or getting the cold shoulder, that's understandable. It's discouraging to follow up and find out that you are not going to be hired or your project isn't going to be purchased. But isn't knowing that information sooner rather than later better in terms of moving forward with your goals?

Don't Follow Up Too Much

There is a difference between being a professional who follows up on meetings and becoming a stalker. In Hollywood in particular, there are people who decide, "If you're not going to call me back, I'm going to call you every ten minutes until you pick up the phone," or "I'm going to write you a letter every day until I get the response I want." This kind of bullying strategy seldom works.

How to Follow Up

First, remember that following up may seem like just a little reminder, but it's a meeting. You can break the deal here just as easily as you can in the room. Remember to go back to Square One and use the guidelines for e-mail and phone communication, and follow these rules:

1. *After a meeting, send a thank-you note within twenty-four hours.* If you've had an in-person meeting or even a phone meeting, handwritten thank-you notes are a good idea. This is because when the assistant comes in with the day's mail, often the handwritten notes are placed on top of the stack.
2. *Follow up three times, then move on.* Suppose you send an e-mail to follow up and you hear nothing. Then, phone one to two weeks later. If you don't get a response, phone again one to two weeks after that. If the buyer responds and requests more time or asks you to follow up in the future, you can continue. If you don't get a response, move on.
3. *Keep a log of your communication.* You want to remember when you spoke with the buyer last and what was said.

Tips for Using the Phone

You will likely be giving a message to an assistant or going directly to voice mail. Have something written down so that you're prepared: "This is _____ calling. We met last week about _____. I sent in _____ and I'm just calling to make sure you received the package."

And, in case the buyer actually does take your call, (1) keep a copy of the materials you sent nearby in case you need to refer to something on it, and (2) make the phone call from a place where you can talk calmly without distractions.

Case Study: Elliot

Elliot has completed the rewrite of his script *The Last All-Nighter*. His friends have all given it a thumbs-up. He paid for coverage (analysis by a professional script reader) of the script and was very pleased when it came back with a "recommend." He decided it was time to send the script out in the hopes of getting an agent or finding a producer who would want to shepherd his project.

Situation 1: Friend of a Friend

Elliot asked Peter, a talented writer in his writer's group, to read his script. Then they met to discuss it. In their meeting, Peter agreed to forward it to Tina, a friend of his who is an assistant to a bigwig at a production company. Elliot sends the following e-mail:

> Peter,
>   Thanks so much for forwarding *The Last All-Nighter* to your friend Tina. I really appreciate your help and I'm going to follow up with her next week.[1] The beers are on me the next time we hang out. Many thanks.
>   Best,
>   Elliot

In a week, Elliot hasn't heard from Tina. Because he hasn't met her before, he decides to follow up initially by phone:

UNDER THE SURFACE

[1] *This tells Peter that he doesn't need to do anything else. Elliot will follow up with Tina and carry the ball from here.*

Tina: Good afternoon, Ms. Cohen's office, this is Tina.

Elliot: Hi, Tina, this is Elliot Forrester. I'm a friend of Peter Cline.

Tina: Oh, yeah, he's great.

Elliot: Do you have a minute to chat?

Tina: Yeah, quickly.

Elliot: I believe that Peter gave you a copy of my script *The Last All-Nighter* recently and I just wanted to make sure you had received it.

Tina: Hang on a sec.

Elliot: Sure.

Tina: Yeah, I have it. What's it about again?[1]

Elliot: It's a thriller about two teen rivals who join forces to solve a murder. During the annual camp treasure hunt, the two leads discover the dead body of the camp director where the treasure should be and realize someone's altered the hunt—but it's up to them to discover who and why.

Tina: Hmm. That sounds pretty good. How old are the leads supposed to be?

Elliot: Seventeen or eighteen. It's set the summer before their senior year in high school.

Tina: This might be something MTV would be interested in. I'll read it this weekend and get back to you.

Elliot: Thanks so much. I look forward to hearing what you think.

Tina: No problem. Bye.

Elliot decides to e-mail Tina on the following Tuesday to check in.

Hi Tina,

I hope you had a good weekend. I just wanted to send you a quick note to check in and see if you had a chance to read *The*

UNDER THE SURFACE

[1] *This is the crucial moment. To get Tina interested, Elliot needs to be ready to deliver a great trailer right here.*

Last All-Nighter. Peter said that you have great taste in material and I look forward to hearing your thoughts.

Best,
Elliot

Elliot—

Things have gotten really busy. I haven't had a chance, but I will read it.

T.

Thanks so much, Tina. I really appreciate it. When would you like me to follow up with you?

Elliot

Next Mon.

T.

The following Monday, Elliot calls Tina.

Tina: Ms. Cohen's office. This is Tina.
Elliot: Hi, Tina, this is Elliot Forrester.
Tina: Oh, hi. I read your script last night and it's good.
Elliot: Thanks so much. Do you have any feedback?
Tina: I do, actually. I thought the premise was good, but it took too long to get into the main story. I would cut five pages from the beginning so we're at the hunt much more quickly. I thought the secondary characters that were adults were great—lots of personality and intrigue. The campers, though, started to blend together and I would take another look at them. Also, I don't

know if you've read it, but there's a movie that Universal is developing that is also a treasure hunt movie. You should keep your eye on it. It's different, but there are some elements that are similar.

Elliot: That's really helpful. What would you recommend I do next?

Tina: When you make these changes, send it to me again. I'll look at it again and I'll forward it to my boss, who usually likes teen thrillers.

Elliot: Okay. That sounds good. I really appreciate you taking the time to read it. I'll get back to you soon.

Tina: Okay.

Elliot: Bye.

Commentary on Situation I

Even though Elliot would like to eventually meet with Ms. Cohen, he relates to Tina as if she's the high-level buyer, and treats her respectfully and professionally. Also, he didn't get defensive when receiving Tina's notes.

Many screenwriters, like most sellers who are passionate about a project of any kind, tend to get defensive when their work is critiqued. To them, either they get the positive feedback they want or they don't want to hear it. This is really too bad. Professionals get notes (and take their advice) all the time. It's just part of the business.

Elliot decides that he's going to do a rewrite for Tina because it's a good opportunity to get his script to Ms. Cohen. He could jump right in, but before he does all that work, he wants to get some more feedback.

This is a major win. If you have asked someone to read a screenplay, business plan, venture capital proposal, or something else, getting helpful notes and a conditional "if you redo it, I'll look at it again" is a big success.

Situation 2: A Good Person to Know

Elliot runs into his neighbor James at the coffee shop down the street from his apartment. From previous conversations with him, Elliot knows that James works in special effects and has relationships with some big-time producers. Elliot asks James if he would be willing to take a look at his script. James agrees and asks if Elliot would read a TV script he's working on.

> James,
>
> It was great to see you at The Beehive this afternoon. As we discussed, here's a copy of *The Last All-Nighter*. I'm open to any suggestions you have, and feel free to send me your pilot whenever you're ready.
>
> Thanks so much,
> Elliot
>
> Elliot—
>
> Good work, man. I liked the chase in the woods and the dialogue was pretty tight. I think you should make one of the main characters a girl and then you can make it sexier. They can start falling for each other as they solve the crime and then they can bang it out in Act III. Get some hot TV actress to play the lead and it could be great.
>
> Peace.
> James

Elliot realizes that he and James have different ideas about where to take the story, so he decides not to work with him on this project.

James,

Thanks so much for taking time out of your weekend to read my script. I really appreciate your feedback and I'll keep your ideas in mind when I'm working on the next draft. I hope to see you again soon.

Best,
Elliot

Commentary on Situation 2

Most people will get especially defensive when they receive unhelpful notes because they feel insulted that the other person didn't get it. Instead, they'll argue for their original vision. This doesn't help.

Whenever you get feedback, keep the quality of the work foremost in your mind. Ego comes second. If notes are helpful, take them. If not, leave them. If you're not sure, file them away and see how they fit into the rest of the feedback you're getting.

If you figure out that someone's notes aren't so helpful, thank that person for his or her time and politely stop pursuing feedback from that person. This way, you preserve your relationship but you don't waste your energy.

Situation 3: The Long-Shot VIP

At a party, Elliot meets Michelle, a well-known screenwriter.

Elliot types a letter on his personal letterhead and sends it in a fancy envelope—he's hoping to break through to the top of the stack.

Hi Michelle,

I saw your film *Unreal* and really enjoyed it—I was completely stunned by the ending. I thought it was so well done; kudos to you and your team. Just to jog your memory about who I am, we met at Scott's barbeque in July. I'm the tall guy with wild sideburns and we talked about Miles Davis.

I really admire your writing and I wondered if you would be willing to read some or all of my latest script. I know that you are incredibly busy, but if you would be open to reading the script, I would love any suggestions or feedback that you have.

The Last All-Nighter is a thriller about two teen rivals who join forces to solve a murder. It's the last week of August, and during the annual Camp Appaloosa treasure hunt, Joe (the brainy athlete) and Aaron (the rugged outdoorsman) discover the dead body of the camp director where the treasure should be. Someone's altered the hunt—but who, and why?

I will call your office on Monday to see if you would like me to send in the script. Thanks so much for your consideration.

Best,
Elliot

Elliot calls on Monday afternoon.

Jennifer: Studio 50. This is Jennifer.
Elliot: Hi, Jennifer. This is Elliot Forrester calling for Michelle.
Jennifer: May I ask what this is regarding?
Elliot: I met Michelle at a barbeque a couple weeks ago[1] and I sent her a note last week. I'm calling to follow up.
Jennifer: Michelle's in a meeting right now. Can I take a message?
Elliot: Sure. Elliot Forrester. 310-555-1498. Would it be possible to see if she received the letter?[2]

UNDER THE SURFACE

[1] When following up, it's good to reference the original event.
[2] Elliot reinforces his message. He just wants to know if she received his letter—he doesn't need to explain any more than that.

Jennifer: I don't see it, but I'll check and call you back.

Elliot: Okay, thanks.

Jennifer: Bye.

Elliot doesn't hear back from Michelle or Jennifer. He waits a week and decides to call back.

Jennifer: Studio 50. This is Jennifer.

Elliot: Hi, Jennifer. This is Elliot Forrester. I'm hoping you can help me. Do you have a minute?

Jennifer: Mm-hmm.

Elliot: We spoke briefly last week. I met Michelle at a barbeque a few weeks ago and sent her a letter after we met. I just wanted to confirm that she received it.

Jennifer: Oh. What's your last name again?

Elliot: Forrester.

Jennifer: No, we never received it.

Elliot: Okay, I'll send another copy today. If I sent the letter to your attention, would that help?

Jennifer: Michelle gets a lot of mail and it won't help if you send it to me.

Elliot: I really appreciate your help, Jennifer. Would it be okay if I called you in a couple days to make sure you received it?

Jennifer: Sure.

Elliot: Bye.

Jennifer: Bye.

Three days later, Elliot calls again.

Jennifer: Studio 50. This is Jennifer.

Elliot: Hi, Jennifer. This is Elliot Forrester checking to see if you received my letter to Michelle.

Jennifer: Yes, we did.

Elliot: And were you able to give it to Michelle?

Jennifer: Yes, it's on her desk. I'll let you know if I hear anything.
Elliot: Great, thanks so much, Jennifer.
Jennifer: No problem. Bye.
Elliot: Bye.

He waits another week and doesn't hear anything. He decides to e-mail Jennifer since she seemed to have the most information.

> Dear Jennifer,
>
> Thanks so much for getting my letter to Michelle last week. I wanted to follow up with you and see if it would be possible for me to send you a copy of my script *The Last All-Nighter*.
>
> Thanks,
> Elliot

Then Elliot receives the following e-mail:

> Dear Mr. Forrester,
>
> Thank you for your correspondence. We're sorry, but we can't accept unsolicited submissions. We wish you the best of luck placing your projects elsewhere.
>
> Sincerely,
> Jennifer

Commentary on Situation 3

So it didn't work out. *C'est la vie.* However, Elliot has acted like a professional, and if he should run into Michelle or Jennifer down the road, he hasn't incurred any ill will.

Situation 4: The VIP Mentor

Elliot calls Ryan, who was his advisor in college and is a successful writer/director. He tells him about the script and asks Ryan to read it. Ryan agrees. Elliot attaches a note to the script:

> Dear Ryan,
>
> It was great to catch up with you and hear about your latest adventures.
>
> As I mentioned on the phone this morning, I've recently completed *The Last All-Nighter* and I would love to get your feedback. I know you are very busy, so please read this at your convenience. My goal is for this script to be good enough to attract a producer or an agent.
>
> I really appreciate your help.
>
> Best,
> Elliot

A month later, Elliot decides to e-mail Ryan.

> Hi Ryan,
>
> I hope the casting sessions for *Pop Culture* are going well.
>
> I wanted to share some good news. I just found out that my script *The Last All-Nighter* is a semifinalist for the Nicholl Fellowship. I'm definitely interested in your feedback on the script whenever you have a chance.
>
> Warmest regards,
> Elliot

He gets an e-mail back:

Congrats, dude! I should be able to get to it soon.
Ryan

Two weeks go by and Elliot doesn't want to be pushy, but he wants to contact Ryan again. He could e-mail him asking him if he's read the script, but Elliot is pretty sure that if Ryan did read it, he would call him. Elliot reads a great interview with Clint Eastwood and he thinks that Ryan would enjoy it too. This is the "indirect" kind of follow-up. Elliot clips out the article and handwrites the following note:

Ryan,

I read this article and it reminded me of your great lecture years ago about Westerns. I thought you'd enjoy this interview.

Talk to you soon,
Elliot

A week later, Elliot receives a call from Ryan. Ryan is enthusiastic about the script and thinks it will have broad commercial appeal. He offers to send it to his agent, Susan, to see if she would be interested. Elliot writes the following handwritten thank-you note:

Dear Ryan,

I really appreciate you recommending me to Susan. I was so happy to get your call and thrilled to hear that you liked the script. You've been a real mentor to me and someone I have looked up to for a long time, so it really means a lot that you see potential in this script. I will follow up with Susan next week, and I just wanted to send you a note to say thanks. Thanks!

Warmest regards,
Elliot

The following Monday morning, Elliot receives a call from Susan's assistant.

Elliot: Hello, this is Elliot.

Susan's assistant: Hi, Elliot, I have Susan from The Red Agency on the line for you.

Elliot: Okay.

Susan's assistant: Can you hold for a minute?

Elliot: Sure.

Susan: Elliot. Nice to meet you. Ryan sent me your script and told me that you were one of his favorite students. He said you were the best writer in his class.

Elliot: Well, that's really nice. Thanks.

Susan: So, enough of the pleasantries. He rarely recommends anything, so even though I'm swamped, I took the time to flip through it this morning, and your writing is good. Very good.

Elliot: Wow, thanks, thanks so much.

Susan: I've given your script to one of my colleagues named Matt. He's a young agent here and he's a real star. I've told him to get together with you this week. You don't have an agent, do you?

Elliot: No, I don't.

Susan: Good. Matt will contact you this week.

Elliot: Okay, thanks.

One minute later, the phone rings.

Elliot: Hello.

Matt: Hi, Elliot. This is Matt from the Red Agency. Susan recommended that I call you.

Elliot: That was fast.

Matt: We don't screw around over here. When we identify talent, we go after it. That's why we have the best client list in the business. Elliot, here's what's going to happen. You're going to come in tomorrow and meet with me. We'll talk about your projects, what you want to do, and how we can make that happen.

Elliot: Okay.

Matt: Ten o'clock. You know where we are, right?

Elliot: Yes, I think so.

Matt: Allyson, pick up and give Elliot directions. She's the best; she'll give you everything you need to know. Look forward to seeing you tomorrow, Elliot.

Elliot: See you tomorrow.

Elliot e-mails Ryan to let him know that he connected with Susan.

> Ryan,
>
> I just wanted to let you know that Susan called me this morning. She connected me with Matt, one of the agents who works with her, and we're meeting tomorrow morning at ten. Thanks again for all your help.
>
> Elliot

The next morning, Elliot meets with Matt, who is full of enthusiasm and uses his BlackBerry throughout the meeting. Matt says that he doesn't usually like teen movies, but *The Last All-Nighter* kept him interested. He knows that Sony and Universal are looking for teen-skewing material. Matt offers to hip-pocket[1] Elliot and send out his script to a couple producers he knows as a test. After the meeting, Elliot writes Matt an e-mail:

UNDER THE SURFACE

[1] *Hip-pocketing means that Matt will work with Elliot on a try-out basis, but Elliot isn't an official client. If someone wants to buy the script, then Matt will become Elliot's agent.*

Dear Matt,

Thanks so much for reading *The Last All-Nighter* and meeting with me this morning. I really appreciate you sending the script to the producers you feel would be a good fit.

Have a great time in Maui and I look forward to talking to you again soon.

Best,
Elliot

He's also going to send a note to Susan since she is the real power-house of the company and it can't hurt to be polite and have his name in front of her one more time.

Dear Susan,

Thanks so much for reading my script *The Last All-Nighter* and forwarding it to Matt. I wanted to let you know that I met with Matt yesterday and he's really impressive. I really appreciate your time and the connection.

Sincerely,
Elliot

Commentary on Situation 4

Success!

What happens now is . . . more of the same. As his script gets more exposure and Elliot meets with more people, he'll continue to follow up with all of them. If his script is purchased, he still keeps following up with the relevant people. No one will take more interest in Elliot's career than Elliot—that makes it his job to stay on top of the process.

Conclusion

Whatever you create, you've got to get it to the right people. This is a process of keeping in touch, getting past the gatekeepers, making requests, and following up. It takes a lot of time and energy. You may be wondering, "Where am I going to find that time?"

Well, I'll tell you. The secret to finding more time is to learn how to protect the time you have. It's time to take a page out of the buyer's playbook. In the next chapter, we'll talk about how to say no.

CHAPTER 35

How to Say No

When I was an assistant, it wasn't uncommon for me to be called in the middle of the night to answer questions, track down someone, or gather some information. Once I even drove a script to a strip club at 3 A.M. I was on my way home when I thought, "You know, maybe I should have let that call go to voice mail."

On one hand, this kind of dedication to my job is part of what helped me get ahead. On the other hand, I could have progressed even more quickly if I'd known how to say no. I didn't learn the value of no until I became an executive, and even then it was hard for me.

Over time, I've learned that in business, the ability to say no is the essential tool that protects you so that you can do your job and get the credit you deserve.

Are You Paying the Price of Nice?

- Do you find yourself doing the work of others?
- Are other people at your level constantly delegating work to you?

- Do you find yourself taking notes in meetings, even if it isn't your responsibility?
- Do you accept more grunt work assignments than other people?

If you answer yes to even a couple of these questions, you are probably the kind of person who cares about other people, works hard, and is a team player. But you're also at a major disadvantage when it comes to getting promoted and being more successful. You're paying the price of nice:

- You have less time for your own work.
- You spend your time on projects that have a lower chance of success.
- Your colleagues and superiors have less respect for you than they should.

The key lesson here is this: *Don't confuse being liked with being respected.* Being agreeable may endear you to your colleagues and superiors—but it won't make them respect you. You can't earn respect at work until you know what your boundaries are and how to protect them. With boundaries and respect come better assignments and more time to do them well.

Ten Ways to Say No

1. *Take a time-out.* If you're not sure how to say no, one of the easiest things you can do is postpone the decision. Here are a few classic time-buying responses that you can use in almost any situation:

    "I'm sorry, but this is not a good time to talk about this. Can we set a time to speak this afternoon?"

    "I need to check my calendar and I'll get back to you tomorrow."

"I need to consult my business partner."

"Let me make a phone call to check something out first."

And, in case of emergency, "Hang on one sec—I'll be right
back."

2. *Have a "policy."* This is an option that diminishes the feeling
that you are personally rejecting the person making the request.
For whatever reason, it's harder to argue against a policy. For
example:

> "I'm sorry I won't be able to attend the fund-raiser. It's our
> policy to have dinner together as a family every Sunday
> night."

> "I have a policy against loaning money to co-workers."

3. *Just say no.* The most powerful and effective nos are the least
complicated. Say no politely and leave it at that. Detailed explanations tend to be seen as fictional even if they're not. Keep
your explanations to a minimum:

> "No, thanks."

> "No, I just don't have time."

> "No, it's not my thing."

> "Unfortunately, I can't make it."

4. *Broaden your definition of what it means to "have plans."* Your plans
could be to get a massage, to walk your dog, or to lie on the
couch watching reruns of *The Wire*. Free time is important—
don't be afraid to claim yours. Give yourself permission to
make plans with yourself, put them in your calendar, and
keep them.

5. *Screen your calls.* Don't answer the phone when it rings. Caller
ID is a great invention for helping you say no. Unless you need
to speak with the caller, let the person leave a message. Once
you listen to it, you can decide how and when to respond. Plus,
if you're not there, often the caller will try someone else.

6. *Don't respond to off-hours e-mails.* The more you respond to e-mails
during off hours, the more people will expect a quick response.

7. *Use voice mail or e-mail to say no.* If you feel that if you say no in person someone may be able to convince you otherwise, use voice mail or write a note.

8. *Cite a higher authority.* If someone tries to give his work to you and if you can't say no directly for some reason, make him get permission from your boss. Say, "I have to finish this assignment for _____ first. Run it by her and if she wants me to handle it, I'll be happy to take care of it for you."

9. *Say that you're busy.* Especially when it comes to social plans, the best excuse is that you're busy with work:

   "I'd like to, I'm just not available."

   "I can't, I'm just so under the gun right now."

   "Unfortunately, I'm swamped. Another time?"

   "I've got a major deadline; I just can't."

   "I have plans."

   "I have an appointment I can't break."

   "I have a previous engagement."

10. *When you say no, don't use upturn phrasing.* This is where your voice lifts up at the end of the word. This gives the impression that your no can be negotiated. Instead, use "downturn phrasing," where your voice goes down in tone at the end of the word. This communicates no in a much firmer way.

Case Study: Liz

Liz has been an excellent salesperson at Tall People Furniture, but she makes some classic mistakes. She often works nonstop without a break. She backs down easily when she has a new idea (or doesn't present it at all). Plus, she's always handling small tasks for the other salespeople. It grates on her, but she's the youngest member of the team and they seem to expect her to do it.

In two weeks, Liz will have her annual review with her boss, George. She knows that there's a management position opening up soon. Liz wants to use her annual review to let him know that she wants to be considered.

Liz knows that she's the underdog candidate for three main reasons: she has the least amount of seniority, she's the youngest, and she's a woman. However, Liz knows the rest of her sales colleagues and she believes that out of all of them, she's the best-qualified person for the job. Now she just has to get George to believe it.

For the next two weeks, she's going to spend any additional time she can find doing research and preparing her presentation. This means that she isn't going to be able to do all the favors and additional work that she's done in the past. Standing up for herself in the office is long overdue, but with the deadline looming, Liz decides to take a stand. Here are some of the requests she gets in the two weeks before her big meeting and how she handles them.

Liz Protects Her Boundaries

1. *Her co-worker Gail stops by her desk on the way to the kitchen.*

Gail: Hi, Liz, could you help me with my PowerPoint presentation? Your presentations always look amazing[1] and mine look like they were designed by a dog. Can you help me figure it out?

Liz: Thanks for the compliment. I'm in the midst of a project right now and I'm not able to help. I know it can be time-consuming to create a PowerPoint presentation, but you can do it.

Gail: But yours always look so much nicer. Are you sure you can't spend ten minutes showing me how to choose colors and animate the graphics?

Liz: I wish I could, but I'm in the midst of a project right now and I'm not able to help.[2]

UNDER THE SURFACE

[1] *Beware of the trap of flattery. Your co-worker knows how to engage your interest. Your ego may want to do it, but this isn't a good use of your time.*

[2] *If they keep pushing, repeat what you've said again in a calm tone of voice.*

Gail: Okay, well, I guess I could ask Justin to show me.

Liz: That's a good idea.

2. Liz's co-worker Nancy instant-messages Liz with a request.

Nancy: Will you make the delivery to Mrs. Duffell since it's on your way?

Liz: No, I'm going in the other direction today.[1]

3. Liz gets home from a long day at work. Her best friend, Melissa, calls.

Melissa: Will you go to this party on Saturday afternoon with me?

Liz: No, but thanks for inviting me.[2]

Melissa: But I have to go and I don't want to go alone.[3]

Liz: I'm sorry, I'm just so busy.[4]

Melissa: That's a bummer.

4. One of Liz's best customers calls to invite her to a basketball game. However, Liz wants to have her weekend to completely relax.

Mrs. Gutstein: Hi, Liz.

Liz: How are you, Mrs. Gutstein?

UNDER THE SURFACE

[1] Yes, she could do it, but it won't help her accomplish what she needs to do. Running errands for other people is a trap. Even if it's on the way, if anything goes awry (whether it's your fault or not), you're likely to be seen as responsible.

[2] Simple and decisive answers are best.

[3] This is a subtle trap. If Liz says anything like, "Sure you can go alone, you'll be fine," then this gives Melissa the chance to explain more about why she's so desperate for company—and it may get harder for Liz to say no. Therefore, always say no on your terms. Your no only has to do with you. This is why the famous breakup line is, "It's not you, it's me." It makes the breakup non-negotiable.

[4] If they start to pry and want to know more, keep it simple. For example, if Melissa asks, "What do you have to do?" Liz can reply, "I'm just swamped with work. Perhaps another time."

Mrs. Gutstein: Very well, thanks. I just found out we have two extra tickets to the basketball game this weekend and I wanted to give them to you since you've been so helpful.

Liz: Wow, that is really thoughtful of you, Mrs. Gutstein. I really appreciate you thinking of me. Unfortunately, I already have a commitment this weekend, so I won't be able to attend.

Mrs. Gutstein: Well, that's too bad. I'll catch you the next time.

Liz: Thanks so much.

5. Liz's boss, George, asks for a favor that is outside of Liz's duties.

George: Liz, sometime today, could you organize the supply closet?

Liz: Hmm. How about if you make it a group project and then everyone will know where the supplies are in the future?

George: Sure, that makes sense. Would you like to be in charge?

Liz: I appreciate being asked,[1] but I'm swamped right now. How about if you assign different parts of the closet to each person on the sales team? Then we can each have a small section that we're in charge of keeping stocked and organized.

George: I like that idea. I'll go check it out now.

Liz: Sure thing.

6. George asks Liz to do a more appropriate task, but one that would distract her.

George: Liz, I just found out that Sam is behind on reconciling the monthly receipts. Since you used to do it and I know you're incredibly fast at it, could you work with him today so it's finished in time?

Liz: You're right. I do know how to reconcile receipts from doing that job previously. However, I have two projects that I'm work-

UNDER THE SURFACE

[1] Acknowledge the request and be polite.

ing on right now. I'm researching and updating the Greene account since we're meeting with them tomorrow morning. Once
I finish that, I'm going to start editing the marketing materials
you gave me on Monday. Which task is more of a priority for
you—reconciling the receipts or having your marketing materials up-to-date?[1]

George: Well, all of those are important. Hmm. You'd better keep
working on your projects and I'll find someone else to help
Sam with the receipts. You know, Jordan could probably help
him. Keep going and I'll see you tomorrow at the meeting.

Small Steps, Big Changes

You know that great feeling when you clean out a closet and donate or
throw away a whole bunch of stuff? Suddenly, it's so much easier to
find the things you need and there is enough space to easily access
what you have. Plus, there's space available for what's new.

The same benefit applies when you learn to say no to the people,
activities, and requests that are cluttering up your life. You have more
time for the people and activities to which you want to say yes.

---

[1] *The mark of a true pro. If you're getting piled on, lay out the priorities and let
your supervisor make the decision.*

Part VI

■

Troubleshooting

L et me begin this section with an adaptation of Murphy's Law:
If you expect a meeting to sail smoothly through all five stages, that will not happen.

Conversely, if you expect a meeting to get derailed in one way or another, you're much more likely to be able to put it back on track. That's what this section is all about. I'll give you specific advice on how to handle the common difficulties we all have with other people and events that are out of our control, like:

- When your meeting is interrupted repeatedly
- When the buyer gives you a hard time
- When your partner doesn't hold up his or her end of the deal
- When things just don't go your way

In the next chapter, we'll talk about how to react when your meeting gets knocked off course by an interruption, mistake, or catastrophe.

CHAPTER 36

Interruptions, Mistakes, and Catastrophes

E very meeting can be expected to have all sorts of imperfections. The secret to handling these imperfections is to (1) expect them and (2) view them as opportunities.

Interruptions

Interruptions are opportunities to show that you respect the buyer.

When the buyer's phone rings, his assistant enters the room, or another type of interruption occurs, this is not a personal slight. This reflects the simple reality that anything that is a speculative project is a lower priority than a project that is actually in progress. If you act offended, the buyer will see that you don't "get it."

In Hollywood, interruptions can range from the mundane to the bizarre. On the mundane side, frequently I would be interrupted by phone calls from my boss or from producers on the set who needed me to handle a production problem. On the bizarre side, every few weeks I'd have a script delivered in a spectacular fashion—wrapped around a machete (a jungle adventure), put inside a cage of white lab rats (a medical thriller), or wrapped in red foil like a box of Valentine chocolates (a romantic comedy).

Professionals understand that interruptions happen, and they use the following strategy:

1. *Give the buyer some space.* Stay in the room and remove your attention from the buyer if that's appropriate. You can busy yourself with your waiting room materials.
2. *If appropriate, give the buyer some privacy.* Offer to step outside the room or even to come back another time.
3. *Provide a summary.* When the interruption is over, recap what's happened so far. An effective summary reinforces your message and demonstrates your competence.

Now, if you've scheduled thirty minutes for a meeting and you get interrupted after twenty-five minutes, that's probably not an interruption. It's likely to be an "interruption." It's typical for an executive to have a secret signal with his assistant. For example, my colleague would buzz his assistant and ask him to "order sandwiches for lunch." That meant to come in and interrupt the meeting in five minutes. This is another reason to try to schedule a little more time for the meeting than you think you need and to end it with time to spare.

Mistakes

Mistakes are opportunities to show that you have poise.

Mistakes include when you lose your place, stumble over your words, fumble with the papers in your briefcase, or stick your foot in your mouth while answering a question. It's normal; we all do it. All you have to do is acknowledge it, if needed, and keep going.

One time, a writer was in my office meeting about a project we were working on together. While he was pitching me the story, he was drinking orange soda. Just as it got to the point where he revealed who the killer was, instead of the character's name, from the depths of his stomach came a dramatic burp. We looked at each other for a moment. Then he said, "Apparently, I had tuna for lunch." We laughed, he blushed, and then he kept right on going.

Catastrophes

Catastrophes are opportunities to show that you can handle anything.

Catastrophes are rare, but they do happen. One time, I was in a meeting with a director that was going really well . . . until his pitch was interrupted by a magnitude 6.7 earthquake.

Luckily, we were in the brand-new MGM Tower, which was built with all sorts of anti-quake safety mechanisms. Basically, the whole building was built on rollers. Even though my office was on the fifteenth floor, we were perfectly safe. Unfortunately, for the next twenty minutes we were oscillating from side to side like a gigantic tuning fork.

It's hard to get back on track in a situation like that. The best you can do is shift gears. While the building continued to sway, he took the opportunity to build rapport and we talked about our shared interests in yoga. When we eventually resumed our meeting, I was interested to hear the rest of his pitch.

Interruptions are common, mistakes are inevitable, and catastrophes will happen from time to time. But don't let anything throw you off your game. Expect these opportunities and use them. Distinguish yourself by adapting to whatever is happening in the moment. And if you have tuna for lunch, skip the orange soda.

CHAPTER 37

Bad Buyers

Most buyers are bad buyers. They are unprepared and distracted. They have trouble remembering basic aspects of your presentation. They ask you off-topic questions and want to talk more about themselves than the business at hand.

You should expect these behaviors and whenever possible give them the benefit of the doubt. After all, even a bad buyer is still a buyer. As long as she doesn't cross the line, it's best to roll with the changes and do your best to keep the meeting on track.

Here are eleven of the most common situations and suggestions for how to handle them.

1. If it is crucially important that the buyer review your materials prior to the meeting:
- Call the day before and say, "I just wanted to confirm that you received the materials last week. Will you have a chance to look at them before we meet?"
- In the actual meeting, take the time to build rapport, and when you start to get down to business, ask, "Have you had a chance to look at the materials?"
- If the buyer hasn't, ask, "Would you prefer that I come back

some other time?" Often, the buyer will say, "No, don't leave. Give me five minutes and I'll read it right now." That's no problem for you—you've got your waiting room materials ready.

2. If the buyer appears to be distracted:

If the buyer is checking her e-mail every few minutes, reading her snail mail, or dealing with other tasks, ask, "Would you like a couple of minutes to take care of what you're working on?" You can also try, "Is now still a good time? We can reschedule if you like." Keep your tone warm and polite—if any irritation creeps into your voice, it's a deal breaker.

3. If the buyer wants to talk a lot about subjects that are unrelated to your proposal:

After engaging with her for a few minutes, you can say, "_____ is so interesting. . . . Just to make sure we stay within your schedule, perhaps we could discuss . . ."

4. If the buyer seems uninterested:

If you don't have the buyer's attention, it's time to shift gears. Suppose you're midway through your pitch and the buyer starts looking around the room, checking her watch, tapping her foot, shifting around in her seat, and so on. What do you do?

The easiest way to get the buyer's attention is to pause, then ask a question. If you're at a point in your presentation where it's hard to come up with a relevant informational question, you can always say, "What questions do you have at this point?" It can also help to change your body position (try leaning forward) and modulate your voice.

If you've built enough rapport, you may also be able to get away with something like, "Okay . . . where did I lose you?" Regardless, you can't continue the presentation until you have the buyer's attention.

If she doesn't seem interested, do not soldier on and try to complete the meeting with your dignity intact. This is an important information-gathering opportunity and you don't want to miss it. You took the trouble to get into this room and deliver a pitch you think the buyer wants to hear. If she isn't interested, you want to find out why.

5. If the buyer contributes a bad idea:

Strange as it may seem, a bad idea is usually good news. It means the buyer is considering buying the product, service, or idea and is attempting to make it better.

Often the buyer has identified a valid problem but may not have the ideal solution. Your goal is to uncover the reason or observation behind their idea. Try saying, "I like where you are going with that. What's the specific issue you're trying to solve?"

6. If the buyer contributes an idea so bad that it makes you want to scream:

There are times when the buyer just wants to assert himself, hear himself talk, or otherwise insert his ideas into your work. In Hollywood, this happens all the time and is the bane of most writers' existences.

When I was a junior exec, one of my supervisors was not exceptionally savvy when it came to casting. Let's just say that he was very accomplished in a traditional business and was brought to my company with the idea that he could make the film division more profitable.

Unfortunately, while this person had business acumen, he was not blessed with artistic taste. For example, he believed that Carmen Electra was the best actress in the world and he would suggest her for every movie—whether it was a comedy, drama, period piece, or war epic.

Not to slight Ms. Electra—there are genres that suit her. However, we would be in a meeting with a director such as Martin Scorsese, discussing a dramatic project such as *The Queen*, and this supervisor would say, "I have a great idea. How about if the role of Queen Elizabeth is played by Carmen Electra?"

The producers and the director would get wide-eyed, and I would jump in and say, "Interesting idea. I'll put her on the list and we'll discuss it."

That's basically the technique. The buyer's excitement is a good thing and you don't want to dampen it. Therefore, in response to a scream-worthy idea, say something like, "I hadn't thought of that. I'll consider it."

7. *If the buyer contributes a whole bunch of bad ideas:*

Find at least one good element and focus on that. You must find at least one thing to compliment, such as "I like the part about ____." Then, if you can, reorient the conversation to the issue the buyer is trying to solve.

8. *If the buyer is adamant about a truly terrible idea:*

A writer came in and told me this story: He was brought into a studio meeting to discuss a rewrite of a generic romantic comedy—you know, guy loses girl, wants to get her back, and all that. This writer had read the original script and brought in some ideas to pitch, but before he got to them the development exec said, "Okay, we want to hear your ideas. But here's what we'd like you to do. Keep everything the same, but make the guy into a chimp."

If this happens, take notes, and follow the meeting through to the conclusion. Once you're home and can consider your options, either write the lead part for a chimp or politely decline the assignment.

9. *If the buyer contributes a really good idea:*

When this happens, you're in luck. If you can actually incorporate a buyer's idea into your project, that buyer will be much more invested in seeing it come to fruition.

Therefore, acknowledge his contribution. Say, "That's a really great idea. What I like especially is ____." Be specific with your compliments.

10. *If the buyer's questions verge on antagonistic:*

Tough questions are to be expected. It's normal for the buyer to play devil's advocate. However, if it seems as though the buyer is trying to break you down or get under your skin, be careful. There is a line, and if he crosses it, you need to be prepared to call him on that. Prior to that point, avoid addressing the antagonism of his tone.

It's hard to do, I know, but keep your cool. Focus on answering the content of the buyer's questions. It's possible that this is a test of some sort. It's also possible that the buyer is a jerk. But unless the buyer crosses the line, it's not to your benefit to take an adversarial position.

11. If the buyer crosses the line:

Basically, we're talking about racism, homophobia, anti-Semitism, violent threats, or sexual impropriety. These circumstances are rare, but they do happen.

Now, we've all got different comfort zones and we're going to have different lines. But when the buyer crosses *your* line, my advice is to respond promptly and directly. If you don't nip this behavior in the bud, it will continue and probably get worse.

However, after you let the buyer know that he's crossed the line, it's possible that he will make amends and conduct himself properly.

Therefore, the way you handle yourself here requires you to be firm in a way that would allow the buyer to recover. So after the buyer crosses the line you might say, "Wow. I'm really surprised to hear you say something like that. That's not okay with me."

If the buyer apologizes, you can proceed with the meeting. If not, make your exit. Then, regardless of what has happened, document everything in writing and save whatever hard evidence you've got. You don't know when you might need some proof that the buyer was the one who conducted himself inappropriately in the room.

Finally, with the exception of those buyers who cross the line, remember that buyers are people, too. Many are overworked and under a great deal of pressure. Just like you, sometimes they have bad days, brain freezes, and moments of weakness. So if you find yourself in the room and the buyer is being uncooperative, don't get frustrated or take it personally. Stay focused and find a way to connect on a personal level. A buyer who likes you is rarely a bad buyer.

CHAPTER 38

Partner Hijinks

Tolstoy wrote, "Happy families are all alike. Unhappy families are each unhappy in their own way." Business partnerships are the same. While each bad partnership has a unique story of "why it didn't work," good partnerships have many aspects in common.

Over the years, I've met with a lot of writing and producing partners and I've got a sense for what works and what doesn't. In general, the way to create and maintain a solid partnership (and avoid hijinks) is to set yourself up to win in the first place.

- Choose a partner who shares your goals and complements your skills.
- Negotiate all the terms of your partnership in the beginning.
- Always meet before the meeting.

Choose Partners Wisely

Partnerships last when the whole is greater than the sum of the parts. If you and your partner have similar skills and perspectives, you may not be adding very much to each other's work. You're supplementing each other, but what you want is to *complement* each other.

When it comes to choosing a business partner, provided that you have similar goals and values, it's to your advantage if each of you has different areas of expertise and capabilities. This way, you each balance the other person's weaknesses with strengths.

Negotiate Before Anything Is at Stake

It's sad, but like most romantic relationships, most business partnerships end. Proceed with that in mind.

So often I hear, "I was working on a project and my partner flaked." "I was starting a business with two other guys and then we just stopped getting along." "I designed this invention with a friend and I want to keep pursuing it and she doesn't."

In the excitement of starting a new venture or project, it's natural to focus on the ideal outcomes. We want to be optimistic. We say to ourselves, "We're going to work on this together and then we'll sell it for a lot of money and we'll both retire early." It's the romantic equivalent of starting to date someone and in the flush of romance thinking, "We'll get married, have kids, and live happily ever after."

In business partnerships, a healthy dose of reality will help both parties in the long run. A big wake-up call for me (and the reason I chose to go it alone) was when I met with my attorney to discuss opening my business with a financing partner. My attorney asked me if my partner died, would I want to be in business with his spouse? If I died, would my half of the business immediately transfer to my partner? Would he buy my portion out? What if the business was in debt? Would my family assume the debt?

I've known a lot of people who don't negotiate terms because they are afraid of spoiling their relationship. As well, working with an attorney can be expensive. The question is whether or not you're serious. Professionals value their investment of time and energy. They choose their projects carefully and they plan for the future. While negotiating an agreement in the beginning can be uncomfortable, it is often far better than negotiating down the road when there's a lot at stake.

Status Versus Success

Often, this happens when there is a clear disparity in status between the partners. The underlying source of the problem is that the lower-status partner doesn't want to fully admit to himself that, yes, he's lower-status. He wants to believe that his partner is really treating him as an equal. Thus, he allows things to move forward without negotiating any terms. In other words, he wants to feel high-status more than he wants to actually be successful.

Mistake!

In Hollywood, it goes like this: A couple of idealistic, up-and-coming producers develop a great script but can't get it to the studio. They meet with a big-name producer, who agrees to partner with them. The big-name producer says, "We'll figure out our agreement once they want to buy it. I'll make sure you're taken care of."

The big producer makes one phone call, has one meeting, and gets an offer for $300,000. Then the big producer calls the up-and-coming producers and says, "Good news. They want it for three hundred. Here's how we're going to divide it up. My quote ("quote" is Hollywood-speak for "standard fee") is $300,000, but I'll be a good guy and give you $50,000. The best part is, you guys will have a movie in development."

The up-and-coming producers are stunned because they assumed they were all equal partners. Because there are two of them, they ask for $200,000. The producer laughs. Then they ask for $100,000. They get stonewalled. Then lawyers get involved. A few months of acrimonious negotiation ensue. Eventually the studio loses interest and the deal dies.

If you want your partnership to last, negotiate first.

Meet Before the Meeting

Pitching in tandem has an equal number of advantages and disadvantages. On one hand, you'll have your combined energy and expertise. On the other hand, the chance that someone will say something stupid doubles. Meeting before the meeting increases your synergy and decreases the chances of stumbling.

When you meet, agree on who will take the lead in what stage of the meeting and how you will handle specific situations. Here are some questions to help you get started:

- What is our main goal for the meeting?
- Do we plan on using notes or visual aids?
- Do we plan on taking notes? If so, how?
- How much "air time" does each of us need?
- Will one of us be the leader in the room?
- In what configuration should we sit?
- How will we handle our introductions?
- How about keeping to a specific schedule?
- Is it okay to interrupt? If so, how?
- Where might we need a transition?
- How will we handle it if we disagree during the meeting?
- How can we support each other?
- Who will have the last word?

Something I like to teach my clients is how to use subtle signals to communicate in the meeting. The two I like to use are "stop talking" and "save me." Come up with your own verbal or nonverbal signals to convey the messages you think are important.

Save Problems for Later

Handle your disagreements after the meeting. Disagreements are injurious in the room. After the meeting, however, discussing your disagreement will often lead to greater understanding and improvements in your presentation for next time.

Now, you may be ready to turn the page, but don't. This isn't a gimmick. The next chapter is something I wrote specifically for when you are totally stuck. The truth is that there's probably nothing wrong with reading it right now, but if you save it for when you need it, it will be even more helpful.

CHAPTER 39

Read This Chapter
When You Get Stuck

have a lot of experience helping my clients get unstuck. However, I'm not a psychologist or a life coach. The suggestions I'm about to make are not the result of training or education. They are just what has evolved from doing what works. So if what I have to say doesn't appeal to you, that's no problem. If it does, that's great. My only goal here is to be helpful by sharing with you what I know has worked for creative professionals at all levels.

Face the Facts

If you're feeling stuck, my heart goes out to you. Feeling stuck is not fun. Perhaps you keep getting uncomfortably nervous in meetings. Perhaps you can't come up with a great pitch that speaks to the buyer's needs. Perhaps you have a great pitch but can't sell your project or your idea no matter how hard you try. Perhaps the line of work you're in just doesn't interest you anymore. Let's not kid ourselves. Being stuck is tough.

To get unstuck, we must face the facts. Here they are:

1. Being stuck is normal.
2. Eventually, you will get stuck again.
3. Being stuck is a valuable opportunity.

Now, hang on a sec before you get upset. I get it that stuckness can be frustrating, maddening, even depressing. I'm not a Pollyanna telling you to turn your frown upside down. My professional and personal experience is that, embraced properly, being stuck helps us learn extraordinarily valuable information that cannot be learned any other way.

Embrace the Benefits

The benefits of being stuck are numerous and profound. Whether you are looking for inspiration with a project or some direction in your own life, when you get stuck you can just about count on achieving one or more of the following benefits:

- Getting rest that you desperately need
- Learning an important lesson
- Making a valuable course correction
- Reconnecting with your passion

Without knowing your specific situation, I can't tell you which of these outcomes you're likely to experience. And I admit that there's the possibility that you'll never climb out of the rut that you're in—it's just a very, very small possibility. The much more likely outcome is that you will benefit from your stuckness in multiple ways. Keep that in mind when things get tough.

Be Curious

No matter how successful a writer may be, confronting the blank page requires a tremendous amount of will and, for lack of a better word, faith. Even my clients who have won Oscars and Emmys still struggle with fear, nerves, and the feeling that they'll never create something worthy again. Even though they have proven that they can do it, it doesn't remove the constant fear that it was a fluke, or the last one, or the peak of what they'll ever do. They have to not only live up to the past success but exceed it. Many of them also have, you know, relationships and families and mortgages and mistakes from their past that haunt them. Everything added up can create a lot of pressure.

Thus, it's understandable that at a certain point in the writing of a script, many writers lose their way. They lose their enthusiasm for the project. They forget why they took the assignment (aside from the money). They forget why they got interested in becoming a writer in the first place. Suddenly, their script is falling apart, their career is on the line, deadlines are looming, and they've got no mojo left.

What do these writers do? First, they maintain a useful attitude by reminding themselves of the following realities:

- As bad as they feel right now, if they don't get unstuck, the eventual outcome will be a catastrophe.
- They've been stuck before and they'll be stuck again. This may feel like the end of the world, but it's not—so they try not to make things worse.
- The only reason they're stuck is because there's something they need to do that they aren't doing. If they can figure out what that is and how to do it, they'll be okay.
- They're a little curious about just what it is that they need to do.

If you can remain curious, you're on the right track. Curiosity is a great sign of health. It means your mind is open and you're courageous enough to face the unknown.

Drift Around the Mountain

As you probably know, *Zen and the Art of Motorcycle Maintenance* is a renowned bestseller. What you might not know is that the manuscript, written by Robert Pirsig, was rejected by 121 publishers before being accepted by Viking.

In the book, Pirsig describes how we get unstuck. He calls it "lateral drift." Here's how it works: Imagine that you're trying to climb a mountain to get to the top—the goal. You try to climb straight up because it's the most efficient way. Eventually, you reach a seemingly insurmountable boulder—the obstacle. Rather than beat your fists into it, you move laterally, that is, you move sideways around the mountain until you find another way to go up.

To adapt this metaphor to life in general, when you get stuck:

1. Stop doing what you are doing.
2. Do something else.
3. Wait until you experience a trickle, flash, or lightning bolt of inspiration.
4. Go back to what you were initially doing and apply what you've learned.

I've read that when Steven Spielberg gets stuck on a movie, he likes to go for long drives in his car. Julia Cameron, author of *The Artist's Way*, likes to bake cakes and pies. Some people pace, doodle, or clean house. Regardless, do something that will take your mind off where you're stuck. Eventually, your unconscious mind will unstick you—

you'll either encounter some new information, learn an important lesson, or muster the wherewithal to make a valuable course correction. Then you can go back to climbing up the mountain.

I know some people who learn what they need to know and then say, "Of course! It was so obvious! Why did I have to suffer just to learn something so simple?" The answer is that sometimes being stuck is the only way to learn. The key is to appreciate it and continue to practice getting unstuck. In this way, you get better at avoiding stuckness in the first place and you unstick yourself more easily.

Give Yourself a Break

If you've been stuck for a while, beating your head against a (hopefully) metaphorical wall, you're probably irritated and exhausted. You might need some serious rest before you can go around the wall, climb over, or break through. That's why sometimes the right thing to do when you're stuck is nothing at all.

If this appeals to you, then I encourage you to stop trying to improve yourself and your situation. Stop trying. Stop doing. Just take a nice, long break.

Doesn't that sound good? And you know what? It's good common sense. If you're stuck because you've been overextending yourself, the first step is to recuperate.

Fill up your tank before you get back in the car.

Be Willing to Ask for Help

As you know, there are people in Hollywood who do not keep it together. They venture into extremely dangerous territory—drinking until they black out, putting on a lot of weight, abusing drugs, or becoming a workaholic. And there's nothing about being self-destructive that's limited to Hollywood. Celebrities are just like everybody else in so many ways—they just have the kind of jobs that make their misfortunes newsworthy.

I'm not here to pass judgment. All I know is that sometimes some of us are not ready to get unstuck, and before things can get better, they may get worse. I wish there was a way around this, but to me this just seems like a part of real life. Sometimes we have to self-destruct in order to re-create ourselves.

However, even in a self-destructive phase, there is still a useful approach, and that is to ask for help. I can tell you that almost all of the creative professionals I know, at some point in their lives, have been in therapy. Many continue to work with therapists, life coaches, mentors, and counselors of all sorts even when they aren't stuck. I do. The results in my life have been significant.

I know that there are a lot of you who don't think that therapy is for you, and I respect that. However, when I get stuck in any aspect of my life or my business, I believe in finding the most qualified person I know who can help. I give my clients the same advice.

A Final Word

Whether personal or professional, being stuck is painful. However, most of us layer additional pain on top of the pain of stuckness because we believe that we're not supposed to be stuck. We believe that if we're stuck, something has gone wrong.

Stuckness hurts, but it's not wrong or bad. It's inevitable and useful. If you approach your stuckness in this way, it will hurt less and you will get more out of it.

And when you finally make it through to the other side, give yourself a cookie.

The Credits

I couldn't have written this book without the wisdom, patience, generosity, and guidance I received from so many people. I wish to thank the following people for their invaluable contributions:

- *For calling me and saying, "This should be a book.":* Richard Abate.
- *For making this book happen:* Roger Scholl, Chris Fortunato, Talia Krohn.
- *For spreading the word:* Elizabeth Hazelton, Meredith McGuinness.
- *For their support and encouragement:* Peter Barnett, Jenny Brill, Iris Dart, Sam Horn, Kate Lee, Al Martella, Melissa Miller.
- *For reading and responding honestly:* Karin Cohen, Steven Haworth, Nancy Miller, Leslie and Brian Olson, Tim Palmer, Gail and Jerry Taxy, and especially Jean Palmer and Ryan Dixon.
- *For everything else:* my extended family, friends, colleagues and clients. Thank you for all that you have given me.

And finally to Ben Taxy: your exceptional dedication, wit, insight, and expertise made this book possible. Working with you has been an incredible experience that I will always treasure.

Epilogue

Fangxiao

Fangxiao rebuilt her practice on her own and she's now managing more assets for more clients than ever before. Recently she ran the New York Marathon in three hours and fifty minutes, a personal best. She also met one potential new client when they nearly tripped over each other at mile thirteen. She's following up with him on Monday.

Liz

Liz got the job as the new sales director and over the next two years increased sales by 43 percent. George promoted her to vice president and gave her a hefty raise. With the extra cash she's got, Liz is thinking about starting a spin-off company devoted to making furniture for shorter people.

J. J.

J.J. started finding new clients quickly. Soon enough, he moved out of his parents' house. Shortly thereafter, he found a girlfriend. She's a Web designer who had a sick iMac and met J.J. through a referral. When he was done fixing her computer, she wrote him a check that in the memo section had her phone number and the words, "Call me."

Elliot

When Elliot's script sold for one-fifty against four, he had to ask his new agent, Matt, what that meant. Matt said, "It means you get $150,000 right now, minus commission, and if they make the movie, you get an additional $250,000, minus commission. Best of all, I'm your agent." To reward himself, Elliot went to a steakhouse for lunch and ordered a New York strip steak and a Manhattan. Then he went home and started working on his next script.

Keep in Touch

I hope you liked the book, and if you have comments or questions, I'd love to hear them. The best way to reach me is via e-mail. My personal e-mail address is: stephanie@stephaniepalmer.com

Thanks so much for reading.

Best,

Stephanie

P.S. For more information, go to www.stephaniepalmer.com.

Index

What this story
needs now is . . .

all alone.

What this story needs
is a pig in a wig,
on a boat,
in a moat,
having fun,
in the sun,
on her own . . .

not a frog,
a dog,
or a goat on a log.

not a rat with a hat,
or a skunk on a trunk,

What this story
needs is a pig
in a wig, on a boat,

not a house,
with a mouse,
or a panda in a blouse,

and a panda
in a blouse.

with a mouse,

in a house,

with a skunk,

on a trunk,

This story also needs a rat.

and a goat on a log.

a dog,

with a frog,

on a boat,

A pig in a wig,

What this story needs is a pig.

WHAT THE STORY NEEDS IS A PIG IN A WIG

By Emma J. Virján

HARPER

An Imprint of HarperCollinsPublishers

set down his coffee cup very hard and looked at her with a frown.

"Cheerleading," he said, "does not have top priority."

And that was that. It was all decided, and there wasn't anything to argue or fuss about. It was too busy a time, anyway. We almost skipped Thanksgiving, except that there were students who couldn't go home for the vacation, and so five of them spent that Thursday with us, and Mom cooked a turkey. But most of the day we packed. The students helped to put books into boxes, and some of them helped Mom, packing dishes and kitchen things. I did all my packing alone that week. I cried when I fitted my new, unused box of oil paints — a gift for my thirteenth birthday the month before — into a box, and I cried again when I packed my camera. But at least those things, the things I cared about most, were going with me. Molly had to give her blue and white cheerleading outfit to one of the substitute cheerleaders, a girl named Lisa Halstead, who pretended to be sad and sympathetic, but you could tell it was phony; she couldn't wait to get home and try on that pleated skirt.

And all of that was only last month. It seems like a hundred years ago.

9

Strange, how the age of a house makes a difference. That shouldn't surprise me, because certainly the age of a person makes a big difference, like with Molly and me. Molly is fifteen, which means that she puts on eyeshadow when Mom doesn't catch her at it, and she spends hours in front of the mirror arranging her hair different ways; she stands sideways there, too, to see what her figure looks like, and she talks on the phone every evening to friends, mostly about boys. It took her about two days to make friends in the new school, two days after that to have boyfriends, and the next week she was chosen as a substitute cheerleader.

Me, I'm only two years younger, and that seems to make such a difference, though I haven't figured out why. It's not only physical, although that's part of it. If I stand sideways in front of a mirror — which I don't bother doing — I might as well be standing backwards, for all the difference it makes. And I couldn't begin to put on eyeshadow even if I wanted to, because I can't see without my glasses. Those are the physical things; the real difference seems to be that I don't care about those things. Will I, two years from now? Or do I care now, and pretend I don't, even to myself? I can't figure it out.

As for friends? Well, the first day at the consolidated school, when the first teacher said, "Margaret Chalmers" and I told him, "Would you

10

call me Meg, please," a boy on the side of the classroom called out, "Nutmeg!" Now, three weeks later, there are 323 people in the Macwahoc Valley Consolidated School who call me Nutmeg Chalmers. You know the old saying about with friends like that, who needs enemies?

But I was talking about the age of houses. As my mother had said, this house was built in 1840. That makes it almost one hundred and forty years old. Our house in town was fifty years old. The difference is that the house in town was big, with a million closets and stairways and windows and an attic, all sorts of places for privacy and escape: places where you could curl up with a book and no one would know you were there for hours. Places that were just mine, like the little alcove at the top of the attic stairs, where I tacked my photographs and watercolors on the wall to make my own private gallery, and no one bugged me about the thumbtack holes in the wall.

It's important, I think, to have places like that in your life, secrets that you share only by choice. I said that to Molly once, and she didn't understand; she said she would like to share everything. It's why she likes cheerleading, she said: because she can throw out her arms and a whole crowd of people responds to her.

Here, in the country, the house is very small. Dad

11

explained that it was built this way because it was so hard to keep it warm way back then. The ceilings are low; the windows are small; the staircase is like a tiny tunnel. Nothing seems to fit right. The floors slant, and there are wide spaces between the pine boards. If you close a door, it falls open again all on its own, when you're not looking. It doesn't matter much, the doors not closing, because there's no place for privacy anyway. Why bother to close the door to your room when it's not even your own room?

When we got here, I ran inside the empty house while the others were all still standing in the yard, trying to help the moving van get turned around in the snowy driveway. I went up the little flight of stairs, looked around, and saw the three bedrooms: two big ones, and the tiny one in the middle, just off the narrow hall. In that room the ceiling was slanted almost down to the floor, and there was one window that looked out over the woods behind the house, and the wallpaper was yellow, very faded and old but still yellow, with a tiny green leaf here and there in the pattern. There was just room for my bed and my desk and my bookcase and the few other things that would make it really mine. I stood for a long time by that one window, looking out at the woods. Across a field to the left of the house, I could see another house far away; it was empty, the outside unpainted, and the windows, some of them broken, black like dark eyes. The rectangle of the window in the little room was like the frame of a painting, and I stood there thinking how I would wake up each morning there, looking out, and each day it would change to a new kind of picture. The snow would get deeper; the wind would blow those last few leaves from the trees; there would be icicles hanging from the edge of the roof; and then, in spring, things would melt, and change, and turn green. There would be rabbits in the field in the early morning. Wild flowers. Maybe someone would come to live in that abandoned house, and light would come from those dark windows at night, across the meadow.

Finally I went downstairs. My mother was in the empty living room, figuring out how to fit in the big couch from the other house. Dad and Molly were still outside, sprinkling salt on the driveway so that the moving men wouldn't slip on the snow.

"Mom," I said, "the little room is mine, isn't it?"

She stopped to think for a minute, remembering the upstairs of the new house. Then she put her arm around me and said, "Meg, the little room is for Dad's study. That's where he'll finish the book. You and Molly will share the big bedroom at the end of the hall, the one with the pretty blue-flowered wallpaper."

13

Mom always tries to make things right with gestures: hugs, quick kisses blown across a room, waves, winks, smiles. Sometimes it helps.

I went back upstairs, to the big room that wasn't going to be all mine. From the windows I could still see the woods, and part of the empty house across the field, but the view was partly blocked by the big gray falling-down barn that was attached to our house on the side. It wasn't the same. I'm pretty good at making the best of things, but it wasn't the same.

Now, just a month later, just two days before Christmas, the house looks lived in. It's warm, and full of the sound of fires in the fireplaces, the sound of Dad's typewriter upstairs, and full of winter smells like wet boots drying, and cinnamon, because my mother is making pumpkin pies and gingerbread. But now Molly, who wants more than anything to throw out her arms and share, has drawn that line, because I can't be like those crowds who smile at her, and share back.

2.

Good things are happening here. That surprises me a little. When we came, I thought it would be a place where I would just have to stick it out, where I would be lonely for a year. Where nothing would ever happen at all.

Now good things are happening to all of us. Well, it's hard to tell with my mother; she's the kind of person who always enjoys everything anyway. Molly and Mom are a lot alike. They get so enthusiastic and excited that you think something wonderful has happened; then, when you stop to think about it, nothing has really happened at all. Every morning, for example, Mom puts fresh birdseed in the bird feeder outside the kitchen window. Two minutes later the first bird stops by for breakfast, and Mom jumps up, says "Shhh" and goes to look, and you forget that 400 birds were there the day before. Or a plant in the kitchen gets a new leaf and she almost sends out birth announcements. So it always seems as if good things are happening to Mom.

Dad is more like me; he waits for the truly good things, as if getting excited about the little ones might keep the big ones from coming. But the book is going well for Dad, and he says it was coming here that did it.

He goes into the little room each morning, closes the door, and sets a brick against it so that it won't fall open while he's working. He's still there when Molly and I get home from school at four, and Mom says he doesn't come out all day, except every now and then when he appears in the kitchen and pours himself a cup of coffee without saying a word, and goes back upstairs. Like a sleepwalker, Mom says. We can hear the typewriter going full speed; every now and then we hear him rip up or crumple a piece of paper, and then roll a fresh one into the typewriter and start clattering away again. He talks

16

to himself, too — we can hear him muttering behind the door — but talking to himself is a good sign. When he's silent, it means things aren't going well, but he's been talking to himself behind the door to the little room ever since we came here.

Last night he came to dinner looking very preoccupied, but smiling to himself now and then. Molly and I were talking about school, and Mom was telling us how she had decided to make a patchwork quilt while we're living in the country, using scraps of material from all the clothes Molly and I wore when we were little. We started remembering our old dresses — we don't even *wear* dresses anymore; I don't think I've worn anything but jeans for two years. Molly said, "Remember that yucky dress I used to have that had butterflies on it? The one I wore at my sixth birthday party?" I didn't remember it, but Mom did; she laughed, and said, "Molly, that was a *beautiful* dress. Those butterflies were hand-embroidered! It's going into a special place on the quilt!"

Dad hadn't heard a word, but he'd been sitting there with a half-smile on his face. All of a sudden he said, "Lydia, I really have a grip on Coleridge!" and he jumped up from his chair, leaving half a piece of apple pie, and went back to the study, taking the stairs two at a time. We could hear the typewriter start up again.

Mom looked after him with that special fond look she gives to things that are slightly foolish and very lovable. She smiles, and her eyes look as if they can see back into her memory, into all the things that have gone into making a person what they are. With Dad, I think she looks back to when she knew him as a student, when he must have been serious and forgetful and very kind, the way he still is, but young, which he isn't anymore. With me, I know her memories go back to all sorts of frustrations and confusions, because I was never an "easy" child; I remember that I questioned and argued and raged. But her look, for me, is still that same caring look that goes beyond all that. As for Molly? I've seen her look at Molly that way, too, and it's a more complicated thing; I think when Mom looks at Molly, her memories go back farther, to her own self as a girl, because they are so alike, and it must be a puzzling thing to see yourself growing up again. It must be like looking through the wrong end of a telescope — seeing yourself young, far away, on your own; the distance is too great for the watcher, really, to do anything more than watch, and remember, and smile.

Molly has a boyfriend. Boys have *always* liked Molly. When she was little, boys in the neighborhood used to come to repair her bike; they loaned her their skate keys, brought her home when she skinned her knees and waited, anxious, while she got a Band-Aid; they shared their trick-or-treat candy with Molly at Halloween. When I was down to the dregs in my paper bag, two weeks later, down to eating the wrinkled apples in the bottom, Molly always had Mounds bars left, gifts from the boys on the block.

How could boys *not* like a girl who looks the way she does? I've gotten used to Molly's looks because I've lived with her for thirteen years. But every now and then I glance at her and see her as if she were a stranger. One night recently she was sitting in front of the fire doing her homework, and I looked over because I wanted to ask her a question about negative numbers. The light from the fire was on her face, all gold, and her blond hair was falling down across her forehead and in waves around her cheeks and onto her shoulders. For a second she looked just like a picture on a Christmas card we had gotten from friends in Boston; it was almost eerie. I held my breath when I looked at her for that moment, because she looked so beautiful. Then she saw me watching her, and stuck her tongue out, so that she was just Molly again, and familiar.

Boys, I think, probably see that part of her all the time, the beautiful part. And now suddenly this one boy, Tierney McGoldrick, who plays on the basketball team and is also president of the junior class, is hanging around her every minute in school. They're always together, and he lets her wear his school jacket with a big MV for Macwahoc Valley on the back. Of course, because we live out here in the middle of the woods, so far from everything, they can't actually date. Tierney's not old enough to drive, even if he wanted to drive all the way from where he lives; half the distance is a dirt road that's usually covered with snow. But he calls her up every single night. Molly takes the phone into the pantry, so that the long cord is stretched all across the kitchen, and my mother and I have to step over it while we're putting the dinner dishes away. Mom thinks it's quite funny. But then Mom has curly hair too, and was probably just as beautiful as Molly once. Maybe it's because I have straight stringy hair and glasses that the whole thing makes me feel a little sad.

So Dad has a grip on Coleridge, whatever that means, and Molly has a grip on Tierney McGoldrick. Me, I can't actually say I have a grip on anything, but good things have been happening to me here, too.

I have a new friend.

Just after New Year's, before school vacation ended, I went out for a walk. It was a walk I'd been meaning to take ever since we moved to the house, but things had been so busy, first with school and fixing up the house, then Christmas, then settling down after Christmas — I don't know, the time just never seemed right for it. I guess I like to think that it was fate that sent me out for this particular walk on this particular day. Fate, and the fact that the sun finally came out after weeks of grayness and snow.

I took my camera — the first time I'd taken my camera out since we came to the country — and went, all bundled up in my down jacket and wearing heavy boots, down the dirt road beyond our house. I walked toward the abandoned house that I could see across the fields from the upstairs window.

The snow kept me from getting close to it. The house is a long distance back from the road and of course the driveway, really a narrow road in its own right, hadn't been plowed. But I stood, stamping my feet to keep warm, and looked at it for a long time. It reminds me of a very honest and kind blind man. That sounds silly. But it looks honest to me because it's so square and straight. It's a very old house — I know that because of the way it's built, with a center chimney and all the other things I've learned about from living in *our* old house — but its corners are all square like a man holding his shoulders straight. Nothing sags on it at all. It's a shabby house, though, with no paint, so that the old boards are all weathered to gray. I guess that's why it seems

21

kind, because it doesn't mind being poor and paintless; it even seems to be proud of it. Blind because it doesn't look back at me. The windows are empty. and dark. Not scary. Just waiting, and thinking about something.

I took a couple of photographs of the house from the road and walked on. I know the dirt road ends a mile beyond our house, but I had never gone to the end. The school bus turns around in our driveway, and no other cars ever come down this road except for one beat-up truck now and then.

That same truck was parked at the end of the road, beside a tiny, weatherbeaten house that looked like a distant, poorer cousin of the one I'd passed. An elderly cousin, frail but very proud. There was smoke coming out of the chimney, and curtains in the two little windows on either side of the door. A dog in the yard, who thumped his tail against a snowbank when he saw me coming. And beside the truck — no, actually in the truck, or at least with his head inside it, under the hood, was a man.

"Hi," I called. It would have been silly to turn around and start walking home without saying anything, even though I've promised my parents all my life that I would never talk to strange men.

He lifted out his head, a gray head, with a bright red woolen cap on it, smiled — a nice smile — and said, "Miss Chalmers. I'm glad you've come to visit."

"Meg," I said automatically. I was puzzled. How did he know who I was? Our name isn't even on the mailbox.

"For Margaret?" he asked, coming over and shaking my hand, or at least my mitten, leaving a smear of grease on it. "Forgive me. My hands are very dirty. My battery dies in this cold weather."

"How did you know?"

"How did I know Meg for Margaret? Because Margaret was my wife's name; therefore, one of my favorite names, of course. And I called her Meg at times, though no one else did."

"They call me Nutmeg at school. I bet no one ever called your wife Nutmeg."

He laughed. He had beautiful blue eyes, and his face moved into a new pattern of wrinkles when he laughed. "No," he admitted, "they didn't. But she wouldn't have minded. Nutmeg was one of her favorite spices. She wouldn't have made an apple pie without it."

"What I meant, though, when I said, 'How did you know?' was how did you know my name was Chalmers?"

He wiped his hands on a greasy rag that was hanging from the door handle of the truck. "My dear, I apologize. I have not even introduced myself. My name is Will Banks. And it's much too cold to stand out here. Your toes must be numb, even in those boots. Come inside, and I'll made us each a cup of tea. And I'll tell you how I know your name."

I briefly envisioned myself telling my mother, "So then I went in his house," and I briefly envisioned my mother saying, "You went in his *house?*"

He saw me hesitate, and smiled. "Meg," he said, "I'm seventy years old. Thoroughly harmless, even to a beautiful young girl like you. Come on in and keep me company for a bit, and get warm."

I laughed, because he knew what I was thinking, and very few people ever know what I'm thinking. Then I went in his house.

What a surprise. It was a tiny house, and very old, and looked on the outside as if it might fall down any minute. For that matter, his truck was also very old, and looked as if *it* might fall down any minute. And Mr. Banks himself was old, although he didn't appear to be falling apart.

But inside, the house was beautiful. Everything was perfect, as if it were a house I'd imagined, or dreamed up with a set of paints. There were only two rooms on the first floor. On one side of the little front hall was the living room: the walls were painted white, and there was an oriental rug on the floor, all shades of blues and reds. A big fireplace, with a painting that was a real painting, not a print, hanging over the mantel. A pewter pitcher standing on a polished table. A large chest of drawers with bright brass handles. A wing chair that was all done in needlepoint — all done by hand, I could tell, because my mother does needlepoint sometimes. Sunlight was pouring in the little windows, through the white curtains, making patterns on the rug and chairs.

On the other side of the hall was the kitchen. That's where Mr. Banks and I went, after he had shown me the living room. A wood stove was burning in the kitchen, and a copper kettle sat on top of it, steaming. A round pine table was laid with woven blue mats, and in the center of it a blue and white bowl held three apples like a still life. Everything was scrubbed and shiny and in the right place.

It made me think of a song that we sang in kindergarten, when we sat at our desks and folded our hands. "We're all in our places with bright shiny faces," we used to sing. I could hear the words in my mind, the little voices of all those five-year-olds, and it was a good memory; Mr. Banks' house was like that, a house warm with memories, of things in their places, and smiling.

He took my jacket and hung it up with his, and

poured tea into two thick pottery mugs. We sat at the table, in pine chairs that gleamed almost yellow from a combination of old wood, polish, and sunlight.

"Is yours the little room at the top of the stairs?" he asked me.

How did he know about the little room? "No," I explained. "I wanted it to be. It's so perfect. You can see the other house across the field, you know" — he nodded; he knew " — but my father needed that room. He's writing a book. So my sister and I have the big room together."

"The little room was mine," he said, "when I was a small boy. Sometime when your father isn't working there, go in and look in the closet. On the closet floor you'll find my name carved, if no one's refinished the floor. My mother spanked me for doing it. I was eight years old at the time, and I'd been shut in my room for being rude to my older sister."

"You lived in my house?" I asked in surprise.

He laughed again. "My dear Meg," he said, "*you* live in *my* house.

"My grandfather built that house. Actually, he built the one across the field, first. Then he built the other one, where you live. In those days families stuck together, of course, and he built the second house for his sister, who never married. Later he

26

gave it to his oldest son — my father — and my sister and I were both born there.

"It became my house when I married Margaret. I took her there to live when she was a bride, eighteen years old. My sister had married and moved to Boston. She's dead now. My parents, of course, are gone. And Margaret and I never had children. So there's no one left but me. Well, that's not entirely true — there's my sister's son, but that's another story.

"Anyway, there's no one left here on the land but me. There were times, when I was young, when Margaret was with me, when I was tempted to leave, to take a job in a city, to make a lot of money, but —" He lit his pipe, was quiet for a minute, looking into the past.

"Well, it was my grandfather's land, and my father's, before it was mine. Not many people understand that today, what that means. But I *know* this land. I know every rock, every tree. I couldn't leave them behind.

"This house used to be the hired man's cottage. I've fixed it up some, and it's a good little house. But the other two houses are still mine. When the taxes went up, I just couldn't afford to keep them going. I moved here after Margaret died, and I've rented the family houses whenever I come across someone who has reason to want to live in this wilderness.

27

"When I heard your parents were looking for a place, I offered the little house to them. It's a perfect place for a writer — the solitude stimulates imagination, I think.

"Other people come now and then, thinking it might be a cheap place to live, but I won't rent to just anyone. That's why the big house is empty now — the right family hasn't come along."

"Do you get lonely here?"

He finished his tea and set the cup down on the table. "No. I've been here all my life. I miss my Margaret, of course. But I have Tip" — the dog looked up at his name, and thumped his tail against the floor — "and I do some carpentry in the village now and then, when people need me. I have books. That's all I need, really.

"Of course," he smiled, "it's nice to have a new friend, like you."

"Mr. Banks?"

"Oh please, please. Call me Will, the way all my friends do."

"Will, then. Would you mind if I took your picture?"

"My dear," he said, straightening his shoulders and buttoning the top button of his plaid shirt. "I would be honored."

The light was coming in through the kitchen window onto his face: soft light now; it had become late afternoon, when all the harsh shadows are gone. He sat right there, smoked his pipe, and talked, and I finished the whole roll of film, just shooting quickly as he gestured and smiled. All those times when I feel awkward and inept — all those times are made up for when I have my camera, when I can look through the viewfinder and feel that I can control the focus and the light and the composition, when I can capture what I see, in a way that no one else is seeing it. I felt that way while I was taking Will's picture.

I unloaded the exposed film and carried it home in my pocket like a secret. When I looked back from the road, Will was by his truck again, waving to me; Tip was back by his snowbank, thumping his tail.

And deep, way deep inside me somewhere was something else that kept me warm on the walk home, even though the sun was going down and the wind was coming over the piles of snow on either side of the road, blowing stinging powder into my eyes. It was the fact that Will Banks had called me beautiful.

3.

February is the worst month, in New England. I think so, anyway. My mother doesn't agree with me. Mom says April is, because everything turns to mud in April; the snow melts, and things that were buried all winter — dog messes, lost mittens, beer bottles tossed from cars — all reappear, still partly frozen into icy mixtures that are half the gray remains of old snow and half the brown beginnings of mud. Lots of the mud, of course, ends up on the kitchen floor, which is why my mother hates April.

My father, even though he always recites a poem that begins "April is the cruelest month" to my mother when she's scrubbing the kitchen floor in the spring, agrees with me that it's February that's worst. Snow, which was fun in December, is just boring, dirty, and downright cold in February. And the same sky that was blue in January is just nothing but white a month later — so white that sometimes you can't tell where the sky ends and the land begins. And it's cold, bitter cold, the kind of cold where you just can't go outside. I haven't been to see Will, because it's too cold to walk a mile up the road. I haven't taken any pictures, because it's too cold to take off my mittens and operate the camera.

And Dad can't write. He goes in the little room and sits, every day, but the typewriter is quiet. It's almost noisy, the quietness, we are all so aware of it. He told me that he sits and looks out the window at all the whiteness and can't get a grip on anything. I understand that; if I were able to go out with my camera in the cold, the film wouldn't be able to grip the edges and corners of things because everything has blended so into the colorless, stark mass of February. For Dad, everything has blended into a mass without any edges in his mind, and he can't write.

I showed him the closet floor, where *William* is carved into the pine.

31

"Will Banks is a fascinating man," Dad said, leaning back in his scruffy leather chair in front of the typewriter. He was having a cup of coffee, and I had tea. It was the first time I had visited him in the little room, and he seemed glad to have company. "You know, he's well educated, and he's a master cabinetmaker. He could have earned a fortune in Boston, or New York, but he wouldn't leave this land. People around here think he's a little crazy. But I don't know, I don't know."

"He's not crazy, Dad. He's nice. But it's too bad he has to live in that teeny house, when he owns both these bigger ones that were his family's."

"Well, he's happy there, Meg, and you can't argue with happiness. Problem is, there's a nephew in Boston who's going to make trouble for Will, I'm afraid."

"What do you mean? How can anyone make trouble for an old man who isn't bothering anybody?"

"I'm not sure. I wish I knew more about law. Seems the nephew is the only relative he has. Will owns all this land, and the houses — they were left to him — but when he dies, they'll go to this nephew, his sister's son. It's valuable property. They may not look like much to you, Meg, but these houses are real antiques, the kind of things that a lot of people from big cities would like to buy. The nephew, apparently, would like to have Will declared what the law calls 'incompetent' — which just means crazy. If he could do that, he'd have control over the property. He'd like to sell it to some people who want to build cottages for tourists, and to turn the big house into an inn."

I stood up and looked out the window, across the field, to where the empty house was standing gray against the whiteness, with its brick chimney tall and straight against the sharp line of the roof. I imagined cute little blue shutters on the windows, and a sign over the door that said "All Major Credit Cards Accepted." I envisioned a parking lot, filled with cars and campers from different states.

"They can't do that, Dad," I said. Then it turned into a question. "Can they?"

My father shrugged. "I didn't think so. But last week the nephew called me, and asked if it were true, what he had heard, that the people in the village call Will 'Loony Willie.'"

"'*Loony Willie*'? What did you say to him?"

"I told him I'd never heard anything so ridiculous in my life, and to stop bothering me, because I was busy writing a book that was going to change the whole history of literature."

That broke us both up. The book that was going to change the whole history of literature was lying in stacks all over my father's desk, on the floor, in at least a hundred crumpled sheets of typing paper in the big wastebasket, and in two pages that he had made into paper airplanes and sailed across the room. We laughed and laughed.

When I was able to stop laughing, I remembered something that I had wanted to tell my father. "You know, last month, when I visited Will, I took his picture."

"Mmmmm?"

"He was sitting in his kitchen, smoking his pipe and looking out the window, and talking. I shot a whole roll. And you know, Dad, his eyes are so bright, and his face is so alive, so full of memories and thoughts. He's interested in everything. I thought of that when you said Loony Willie."

"Could I see the pictures?"

I felt a little silly. "Well, I haven't been able to develop them yet, Dad. I can't use the darkroom at school because I have to catch the early bus to get home. It's just that I *remember* his face looking like that when I photographed him."

My father sat up straight in his chair very suddenly. "Meg," he said, "I have a *great* idea!" He sounded like a little boy. Once Mom told Molly and me that she didn't mind not having sons, because often Dad is like a little boy, and now I could see exactly what she meant. He looked as if he were ten years old, on a Saturday morning, with an ex-

34

citing and probably impossible project in mind.

"Let's build a darkroom!" he said.

I could hardly believe it. "*Here?*" I asked.

"Why not? Now look, I don't know anything about photography. You'll be the expert consultant. But I *do* know how to build. And I need a little vacation from writing. Could I do it in a week?"

"Sure, I think so."

"What would you need?"

"A space, first of all."

"How about that little storeroom in the passageway between the house and the barn? That's big enough, isn't it?"

"Sure. But it's too cold, Dad."

"Aha. You're not thinking, Consultant. We need a heater." He turned to his desk, found a fresh sheet of paper, and wrote, "1. Heater." My father loves to make lists. "What next?"

"Let's see. There are already shelves in there. But I'd need a counter top of some sort." He wrote that down.

"And special lights. They're called safelights. You know, so you won't expose the photographic paper accidentally."

"No problem. There's electricity out there. What else? You'll need lots of equipment, won't you? If you're going to have a darkroom, it might as well be the best darkroom around."

35

I sighed. I could already tell what the problem was going to be. But, as I said, my father loves making lists. What the heck. I started telling him everything a darkroom would need: an enlarger, a timer, trays, chemicals, paper, developing tanks, special thermometers, filters, a focuser. The list grew very long and he started on a second sheet of paper. It was kind of fun, listing it, even though I knew it was just a dream. It was a dream I'd had for a long time, one that I'd never told anyone.

"Where can you get this kind of stuff?" he asked.

I went to my room, picked out one of my photography magazines, and brought it back. We looked through the ads in the back pages: New York. California. Boston.

"Boston," he said triumphantly. "Terrific. I have to go down there to see my publisher anyway; might as well do it this week." He wrote down the name and address of the company. "Now. How much is all of this going to cost?"

I started to laugh, even though I didn't really feel like laughing. It was so typical of my father, that he didn't think of the obvious problem till last. We looked through the Boston company's price list, wrote the prices on my father's paper, and finally added them up. His face fell. Good thing I'd realized all along it was a dream; that made it less disappointing. Poor Dad; he'd thought it was real, and it took him by surprise that it wasn't.

We both kept smiling very hard, because neither of us wanted the other to be sad.

"Listen, Meg," he said slowly, folding the list up and putting it on a corner of his desk. "Sometimes when I'm sitting here working on the book, I come to a problem that seems insurmountable. When that happens, I just let it go for a while. I keep it in the back of my mind, but I don't *agonize* over it. Do you know what I mean?"

I nodded. I'm pretty good at not agonizing.

"So far," he explained, "all of those problems have resolved themselves. Out of nowhere, all of a sudden, the solutions appear. Now here's what I want you to do." He tapped the folded darkroom list with his finger. "I want you to put this out of your mind for a while, but keep it somewhere in the back where your subconscious will be working on it."

"Okay," I agreed.

"And before long, the solution will come. I'm absolutely sure of it. Probably soon, too, because *both* of our subconsciouses will be working."

I laughed. He was so sure, and I didn't believe it for a minute. "All right," I promised.

"Or would that be 'subconsciese'? The plural, I mean?"

"Dad," I said, picking up our empty cups to take

them to the kitchen, *"you're* the English professor."

Mom was in the kitchen, sitting by the fireplace stitching on her quilt. She was so excited about that quilt, and it *was* pretty, what she had done so far. But Molly and I cringed when we looked at it too closely, I suppose because it was full of memories; let's face it, some memories are better off forgotten, especially when you haven't lived far enough beyond them yet. There was the dress with the butterflies, which Molly always hated, right near the center. Near it was a blue-and-white-striped piece that I didn't want to be reminded of. It was the dress that I wore to my fifth birthday party, the day when I threw up all over the table, just after the cake was served. There was the pink with little white flowers, that I wore to Sunday School on Easter when I was supposed to say a poem to a roomful of people, forgot every word of it, and cried instead, when I was maybe six. There was the blue plaid that Molly wore her first day in junior high, when she didn't realize that every other girl would be wearing jeans. And there was a piece of my old Brownie uniform; I hated Brownies, always spent my dues on candy before I got there, and was scolded every week.

"What's that white piece with the embroidery?" I asked Mom. She really liked it when Molly and I took an interest in the quilt.

She turned the quilt around and held it toward the window so that she could see the piece I meant. Then her face got all nostalgic. "Oh," she said affectionately. "That's Molly's first bra."

"*What?*"

I hadn't even noticed Molly until she burst out with "*What?*" She was lying on a couch in the corner. (Old houses are neat, in many ways. How many houses have a couch in the kitchen?) Actually, it didn't surprise me that she was there. Molly's had the flu all of February, and she's kind of like a fixture, or a piece of furniture herself now, lying there with a box of Kleenex.

In a way, it's fun having Molly sick, because she's home all the time, instead of off with her friends after school and on weekends. We've been doing things we hadn't done since we were little, like playing Monopoly. It's fun to play with Molly, silly games like that, because she doesn't take them seriously. I build hotels all over everything, even on stupid old Baltic Avenue, and when she throws the dice and realizes she's going to land where I have hotels, she starts giggling. She moves her piece along, closer and closer, and laughs harder and harder till she gets there, and then sits him down, thump, by the hotel, and just starts counting out all her money. "You got me," she says. "I'm absolutely wiped out!" Then she hands over all her money, laughing, and says right away, "Let's play again."

I'm a terrible loser. I go around muttering "It isn't fair" after I lose. I thought about it once, about what makes the difference, when I was feeling stupid and childish because I had cried after I lost a game of gin rummy, and said, "You cheated!" to Molly, even though I knew she hadn't. I think it's because Molly has always won at important things, or the things that are important to her, like making cheerleader, and having the best-looking boyfriend; so the little things, like Monopoly games, don't matter to her. Maybe someday, if I succeed at something, I'll stop saying "It isn't fair" about everything else.

It's also a nuisance, Molly being sick. She's grouchy, which isn't like her, because she's missing school — which means missing Tierney McGoldrick, even though he calls every day — and because she worries about how she looks. She can't be feeling *too* bad, because she spends a lot of time in front of the mirror in our room, trying to fix her hair which has gotten kind of scroungy looking, and putting rouge on her face, because it's so pale.

Sometimes, when Molly is messing around with a hairbrush and bobby pins, making herself even more beautiful, which isn't necessary, I kind of wish that she would notice *my* hair and offer to do something about *it*. I can't quite get up the nerve to ask her to. I'm almost positive she wouldn't laugh at me, but I can't bring myself to take the chance.

"Molly, don't get up," sighed Mom, because Molly was about to charge across the room to examine the piece of her bra. "Your nose will start up again."

Molly's flu consists mainly of nosebleeds. Mom says that's because she's an adolescent; Mom says that about almost everything. The doctor from the village says it's because of the cold weather, which damages the nasal membranes. Whichever it is, it's downright messy. Even though her side of our room is still nasty neat, the rug is spattered with Molly's dumb nosebleeds, which to my mind is a good deal more disgusting than anything I leave lying around on my side.

It was time for dinner anyway. Mom put the quilt away, which ended the argument they were about to have about the bra, and served pork chops and applesauce at the kitchen table. I had to move my salad plate over to the side to make room for Molly's box of Kleenex. Dad didn't say anything, even though he likes a tidy-looking table at dinner, because we've had a couple of unpleasant meals when Molly *didn't* bring her Kleenex.

It was a quiet meal, with Molly eating very carefully because of her nose, and Dad and I both a little preoccupied because it isn't all that easy to tuck something into your subconscious and keep it back there. Mom kept starting conversations that ended because nobody joined them. Finally she put down her fork, sighed, and said, "You know, much as I love this place, even in winter, I'll be glad when summer comes. You'll be feeling better about the book, Charles, because it'll be almost finished, and you girls can go to camp and you won't be so bored —"

"Camp," I said suddenly. "*Camp.*" My mother stared at me. Molly and I have gone to the same camp every summer since I was eight and she was ten.

"*Camp,*" said my father suddenly, looking at me with a grin starting.

"How much does camp cost?" I asked my mother.

She groaned good-naturedly. "Plenty," she said. "But don't worry about that all of a sudden. Your father and I have always felt it was important enough that we've kept the money put aside each month. You girls will be able to go to camp."

"Mom," I said slowly, "do I *have* to go to camp?"

She was amazed. I've won the Best Camper Award for two years running for my age group. "Of course you don't have to go to camp, Meg. But I thought —"

"Lydia," announced my father. "I'm going to Boston tomorrow. I have to see my publisher, and I'm going to do some shopping. Meg and I are building a darkroom in the storeroom by the barn, if

Will Banks doesn't mind. I'll call him tonight, Meg."

My mother was sitting there with a piece of lettuce on the end of her fork, shaking her head. She started to laugh. "This family is absolutely nuts," she said. "I haven't the slightest idea what anyone is talking about. Molly, your nose."

Molly grabbed a piece of Kleenex and clutched her nose. From behind her Kleenex she said haughtily, "*I* don'd know whad anyone is talking aboud either. Bud *I'm* going to camp, whether Meg does or nod."

Then she giggled. Even Molly realized how silly she looked and sounded, talking from behind a wad of tissues. "Thad is," she added, "if by dose ever stobs bleeding."

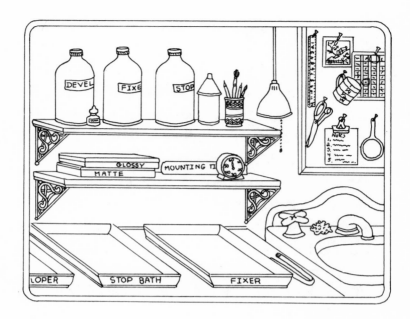

4.

All of a sudden I know how Dad feels when he completes a chapter of the book. Or Mom, when one of her plants suddenly blossoms, or she finishes a new section of the quilt, and goes around with a smile on her face all day, even when no one's looking. I know how Molly must have felt when Tierney McGoldrick asked her to go steady, which is what happened two weeks ago. She came home wearing his tiny gold basketball on a chain around

44

her neck, and was so giggly and cheerful and bounced around so much that Mom finally had to tell her to calm down so that her newly normal nose wouldn't have a relapse.

Molly's nose had finally stopped bleeding at the beginning of March, which is about the same time that the sun came out after a month of gray cold; Dr. Putnam in the village said that proved what he had thought, that the bad weather was causing her nosebleeds. Molly said she didn't care *what* caused them, she was just glad they were over, glad she could go back to school. Dad said he was sorry he hadn't bought stock in the Kleenex company.

I've hardly seen the sun at all because I've been in my darkroom. My darkroom! It's finished; it's all finished, and perfect. My father did it, just the way he said he would, and everything is just the way I dreamed of it. There is *nothing* that my father can't do.

The first pictures I developed were the ones of Will Banks. I'd had that roll of film tucked away in a drawer under my knee socks for almost two months. I was scared stiff when I developed it — scared that I had forgotten how, that I would do something wrong. But when I took the strip of negatives out of the tank and held it to the light, there were two pictures of the old house across the field, and then thirty-four pictures of Will, looking at me in thirty-four different ways. I felt like a genius, like an artist.

When the negatives were dry, I printed them all on one sheet. It's hard to see, from the negatives, exactly how a print will look, so I crossed my fingers again when I developed the contact sheet that would show me the real pictures for the first time. I stood there over the tray of developer and watched in the dim red light as the sheet changed from white to gray, and then saw the grays change to blacks and the shades become the faces of Will; after two minutes, there he was, looking up at me from the tray, thirty-four of him, still tiny, but complete.

When it was ready I took it, still dripping wet, into the kitchen and laid it on the counter beside the sink. Mom was there, peeling potatoes, and she looked over, first curiously, and then as if she were really surprised.

"That's Will Banks!" she said.

"Of *course* it's Will Banks," I told her, grinning. "Isn't he beautiful?"

She and I looked for a long time at all the tiny prints on the paper. There he was, lighting his pipe, and then smoking it, looking at me, half laughing. Then he leaned back in his chair — I had blown the focus on that one a little, when he leaned back, out of the range of focus. I should have realized that. But then there he was, sitting up straight, back in sharp focus again, looking at me with his eyes bright with interest; I remembered that he had been asking me questions about the camera, how I determined what settings to use. Toward the end of the roll, his eyes were looking past me and far off, as if he were thinking about something in the distance. He had been telling me about a camera that he had once, that he still had, if he could find it in the attic of the little house. He had bought it in Germany, he said, after the Second World War, when he was stationed there with the army. That surprised me.

"You were in the *army?*" I had asked him. The only people I knew who were in the army were boys who had flunked out of the university and didn't know what to do with themselves. Sometimes they would come back to see Dad in the house in town, with funny haircuts.

Will had laughed. "I was an officer," he said. "Would you believe it? People *saluted* me!" He put a stern look on his face and made a rigid salute. It was there, in the pictures.

Then he had laughed again, and puffed on his pipe. "In those days we all joined the army. It seemed important, then. For me, the best part was coming home. It was in summer, when I came home, and Margaret had made ten blueberry pies, to celebrate. We ate blueberry pie for three days and then we were sick of blueberry pie and there were still six left over. I think she gave them away."

He had closed his eyes, remembering, still smiling. It was the last picture on the sheet. His eyes were closed, and the smoke from his pipe was a thin white line beside his head and circling across the top of the photograph.

I marked six of the tiny prints with a marking pen: my six favorites, each one a little different. Then I went back into the darkroom and spent the rest of the day enlarging those. I made two sets of them, so that I could give one of each to Will. I wondered if he'd be pleased. They were good pictures; I knew that, and both my parents had said so, too, and they never lie to me. But it must be a funny feeling, I think, to see your own face like that, caught by someone else, with all your feelings showing in it.

I took my own set of Will's pictures up to my room and taped them to the wall very neatly, with three above and three below. I've been trying to keep my half of the room neater ever since Molly drew the chalk line; every time my things start piling up and getting messy, Molly draws it over again, just to let me know it's still there.

She was on her bed, drawing pictures in her school notebook, when I went in and put the pictures on the wall.

48

"Mom'll kill you if you tear the wallpaper," she said, glancing over at me.

"I know it." We both knew it wasn't true. My mother hardly ever gets mad. She scolds us sometimes, but the thought of Mom killing somebody is ridiculous. She doesn't even step on ants.

"Hey," said Molly suddenly, sitting up and looking over at the wall. "Those are really *good.*"

I looked over to see if she was joking, and she wasn't. She was looking at Will's pictures with interest, and I could tell that she meant it, that she thought they were good.

"I like that one there, where he's looking off in the distance and smiling," she decided, pointing to one in the bottom row.

"He was talking about his wife," I remembered, looking at the photograph with her.

Molly sat there for a minute, thinking. She looked pretty again, now that she was feeling better. Her hair had gotten its curl back. "Wouldn't it be great," she said slowly, "to be married to someone who felt that way about you, so that he smiled like that whenever he thought of you?"

I hadn't ever really thought about it in such personal terms. To be honest, I find the whole idea of marriage intensely boring. But right at that moment I knew what Molly meant, and I could feel how important it was to her. "Tierney looks that way at you all the time," I told her.

"Really?"

"Sure. Sometimes when you don't even know he's looking at you. I saw him in assembly last Friday, looking over at you. Remember, you were sitting with the cheerleaders? He was watching you, and that's the way he looked, almost like Will is looking in the picture."

"*Really?*" Molly curled up on her bed and grinned. "I'm glad you told me that, Meg. Sometimes I don't know what's going on in Tierney's head at all. Sometimes it seems as if basketball is all he cares about."

"Well, he's only sixteen, Molly." All of a sudden I realized that I sounded like Mom, and I giggled. So did Molly.

"Hey, look, Meg," she said, handing her notebook to me. "You're such a good artist, and I can't draw at all. Can you help me make these look better?"

She'd been drawing brides. Good old Molly. She's been drawing brides since she was five. Her drawing ability hadn't improved much in ten years, either, to tell the truth. But suddenly the idea of her drawing brides was kind of scary.

I took the ball-point pen. "Look," I told her. "Your proportions are all off. The arms are too short, even though you've tried to hide it with all those big bouquets of flowers. Just keep in mind that a woman's arms reach down to the middle of her thighs when she's standing up. Her elbows should reach her waist — look, your drawings all have elbows up by the bosom; that's why they look wrong. The necks are too long, too, but that's probably all right, because it makes them look glamorous. Fashion designers usually draw necks too long. If you look at the ads in Sunday's *New York Times,* you'll see — Molly?"

"What?"

"You're not thinking about getting *married?*"

Molly got huffy and took back her drawings. "Of course I'm thinking about getting married. Not now, stupid. But someday. Don't you think about it?"

I shook my head. "No, I guess I don't. I think about being a writer, or an artist, or a photographer. But I always think about myself alone, not with someone else. Do you think there's something wrong with me?" I meant the question seriously, but it was a hard question to ask, so I crossed my eyes and made a face when I asked it, and laughed.

"No," she said thoughtfully, ignoring my face-making, which was nice of her. "We're just different, I guess." She tucked the drawings into her notebook and put them on her desk very neatly, in line with her schoolbooks.

"Like you're pretty, and I'm not," I pointed out. What a dumb thing to say.

But I'll give Molly credit. She didn't try to pretend that it wasn't true. "You'll be pretty, Meg, when you get a little older," she said. "And I'm not sure it makes that much difference anyway, especially for you. Look at all the talent you have. And brains. I'm so *stupid*. What do I have, really, except curls and long eyelashes?"

I ruin everything. I should have known that she meant it sincerely. Molly is never intentionally snide. But she doesn't realize how it feels, for someone with stringy hair and astigmatism to hear something like that. How could she? I can't imagine how it would feel to be beautiful; how could Molly know how it feels *not* to be?

And I blew up, as usual. I struck a phony model's pose in front of the mirror and said sarcastically, "Oh, poor me, what do I have except curls and long eyelashes?"

She looked surprised, and hurt. Then embarrassed, and angry. Finally, because she didn't know what else to do, she picked up a pile of her school papers and threw them at me: a typical Molly gesture; even in anger, she does things that can't possibly hurt. The papers flew all over, and landed on my bed and the floor. She stood there a moment looking at the mess, and then said, "There, now you should feel right at home, with stuff all over so it looks like a pigpen." And she stormed out of the room, slamming the door, which was useless, because it fell open again.

I left the papers where they were, and Molly and I didn't talk to each other when we went to bed that night. Neither of us is very good at apologizing. Molly just waits a while after a fight, and then she smiles. Me, I wait until the other person smiles first. I always seem to be the first one in and the last one out of an argument. But that night neither of us was ready to call it quits, and Molly didn't even smile when I climbed into bed very carefully so that all her exercises in past participles stayed where she'd thrown them, and I went to sleep underneath the pile.

I don't know what time it was when something woke me up. I wasn't sure what it was, but something was happening that made me afraid; I had that feeling along the edge of my back, that cold feeling you get when things aren't right. And it wasn't a dream. I sat up in bed and looked around in the dark, shaking off whatever was left of sleep, and the feeling was still there, that something was very wrong. The French papers slid to the floor; I could hear the sound of them fluttering off the bed.

Quietly I got up and went to the window. The first day of spring wasn't very far away, but dates like that don't mean much in New England; it was still very cold, and there was snow, still, in the fields. I could see the whiteness of it as I looked out the window. Beyond the corner of the barn, far across, beyond the pine trees, there was a light in the window of the empty house. I looked up to find the moon, to see if it could be reflecting in one window, but there was no moon. The sky was cloudy and dark. But the light was there, a bright rectangle in one corner of the old house, and it was reflected in another rectangle on the snow.

"Molly," I whispered. Stupid to whisper, if you want to wake someone up.

But she answered, as if she were already awake. Her voice was strange. Frightened, and puzzled. "Meg," she said, in an odd voice, as if she were captured by something, as if she couldn't move. "Call Mom and Dad quick."

Ordinarily I argue with Molly if she tells me to do something, just on general principles. But everything felt wrong. She wasn't just telling me; she was ordering me, and she was very scared. I ran from the room, through the darkness, through the shadows in the hall, and woke my parents.

"Something's wrong," I told them. "Something's wrong with Molly."

Usually, when you turn a light on in the night, everything that you're afraid of goes away. At least

54

that's what I thought once, when I was younger. Now I know it isn't true. When my father turned on the light in my bedroom, everything was there, it was so much there, and so bright, so horrible, that I turned and hid my face against the wall. And in the corner of the wall, with my face buried, my eyes closed tight and tears starting, I could still see it.

Molly was covered with blood. Her pillow, her hair, her face were all wet with it. Her eyes were open, frightened, and her hands were at her face, trying to stop it, trying to hold it back, but it was still coming, pouring from her nose onto the sheet and blanket in moving streams, and spattering on the wall behind her bed.

I could hear my parents moving very fast. I heard my mother go to the hall linen closet, and I knew she was getting towels. I could hear my father's low voice, talking to Molly very calmly, telling her everything was all right. My mother went to the phone in their bedroom, and I could hear her dial and talk. Then she moved down the stairs, and outside I heard the car start. "It's okay, it's okay," I heard my father say again and again, reassuring Molly in his steady voice. I could hear Molly choke and whimper.

Mom came back in the house and up the stairs, and came to where I was still standing with my back to the room. "Meg," she said, and I turned around. My father was in the doorway of the bedroom, with Molly in his arms like a small child. There were towels, already drenched with blood, around her face and head; they had wrapped her in the blanket from her bed, and the blood was moving on it slowly. My father was still talking to her, telling her it was all right, it was all right, it was all right.

"Meg," said my mother again. I nodded. "We have to take Molly to the hospital. Don't be scared. It's just another of those nosebleeds, but it's a bad one, as you can see. We have to hurry. Do you want to come with us?"

My father was moving down the stairs, carrying Molly. I shook my head. "I'll stay here," I said. My voice was shaking, and I felt as if I were going to be sick.

"Are you sure?" asked my mother. "We may be gone for quite a while. Do you want me to call Will and ask him to come up and stay with you?"

I shook my head again and my voice got a little better. "I'll be okay," I told her.

I could tell she wasn't sure, but my father was already in the car waiting for her. "Really, Mom, I'll be fine. Go on; I'll stay here."

She hugged me. "Meg, try not to worry. She'll be okay."

I nodded and walked with her to the stairs, and

56

then she went down, and they were gone. I could hear the car driving very fast away from the house.

The only light on in the house was in my room, mine and Molly's, and I couldn't go back there. I walked to the doorway without looking inside, reached in and turned off the switch so that the whole house was dark. But the beginning of morning was coming; outside there was a very faint light in the sky. I took a blanket from my parents' bed, wrapped it around me, and went into my father's study, the little room that I had wanted to be mine. I curled up in his big comfortable chair, tucked the blue blanket around my bare feet, looked out the window, and began to cry.

If I hadn't fought with Molly this afternoon, none of this would have happened, I thought miserably, and knew that it wasn't true. If I had just said "I'm sorry" before we went to bed, it wouldn't have happened, I thought, and knew that that wasn't true, either. If we hadn't come here to live. If I'd kept my side of the room neater.

None of that makes any sense, I told myself.

The fields were slowly beginning to turn pink as the first streaks of sun came from behind the hills and colored the snow. It startled me that morning was coming; it seemed too soon. For the first time since I had heard Molly's frightened voice in our dark bedroom, I remembered the light in the old house. Had I really seen it? Now everything seemed unreal, as if it had all been a nightmare. On the far side of the pink fields the gray house was very dark against the gradually lightening sky, and its windows were silent and black, like the eyes of guardians.

But I knew that back in the blue-flowered bedroom the blood was still there, that it had not been a dream. I was alone in the house; my parents were gone, with Molly, with Molly's hair sticky from blood, and the stain spreading on the blanket around her. Those moments when I had stood shaking and terrified, with my eyes tightly closed against the corner of the wall, moments which may have been hours — I couldn't tell anymore — had really happened. I had seen the light in the window across the fields, as well. I remembered standing and watching its reflection on the snow, and I knew it was real, too, though it didn't seem important anymore. I closed my eyes and fell asleep in my father's chair.

5.

I made two Easter eggs, one for Will and one for
Molly. Not just plain old hard-boiled eggs that you
dye with those vinegar-smelling colors that never
come out looking the way you hoped they would.
Molly and I used to do that when we were little —
dozens of them, and then we wouldn't eat them,
and they turned rotten.

No, these were special, and there were only two
of them. I blew the insides out of two white eggs, so
that only the shells were left, very fragile and light.

Then I spent hours in my room, painting them.

Molly's was yellow, partly I guess because it reminded me of her blond hair, and partly because my parents told me that her hospital room was depressingly gray-colored, and I thought that yellow would cheer it up a bit. Then, over the pale yellow egg, I used my tiniest brush and painted narrow, curving lines in gold, and between the lines, miniature blue flowers with gold and white centers. It took a long time, because the eggshell was so delicate and the painting so small and intricate; but it was worth it: when it was finished, the egg was truly beautiful. I varnished it to make it shiny and permanent, and when it was dry, I packed it in cotton in a box to protect it, and Mom took it with her when she drove to Portland to visit Molly. It worked, too; I mean it did make the room more cheerful, Mom said.

Molly was lots better, and coming home the next week. In the beginning she had been very sick. They had, first thing, given her blood transfusions; then, when she was feeling better, they decided to do a lot of tests to find out what was wrong, so that her nose wouldn't bleed anymore. They even had specialists see her.

You'd *think* that with medical science as advanced as it's supposed to be, that they could figure out what the trouble was and fix her up pretty quickly. I mean, *nosebleeds!* What's the big deal about that? It's not as if she had a mysterious tropical disease, or something.

But first, Mom said, after they put all that new blood into her, they started taking blood out, to test it. Then they did tests on the inside of her *bones.* Then they x-rayed her. Then, when they thought they knew what was causing the nosebleeds, they started fooling around with all different kinds of medicines, to see what would work best. One day Mom and Dad went in, and when they came home, they told me that special medicine had been injected into Molly's spine. That gave me the creeps. It made me mad, too, because it seemed to me that they were just experimenting on her, for pete's sake. By that time they knew what the trouble was — her blood didn't clot right — so they just should have given her whatever medicine would fix that and sent her home. But no, instead they started fooling around, trying different things, keeping her there longer.

And my parents were very strange about the whole thing. They were just like the doctors; they didn't even think of Molly as a person anymore. They talked about her as if she were a clinical specimen. They came home from the hospital and talked very coldly about different drugs with long names: whether this one was better than that one.

They talked about reactions, side effects, contraindications; it was hard to believe they were talking about Molly.

I kept my mouth shut as long as I could. But then one night at dinner, the only thing they talked about was something called cyclophosphamide. There I was, sitting there with them, and I wanted to talk about other things: my darkroom, my Easter eggs that I was working so hard on, what I was going to do during spring vacation from school. *Anything.* Anything, that is, except cyclophosphamide, which I didn't know anything about and couldn't pronounce.

"Stop it!" I said angrily. "Stop talking about it! If you want to talk about Molly, then talk about *Molly,* not her stupid medicine! You haven't even sent in her camp application, Mom. It's still on your desk!"

They both looked as if I had thrown something at them. But it worked. I don't think I heard the word "cyclophosphamide" again, and for a while they talked of other things, and life was somewhat normal. And now Molly will be home soon, all better — and no more nosebleeds — and after all that business with the fancy drugs, it turned out that what she ended up with is pills. When she comes home, she'll have to take pills for a while. Big deal. They could have found that out when she got there, and sent her home sooner.

But since they didn't, I made the Easter egg for Molly, to cheer her up, and I made another one for Will. Will's egg was blue, and special in a different way. I thought and thought about how to paint it, and finally I looked up spices in the encyclopedia, and found a picture of nutmeg. I painted tiny nutmeg blossoms all over his eggshell, intertwined so that they formed a complicated pattern of orange, brown, and green over the blue background. I varnished and packed it, and on Easter Sunday I took the box with his egg, and the envelope with his pictures, and walked down the road to his house.

I hadn't seen Will since Molly got sick. Things were just too complicated at first. My parents spent a lot of time at the hospital, and I had to do most of the cooking. Then, when she was getting better, my father had to work doubly hard on the book because he hadn't been able to concentrate on it when she was so sick. I realized that I hadn't been concentrating on my schoolwork, either, for the same reason, so I had a lot of catching up to do too.

But finally things were calming down. It was school vacation, Molly was getting better, and even the mud outside had dried up a little. At night it would still freeze, and in fact I noticed, as I walked past, that there were tire tracks frozen into the driveway of the big house across the field.

That was another reason I wanted to see Will

After that first awful night, when I had seen the light in the window, other things had been happening at the house. Nothing seemed as mysterious as that light in the middle of the night; still, I was curious. There was a car at the house occasionally, and the driveway had been cleared of the last spring-muddied bits of snow. Sometimes when the day was very quiet I could hear the sound of saws and hammers coming from the house. Once I had seen the figure of a man on the roof, working. It certainly looked as if someone were getting ready to move in. I asked my father if the nephew had gotten permission to turn the house into an inn, but Dad said he hadn't heard anything about it; on the other hand, Dad pointed out, he'd been so distracted and so busy that he probably wouldn't have noticed if spaceships had landed in the field.

Will was under the hood of his truck again. I should have taken my camera with me. If there is one way in which I will always remember Will, it is under the hood of that old truck.

"Is it your battery again, Will?" I called as I approached him.

He straightened up and grinned. "Meg! I was hoping someone would drop in for tea. In fact, I have the kettle on. I'm so glad fate sent you instead of Clarice Callaway. She's been hinting for years that she'll come to call someday, and I live in perpetual fear of seeing her heading down this road with her Sunday hat on and a fistful of overdue library slips to deliver."

I giggled. Clarice Callaway is the village librarian. She's eighty-two years old, and I'm not giving away any secrets when I say that, because she tells everyone that herself as soon as they're introduced to her. She's also the president of the Historical Preservation Society, and my father says that's a real exercise in irony, because Clarice herself is the best-preserved historical monument for miles around. Also, she has a crush on Will. He told me that whenever he goes to the library, she disappears into the ladies' room, and then comes out again with bright pink rouge on her cheeks, so that she looks like a French doll his sister had when she was a child.

He sighed and wiped his hands on a rag. "It's the radiator this time. In the winter it's the battery, and when spring comes it's the radiator. The tires go flat in summer. Sometimes I think I'll buy a new truck, but then I figure I'd have to learn to deal with a whole new set of disasters. At least now I *know* that every April the radiator hoses will break and the engine will overheat. Better to know what your enemy is before you confront him; right, Meg?"

"Right," I agreed, even though I wasn't at all sure I wanted to be confronted by enemies or disasters, whether I knew them or not.

"Come inside," Will said. "I have a surprise for you."

But my surprise was first. After Will had poured tea for both of us, I opened the big envelope and took out the pictures. I laid the six of them on the kitchen table and watched as Will picked them up one at a time. He didn't laugh or blush or say "Oh, I look *terrible*" the way kids do when they see pictures of themselves. I knew he wouldn't. He picked up each one and studied it, smiling at some, looking thoughtfully at others. Finally he chose the same one that was my favorite: the one where his eyes were closed, and the smoke from his pipe was a thin line along the side and the top of the photograph. He took it to the window and looked at it in better light.

"Meg," he said at last, "all of these are very, very good. You know that already, I'm sure. This is the best one, I think, because of the composition, and also because you hit on just the right combination of shutter speed and aperture setting. You see how the lines in the face are perfectly sharp — you must have a pretty good lens on that little camera of yours — but you slowed it just enough so that the line of smoke has a slight blur to it, as it should.

Smoke has an ephemeral quality, and you caught that, but you didn't sacrifice the clarity of the face. It's a *fine* photograph."

Why did I want to cry when he finished talking? I don't even know what ephemeral means. But something inside me welled up like hot fudge sauce — sweet, and warm, and so rich that you can't bear to have very much. It was because someone who was a real friend was having the exact same feelings I was having, about something that was more important to me than anything else. I bet there are people who go through a whole life and never experience that. I sat there with my hand around the warm mug of tea, and smiled at Will.

"Meg," he said suddenly, gulping his own tea. "I'll make a deal with you!"

I laughed. People say that to me at school, and it means that they want to copy my algebra home-work, and in return I get the Hostess Twinkie from their lunch.

"Remember I told you that I had bought a camera in Germany?"

I nodded.

"It's a fine camera," Will said. "The best made, and of course something like that doesn't diminish with age. I don't know why I haven't used it in so long, except that I lost my enthusiasm for a lot of things when Margaret died. And that," he said

67

gruffly, "is the last thing she would have wanted.

"But I'm going to get it out of the attic. The camera, and four lenses, and a set of filters that go with it. I want you to use it."

The hot fudge started up again. My own camera has just one lens, which can't be removed. I've read about using other kinds of lenses and filters, but I've never had a chance to try.

"I don't know what to say," I told him, and it was true. "What could I possibly do in return?"

"Oh, don't worry about *that!*" laughed Will. "I said I'd make a deal with you. I'm not going to let you off easily, either. In return, I want you to teach me to use the darkroom. Let me borrow your little camera while you're using mine, and we'll set up a regular schedule for lessons. I'll warn you that it's been a long time since I've undertaken to learn anything new. But my eyesight is good, and my hands are steady, still."

"But, Will," I wailed. "I'm only thirteen years old! I've never taught anybody anything!"

Will looked at me very sternly. "My dear Meg," he said, "Mozart wrote his first composition when he was five. Age is a meaningless commodity in most instances. Don't underrate yourself. Now is it a deal?"

I sat there for a moment, looking at my empty mug. Then I shook his hand. He was right; his hands were firm and strong and steady. "It's a deal, Will," I said.

I remembered the Easter egg. In a way it seemed almost silly, now, but I brought out the little box and gave it to him. He held the egg up gravely and examined the design; his eyes lit up with recognition.

"*Myristica fragrans*," he pronounced solemnly. "Nutmeg. Am I right?"

I grinned at him and nodded. "I don't know about the mistica, or whatever you said, but it's nutmeg. You're right."

He put the egg into a shallow pewter bowl, and took it to the living room. After he had put the bowl on a small pine table by the window, both of us stood in the room and looked at it. The blue of the egg was the same muted blue as the oriental rug; the rust and green shades seemed to reflect the colors of the old wood and the hanging, well-tended plants. It was perfect there; Will didn't even have to say so. We just looked at it together as the April sunlight from the window fell onto the bowl and the fragile oval shell, outlined their shadows on the polished table, and then brightened a rectangle on the pattern of the carpet.

"Now, scoot," said Will. "I have to deal with my radiator."

I was just at the end of his muddy driveway, and

his head was back under the hood of the truck, when I remembered. I turned and called to him.

"Will? I forgot to ask you about the big house!"

He brought his head out and groaned. "And I forgot to tell you my surprise!"

So I went back for a minute. I sat on the front steps and scratched Tip beside his ear, while Will pulled the radiator hoses off — "rotten old things," he said to them. "Why do you do this to me every spring?" — and told me about the house. My question, it turned out, was the same as his surprise.

"I was right here last month," he said, "with my head under the hood, as usual. The battery then, of course. And a car drove up with a young couple in it. They asked if I knew anything about that house.

"In the past year, at least ten people have asked me about the house, but they've always been the wrong people. Don't ask me how I know that. It's just something I can feel. And when this young couple — Ben and Maria, their names are — got out of their car, I could tell they were the right ones.

"Ben helped me clean the leads to the battery, and Maria went in the kitchen and made tea for the three of us. By the time Ben and I had washed our hands and finished our tea, I had rented the house to them. When you know it's the right people, it's as easy as that.

"They don't have much money. He's a student

70

still, at Harvard, and he said he was looking for a quiet place for the summer, to write his thesis."

I groaned. Next thing you knew, this whole valley would be noisy from the sound of typewriters. Will laughed; he'd had the same thought.

"But in return for the summer in the house, they're going to fix the place up. He's been working weekends ever since I told them they could have the house. The roof needs work; the wiring needs work; the plumbing needs work. Well, you know what it's like when you get old with no one to take care of you!"

We laughed together. I could tell already that I would like Ben and Maria, because Will did.

"And Maria's going to put in a garden when the ground thaws," he continued. "They'll be moving in officially quite soon, I think. And I've told them about you. They're looking forward to having you stop in, Meg."

Then Will looked a little sheepish, the first time I'd ever seen him look that way. "But I forgot to ask them something," he confessed.

"What?"

He looked in several other directions before he answered. He was embarrassed. Finally he explained, "I forgot to ask them if they're married."

I burst out laughing. "Oh, Will," I said, "do you think it matters?"

He looked as if it hadn't occurred to him that it might not matter. "Well," he said finally, "I can tell you that it would have mattered to *Margaret*. But, well, I guess maybe you're right, Meg. I guess it doesn't really matter to me."

Then he wiped his hands on his rag and grinned. "It might matter to their child, though. From the looks of it, there's going to be a baby coming this summer."

A baby. That was a strange thing to think about. I'm not overly fond of babies. Molly adores them. She says she's going to have at least six someday herself, even though I keep telling her that's environmentally absurd.

I told Molly about it on the phone that night, and she was thrilled at the thought of having a baby in the house across the field. Her voice sounded good, stronger than it has since she got sick. I've talked to her on the phone a lot, and sometimes she's sounded tired and depressed. But now she's feeling well again, and she's looking forward to coming home.

"It's a drag, being here," she said. "Even though there are some good-looking doctors."

That made me laugh. I knew she was feeling normal again if she was noticing the doctors.

I told her how much Will liked his photographs, and that he was going to let me use his German camera.

"Hey, Meg?" she asked. "Do me a favor?"

"Sure." Usually I wouldn't say "sure" without knowing what the favor was; but what the heck, she'd been pretty sick.

"Would you take my picture when I get home? I want a really good one, to give Tierney for his birthday this summer."

"Molly, I'll make you look like a movie star," I told her, and she giggled before she hung up.

6.

Will Banks is learning to use the darkroom, and he's fantastic. Ben and Maria have moved into the house, and they're terrific. Molly is home, and she's being thoroughly unbearable.

Well, as they say, two out of three isn't bad.

I suppose you can't really blame Molly for being a pain. She was awfully sick; no one knows that better than I do. I don't think the sight of her lying there in all that blood will ever go out of my mind.

But apparently she got used to being the center of

attention in the hospital. Who wouldn't, with all those specialists around? Still, here she is at home, and supposedly well — or why would they have discharged her from the hospital? — and she acts as if everyone should still be at her beck and call. And my parents put up with it; that's the amazing thing.

"Could I have a tuna fish sandwich?" asked Molly at lunchtime, the day after she came home. She was lying on the couch in the kitchen, in a pose like Playmate of the Month, except that she was wearing jeans and a sweatshirt.

"Do you want lettuce?" my mother asked her, scurrying to get the bread and mayonnaise. For pete's sake. Do you want lettuce. Two months ago she would have said, "Make it yourself, madam." That's what she would *still* say, to me.

And after all that, Molly didn't even eat the sandwich. She came to the table, ate two bites, and then drifted back to the couch and said she wasn't hungry after all.

"Are you sure you're feeling all right, dear?" asked Mom.

"Quit bugging me, will you?" said Molly, and she stormed off to our room, slammed the door (which fell open again; Molly will never learn that the door to our room is totally useless in a tantrum) and took a nap for the rest of the afternoon.

Molly never used to be like that. *I* used to be like

75

that, sometimes, and I hated myself when I was. Now Molly is that way, and I find myself hating her, or at least hating what has happened to her to make her different.

My parents don't say a word. That's different, too. In the past, when one of us was grouchy, my mother always said and did things that were both understanding and funny, so that we would start to laugh and whatever was making us irritable would just disappear in a comfortable way. Or Dad would be very stern. He says he doesn't have time to waste on rudeness. "Shape up," he would say. And we would shape up, because he didn't leave any choice.

But now Mom doesn't chuckle and tease when Molly is awful. Dad doesn't lay down the law. Instead, Mom gets worried and confused, which makes things worse. Dad gets tense and silent and goes off to his study without saying anything. It's as if an upsetting stranger has moved in with us, and no one knows what to do about it.

Part of why Molly is being so obnoxious, I think, is because she doesn't look very good, and it was always so important to Molly to look pretty. But she lost weight while she was in the hospital (because the food was so dreadful, she says), so that now her face is thinner than it used to be. And more pale. The paleness, I guess, is because she had to have the blood transfusions, and it probably takes the red blood cells a while to build up again.

Worst of all, for Molly, her hair is falling out. That's because of the pills she has to take, my parents said. One of the side effects is that your hair falls out! I told her that there might be medicines with *worse* side effects, like making your nose fall off, but no one thought that was very funny. My mother told her that when she is able to stop taking the medicine, after a while, her hair will grow back thicker and curlier than it was before, but when Mom said that, Molly just said, "Great," very sarcastically and kept staring at her comb full of blond strands. Then Mom said that if it got worse, they would buy her a wig, and Molly said, "Oh, *gross!*" and stomped off to our bedroom.

So things are kind of difficult at our house now. Molly can't go back to school until she gains a little weight and gets her color back. She says she won't go back to school *anyway* if her hair keeps falling out. Mom and Dad don't say much about school. They're depressed about the whole thing, I can tell.

It will just take time. If we're all patient and wait, everything will be the same as it used to be, I know.

Will Banks is very kind to Molly. He comes to the house three evenings a week to work in the darkroom, and he always brings something for her:

a library book to read, or a candy bar, some little thing like that. One night he brought a handful of pussy willows that he had found behind his house: the first ones of spring, and Molly was thrilled. It was the first time I'd seen her really happy about something for a long time.

"Oh, Will," she said softly, "they're beautiful." She held them against her cheek and rubbed the softness like a kitten. We were sitting in the kitchen, and I took a small vase and ran some water into it.

"No water, Meg," said Will. "If you put pussy willows in water, they'll blossom and then die. Just put them in the vase alone, and they'll stay beautiful forever."

There's so much I don't know. I gave Molly the vase, without water, and she arranged the pussy willows in it; she took them up to our room and put them on the table beside her bed. That night, after we were in bed and Molly was already asleep, I looked over, and the moonlight was across the table and across Molly; behind her, on the wall, was the shadow of pussy willows.

It's not surprising that Will knows so much about so many things, because he has an incredible memory. When we began working together in the darkroom, I showed him, first, the basic procedures for developing film. I only showed him once. Then he did it himself, developing a roll that he had shot of his truck and his dog, using his own camera to make sure it was working properly before he gave it to me. He remembered everything: the temperatures, the proportions of chemicals, the timing right down to the second. His negatives were perfect. The pictures weren't great, because, as he said, he'd been "just fooling around, wanting to get the feel of the camera again," but they were technically perfect, developed exactly right.

And he's immensely curious. When I could see that he'd learned to develop film properly, I wanted to go on to the next step: printing the pictures. But Will said, "Wait. What would happen if, when I was developing the film, I purposely made the chemicals too warm? What would happen if I agitated them less? Or more? And what if I had underexposed the film, Meg, when I took the pictures? Couldn't I compensate for that when I developed the film, maybe by prolonging the developing time?"

I thought for a minute. Those things had never occurred to me, and they should have. Of *course* you could compensate.

"I never tried," I said, thinking. "But I bet you could. There must be a book that tells how. Let me —"

He interrupted me. He's also impatient, I've

found, and very independent. "Oh, the heck with books, Meg. Let's figure it out for ourselves. Let's experiment. Someone must have figured it out once, in order to write a book. Why can't we do the same thing?"

So we did. That was a Monday night, and on Tuesday and Wednesday, each of us shot several rolls of film, purposely underexposing and overexposing them. On Wednesday night we developed them, each one a different way. We changed the temperatures on some, the developing time on some, the amount of agitation on some. And we did it! We figured out exactly how to compensate for all sorts of things, how to build up contrast, how to reduce it. We felt like a couple of miracle workers.

When we came out of the darkroom after three hours, Mom was in the kitchen, working on her quilt. She looked up and laughed. "You two sounded like a couple of crazy people in there," she said, "shouting at each other."

I giggled. We *had* been shouting. "Don't leave it in the developer so long, you moron!" I had shouted at Will. "You'll ruin it!"

"I'm *trying* to ruin it!" Will had bellowed back. "So I can figure out how to do it perfectly! How can you learn anything if you won't take risks?"

And *I* was supposed to be teaching *him*.

"Lydia," Will explained to Mom that night,

sitting down to have a cup of tea before he went home, "genius disregards the boundaries of propriety. Genius is permitted to shout if shouting is productive."

Mom laughed again and snipped off the thread as she completed a red-and-white-striped square from a sunsuit I wore when I was three years old. She likes Will. "Well," she said, "I've been living with creative genius long enough that I should know that by now. Charles has been known to shout at his typewriter, if you can believe that."

Will nodded very seriously, chewing on the stem of his pipe. "Oh my, yes. It would be necessary to shout at one's typewriter now and then, I would think. Machinery needs that kind of discipline occasionally. Just today I was shouting at my truck radiator."

Mom was smiling as she measured off a new square in the quilt. It was good to see her relaxed and smiling, the way she used to be, for a change. "How about your homework, Meg?" she asked. "You're not disregarding the boundaries of your homework too, are you?"

I groaned. But I'm keeping up with school, same as always. Suddenly, though, algebra and American history seem pretty dull compared to other things that are happening. I'll be glad when the term ends next month so that I can spend more time on photography. Molly will be completely well by then, too, and things will be easier. And I'll be able to see a lot of Ben and Maria.

Will took me to meet them just after they moved in. Molly came, too; I was surprised that she wanted to, because she's been so miserable and self-conscious about the way she looks that mostly she stays in our room. But when I asked her, she said what the heck, there wasn't anything better to do.

The three of us walked across the field on a hot, sunny Saturday afternoon that smelled like new growing things. We could have gone down the road, of course, but it seemed like the sort of day when walking across a field would be a nice thing to do. Wild flowers were just beginning to appear. They always take me by surprise. It seems, each year, as if winter will go on forever, even back in town. Then when you've resigned yourself to a whole lifetime of grayness, suddenly bright bursts of yellow and purple and white spring up in the fields, and you realize they've been hiding there all along, waiting.

Will was carrying a heavy stick that he sometimes uses when he's walking, especially in the rocky fields. He pointed here and there with the stick, at the little blossoms in the field and the shady border of the woods, as we walked along.

"*Anemonella thalictroides, Cerastium arvense, Cornus*

82

canadensis, Oakesia sessilifolia," he said. Molly and I glanced at him, grinned at each other, and didn't say anything.

"*Uvularia perfoliata,*" Will went on, pointing with his stick to a light yellow, tiny, bell-shaped flower.

"Can you say that three times fast?" asked Molly, laughing.

"Yes," grinned Will back at her.

Suddenly I decided that he was really putting us on. "You're making all that up, Will!" I hooted. "You big phony! You had me fooled for a minute, too!"

He looked down his nose at me in a haughty sort of way, but his eyes were twinkling.

Then he pushed aside some underbrush with his stick, and pointed to a clump of small purple flowers. "*Viola pedata,*" he said, talking to Molly, ignoring me. "So called because the leaves resemble the foot of a bird. You believe me, don't you, Molly?"

Molly was laughing. The sun was shining through her thin hair, and for the first time since she'd been sick, there was color in her cheeks. "I don't know for sure, Will," she smiled. "I *think* I believe you, but the only wild flower I recognize is goldenrod."

He nodded. "*Solidago,*" he said. "Very common around here, a remarkable plant. But we won't see it

83

bloom until the end of July. In the meantime, you should investigate some of these others, Molly. It would keep you busy until you can go back to school, and it would be good for you, being in the fresh air."

Molly shrugged. She didn't like being reminded of her problems. We walked on.

Ben and Maria were behind the house, starting a garden. They had a patch of ground dug up, and Ben was standing in the middle of the turned earth, chopping at the lumps with a hoe. There was sweat all over his bare back — he wasn't wearing anything but faded, patched jeans — and even though there was a handkerchief tied around his head, his hair and beard were wet with sweat too. He smiled when he saw us.

"Ah, saviors!" he called. "You're coming to rescue me from this slave labor, right?"

"Wrong," called the girl who was sitting in the grass at the corner of the garden patch. "No rescue! I want to get my peas planted. Hi, Will!"

I burst out laughing. Will had told me very casually that there seemed to be a baby coming. That was the understatement of the year. Sometimes I forget that Will is seventy years old, and that he's a little shy about some things. Maria was so thoroughly pregnant that I thought we would do well to start boiling water immediately.

She was sitting with her legs crossed, and her middle was resting on her knees. She was wearing a man's shirt with the sleeves ripped out; her arms were bare and very tan, the same as her legs. The shirt was buttoned around her, but just barely; the middle button was pulled sideways by her stomach, and it was going to pop off very soon. I hoped she had a bigger shirt ready; either that, or that the baby would be born before long. It looked like it was going to be a race between the baby and the button, and I didn't know enough about either pregnancy or the art of mending to be able to predict which was going to detach itself first.

Maria had one long dark braid down her back, and a smile that included all three of us, as well as Ben, who was still leaning on his hoe.

"I'd like you to meet my two friends, Meg and Molly Chalmers," Will said. "Meg is the photographer I've been telling you about. And Molly is the cheerleader, but I'm going to try to turn her into a botanist. Girls, this is Ben Brady. And Maria."

Maria reached up to shake our hands, and said, "Maria Abbott." Out of the corner of my eye I could see Will flinch slightly. It all went right over Molly's head. She was so interested in the baby.

"When is the baby due?" asked Molly. "Do you mind my asking? I just love babies."

From the garden, where he had started to hack at

a clod of earth that obviously had a rock in the middle of it, Ben looked up and chuckled. He rolled his eyes. "Does she *mind* your asking? Prepare yourself, Molly, for an hour . . . two hours, *three* hours . . . of conversation. That's all she talks about! I remember a time — it wasn't so long ago, either, come to think of it — when Maria and I used to talk about books. Music. The weather. Politics. Little things like that. Now we sit down in the evening after supper, and we pour a couple cups of tea, put some Beethoven on the stereo, and talk about diapers." He groaned, but he was looking at Maria affectionately.

We were all laughing, even Maria. She threw a handful of weeds at him lightly, and said, "Just hoe your row, Daddy. Molly, come in the house with me. I'll show you the cradle I've been refinishing."

She got to her feet awkwardly, and, standing, said, "Look!" She smoothed the shirt over her middle so we could see how round she was. "It isn't due until July. Can you believe that? It's incredible how big I am, but I'm sure July is right. Do you know how you figure out your due date? It's really easy. You add seven days to the date that your last period started, and —"

I started talking quickly to Will, because I could see how embarrassed he was by the conversation. Maria and Molly went in the house, and Ben put down the hoe. He showed Will and me how he had hauled rocks from the field to make a small wall beside the driveway, and the work he'd been doing on the roof. We wandered around for a long time, talking about what needed to be done to the old house; Will explained how things had been when he was a child, and Ben thought of how to make them that way again. We stood, finally, by a bare patch of earth beside the kitchen door, and Will described the flowers that had been there once, how his grandmother had emptied her dishwater there, over the flowers, and they had grown bigger and healthier than the other plants.

"Of course!" said Ben. "It probably had little scraped-off bits of food, organic stuff, in it. She was mulching the flowers without even realizing it. That's cool; that's really cool. We should try that. I bet we could grow herbs there; Maria's dying to have an herb garden. 'Parsley, sage, rosemary, and thyme,'" he sang, off-key.

Will looked somewhat nonplused by Ben, Maria, the whole thing. But he liked them; I could tell. And he was happy about the house; I could tell that, too.

Maria made iced tea for everyone, and we went inside. The house was furnished with odds and ends of things, most of them with the paint partly removed. Maria was busy refinishing everything.

There was an old spinning wheel, and she said she was going to learn to spin. The cradle, which was almost finished. A rocking chair, partly done, with a pile of sandpaper on the seat. Ben's typewriter and books stood on a desk made from an old door balanced on two sawhorses. Will sat down in the only real chair, a big comfortable one with its stuffing popping out like milkweed from the pods in fall.

"Hope no one has hay fever," laughed Maria as Will sat down. "Every time anyone sits in that chair, feathers and dust fly all over the room. But I'm going to reupholster it after the baby's born."

Ben groaned. "She's gone mad, really mad," he teased. "I live in constant fear that some morning I'll wake up and find that she's sanded and scrubbed and peeled and painted me in the night!"

Maria leaned over and examined his bare foot. "Come to think of it," she mused, "that's not a bad idea. You could use a little work." Then she leaned her head for a moment against his blue-jeaned leg, and he rumpled the top of her hair with his hand.

I didn't say much. I was very happy, being there. The sun had gotten lower in the sky, and as it came through the windows it fell on Maria as she sat there on the floor leaning against Ben, in gold patterns on her shoulders and the thick braid of hair. I was making a photograph in my mind.

But Molly chattered on and on. It was good to hear her; all the tenseness and anger were gone. She and Ben and Maria talked about what the inside of the house needed: hanging plants in the sunny windows; fresh white paint on the old plaster walls; just the right kind of curtains. "I'll weave them myself!" Maria exclaimed; Ben sighed, smiled, and stroked her head.

On the way home, Molly lagged behind Will and me. She was gathering wild flowers, one of each kind. She said she'd press them, and Will told her he would help her to identify each one, that he had a book she could use.

"You know," I said slowly to Will, as we walked back through the field together, "I wish I were more like Molly. I mean, I wish I knew the right things to say to people. Sometimes I seem to just *sit* there."

"Meg," Will said, and he put his arm around me as we walked, "do you see that section of the woods over there, where the spruce tree is beside the birches?"

"Yes," I said, looking where he pointed.

"Not far into the woods, beyond the spruce, at the right time of year, there's a clump of fringed gentians. Have you ever seen a fringed gentian?"

How do you like that? When I said something really serious, really personal, for pete's sake, to my best friend, he wasn't even listening. He was still thinking about his plants.

"No," I told him, a little sarcastically. "I've never seen a fringed gentian."

"It will be after you've moved back to town," he said. "It won't bloom until the end of September, maybe even October. But I want you to come back, so I can show it to you."

"Okay," I sighed. I didn't care about his old fringed gentian.

"It's important, Meg," Will said. "You promise?"

Well, if it was important to him, all right. I would want to come back, anyway, and I didn't mind looking at his flower. Maybe he wanted to photograph it or something.

"I promise, Will," I said.

7.

Finally Molly has stopped being a grouch. It was gradual, and I'm not even sure the change is a good one. She hasn't gone back to being the old Molly she was before she was sick. She isn't giggly, funny Molly anymore, full of smiles and ideas and silly enthusiasms.

I don't know what she is, now. A stranger, mostly. It's as if she has become part of a different world, one that doesn't include me anymore, or even Mom and Dad. She's quieter, more serious, almost withdrawn. When I tell her about things that are happening at school, she listens, and asks questions, but it's as if she doesn't really care much; she's only listening to be polite.

Only a few things interest her now. She spends a lot of time with the flowers. In the past, for Molly, flowers were things to run through in a field, to pick, to bury your nose in, to arrange in a vase on the table. Now, with Will's help, she's learning about them; she reads the books he's brought to her, and identifies the wild flowers she's found in the fields. She classifies them, labels them, arranges them in order in a book that she's putting together. It takes most of her time. She's very careful, and very serious, about her flowers. We don't dare, ever, to tease her about them.

It's as if she has become, suddenly, old.

The other thing that still interests her is the baby. She visits Maria often, and they talk and talk about the baby. Molly is helping Maria to make clothes for it; they sew together, and when she finishes something, Molly smoothes it with such care, folds it neatly, and puts it away in the drawer they're filling with little things.

Even Ben and Maria seem a little puzzled by the concern Molly has for all those tiny nightgowns and sweaters. Once I heard Ben say to her, "Hey, Moll. It's *already* going to be the best-dressed kid in the valley. Quit sewing for a while, will you? Come with me to see if we can find some wild strawberries."

But Molly just smiled at him and shook her head. "You go ahead, Ben," she said. "Take Meg. I want to finish this. I want everything to be perfect when the baby comes."

Ben groaned. "Molly, don't you *know* what babies are like? It's just going to pee on those clothes. Why do they need to be perfect with that kind of future in store for them?"

Molly smiled at him and went on stitching.

And sometimes, for no reason, Molly is like a baby, herself. One night after supper, when it was raining outside, we were sitting in front of the fireplace. Mom was working on the quilt, Dad was reading, and Molly and I were just watching the logs shift and send sparks into the chimney as they burned. We had our pajamas on.

Suddenly, very quietly, Molly got up, went over to Dad, and climbed onto his lap. He didn't say anything. He just put his book down, put his arms around her, held her, and watched the fire. She put her head on his shoulder like a sleepy two-year-old, and with one hand he stroked the fine, wispy, babylike hair she has left.

I could understand, I guess, the change in Molly if she were still sick. But she isn't; she's perfectly well.

93

She is still taking the pills, and every few weeks
Mom takes her to Portland to the hospital, for tests,
to make sure everything is okay. Soon, the doctors
said, she'll be able to stop taking the pills altogether,
and then her hair will grow back. She'll win a
beauty contest, the specialist told her, when she has
her curls again.

Mom told us that at dinner, after they had come
back from the hospital, and Molly just smiled, the
casual and tolerant kind of smile that most people
give to small children who say foolish things. But
there was a time when it would have meant
something to Molly, to be told she was beautiful.

Well, things change. I just have to learn to adjust
to what they change to.

One morning early in June, my father came into
the kitchen, poured himself a cup of coffee, and
sighed. I was just finishing my breakfast and had
planned to spend all of Saturday morning in the
darkroom. I had photographed Maria by her kitch-
en window, and Will and I were experimenting
with different kinds of paper for the finished prints.
I could hardly wait to try printing Maria in
different contrasts, textures, and tones.

But when Dad pours a cup of coffee, sits down in
the kitchen, and sighs, I know I'd better stick
around because something's up.

"I just got a phone call," he said, "from Clarice Callaway."

"Are your books overdue?" I asked. "She's a real stickler about overdue books."

He laughed. "No, she and I have achieved a pretty good understanding about my overdue books. I wish that's all it were. She started the conversation by saying, 'I don't want to meddle, but —' You know what that means."

"It means she wants to meddle. Sometimes she starts with, 'I don't mean to be inquisitive, but —.'"

"Right. And that means she means to be inquisitive. I can see you have Clarice figured out, Meg. Well, this time she's upset about Will renting the house. She says the whole village is up in arms — which I assume is a Callaway exaggeration — because there are hippies living in Will's house."

"Hippies? What's that supposed to mean?"

Dad frowned. "*I* don't know. Ben has a beard, and I guess by Clarice's definition that makes him a hippie. But maybe you can shed some light on the things she brought up. Is it true that Ben and Maria are growing marijuana behind the house?"

I started to laugh. "Dad, of course not. They've put in peas and strawberries so far. Ben wants to plant squash, but he hasn't decided what varieties yet. And his tomatoes and beans go in this week."

95

"Is it true that they walk around nude?"

"Good grief, Dad. No, it isn't true, but even if it were, whose business would it be? They're out in the middle of nowhere. One afternoon Maria took off her shirt and lay in the sun. When I came along, she had her shirt off, and she asked me if I minded. I said I didn't, and she left it off for a while. She gets so hot and uncomfortable, because the baby's due soon."

"Well, that was another of Clarice's topics. Is it true that they're planning to have that baby by themselves, in the house?"

"Yes. But they've both been reading everything they can find about delivering a baby. Maria's doing all sorts of exercises, and they took a course together in Boston. And Dr. Putnam in the village has agreed to come if they need him."

Dad scratched his head. "No chance that they'll change their minds about that?"

"I don't think so, Dad. It's very important to them. They're really excited about doing it them-selves, about having the baby born there in the house, instead of in a hospital. They don't like the impersonal qualities of a hospital. But the baby's important to them, too. They're doing everything they can to be sure the baby will be safe and healthy."

"Well, I guess I can try to convince Clarice of

that. So that leaves only one thing. They *are* married, aren't they?"

I stirred the last soggy Rice Krispies in the bottom of my bowl. "They love each other. They talk about being old together, sitting in rocking chairs on their porch, and what it will feel like to kiss each other when they have false teeth and bifocals."

"That's not what I asked. Are they married?"

Funny how Rice Krispies stick to a bowl when they're wet. I really had to pry them loose from the sides of the bowl with my spoon. "I don't think so, Dad. Maria doesn't wear a wedding ring, and her last name is different from Ben's."

My father winced. "That's what I was afraid of. I don't quite know how to deal with that one. And Clarice has already called Will's nephew in Boston. Well, maybe you should talk to Ben and Maria about it, Meg. They might as well be prepared."

Great. What was I supposed to do, go tell my friends who were going to have a baby next month that I thought they ought to get married? What business was it of mine?

Still, my father was right. They ought to know what was going on. I gave up my plans for working in the darkroom that morning. Ben and Maria had asked if they could see some of my photographs, so I took the ones I'd done of Will, and two that I'd just finished of Molly. She hadn't even noticed my taking them; she'd been sitting on the front steps, working on some of her wild flowers. With Will's help, she'd mounted each of the flowers she'd pressed, and labeled them with their Latin names. One of the pictures showed Molly holding a blossom of Queen Anne's lace up against the sunlight; both she and the blossom were in silhouette. The other photograph was of her bent head, with what was left of her curly hair falling down over her face as she arranged some tiny flowers on a page.

Ben and Maria were hanging sheets and towels on the clothesline behind their house when I got there. They did their wash together every Saturday, using an old wringer machine that they'd bought at a garage sale. Ben always teased Maria that if she didn't have the baby on time, he would put her through the wringer and squeeze it out; just thinking about it makes my stomach lurch, but Maria thought it was funny.

"Hey, Meg!" Ben called cheerfully when he saw me coming. "This time next month, we'll be hanging diapers!"

"You mean *you'll* be hanging diapers," laughed Maria, as she snapped a wet dish towel into the air to get the wrinkles out. "*I'm* going to be lying in bed, being waited on. Having tea brought to me on a tray, while I recover!"

Knowing Maria, I didn't think she was going to be spending much time in bed recovering. She'd probably be up and around the day after the baby arrived, sanding the floors, building a bookcase, making raspberry jam. I talked her into letting me help Ben with the rest of the laundry, and she went inside to make a pot of tea.

We sat around their little painted kitchen table and shared tea with fresh mint in it. I took out the photographs to show them. They loved the ones of Will, because they love Will. But the two of Molly were better. They thought that, and I could see the difference, too. Partly it was because I have been learning so much from working with Will; partly it was because I was using his German camera now. He had taught me to use the different lenses; I had shot these two of Molly with the 90mm lens, and I'd been able, that way, to do it from a distance, so that she hadn't known I was doing it. The look on her face was absorbed, preoccupied with her flowers; the fine lens caught the sharp outline of sunlight on her hair and the shadows across her face and hands.

"I asked Molly if she wanted to come with me this morning," I explained, "but she wasn't feeling well. She said to say hi, though, and to see how you're coming with the cradle."

Maria grinned with pride and pointed into the living room, where the cradle stood, finished. It glowed with wax; folded over one side was a soft yellow crocheted blanket.

"Meg," asked Ben hesitantly, "what's wrong with Molly?"

I told them about her illness, about the nosebleeds, the hospital, the transfusions, and the pills that were making her hair fall out. They were both very quiet. Ben reached over and ran his hand gently over the top of my head. "That's rough," he said. "That's very rough."

"Well," I explained, "it's not that big a deal. And she's lots better. Look." I pointed to one of the photographs. "See how round her face is getting? She's gained ten pounds since she came home from the hospital."

Maria poured more tea into our cups. "I'm glad we came here, Ben," she said suddenly, "for Molly. She's so excited about the baby."

That reminded me why I had come to see them. "Ben? Maria?" I said. "You know the little church in the village?"

"Sure," Ben said. "The white steeple. It looks like a postcard picture. Why? You going to photograph it?"

"No," I said. "But last Saturday, when I was in town with Mom to buy groceries, there was a wedding there. It was really neat. The bride came out and threw her bouquet from the step. The

100

bridesmaids all had light blue dresses on, and —" I hesitated. "Well, I don't know. It was just nice."

Ben and Maria were both making faces. Ben is quite good at making faces; he screwed his mouth up sideways and crossed his eyes. "Weddings," he said. "Yuck."

Maria rolled her eyes and agreed with him. "Yuck," she said.

"*Why?*" I asked. "What's wrong with getting married, darn it?"

They both looked surprised. "Nothing's wrong with getting *married*," Ben said. "It's weddings that are so awful. What do you think, Maria, shall we show her?"

Maria grinned and nodded. "Yeah," she said. "She's a good kid."

Ben went into the living room and took a box out of the closet. He brought it back to the kitchen table and set it down. He leered, fingered his beard, and said in a diabolical voice, "Ya wanna see some feelthy pictures, lady?" Then he opened the box.

I started to laugh. They weren't bad photographs; in fact, technically, they were very good photographs, even though I'm not crazy about color.

But they were *awful.* And they were of Ben and Maria's wedding, for pete's sake. They were in a thick white leather album that said *Our Wedding* on the cover in gold letters. And I could see, while I

101

looked at them, what Ben and Maria meant about yucky weddings.

There were the tuxedos, and the tails, and the top hats. There was Maria with her dress pulled up to show a lacy blue garter. There were the huge baskets of flowers beside the altar of the church. "Know what happened to those flowers?" Maria asked. "Two hundred dollars' worth of flowers? They got thrown away as soon as the service was over."

There was the wedding cake, about three feet high, decorated with birds and flowers and frosting ribbons. "Know how much that cake cost?" grinned Ben. "A hundred bucks. Know what it tasted like? Cardboard."

There were hundreds of people drinking champagne. "Know who those people are?" asked Maria. "My parents' friends. Ben's parents' friends. Know what they're doing? Getting drunk, on five hundred dollars' worth of champagne."

And there were Ben and Maria, surrounded by people, flowers, food. They were smiling at the camera, but they both looked as if they didn't mean it much.

"Know who that is?" Ben asked. I nodded. "That's Ben Brady and Maria Abbott, who wanted to get married in a field full of daisies beside a stream. Who wanted to have guitar music instead of a five-piece band; homemade wine instead of champagne," he said. He slammed the book closed and put it back in the box.

"Why didn't you?" I asked.

They shrugged. "Oh, sometimes it's just easier to please people," Maria said finally. "Ben's parents wanted a big wedding. My parents wanted a big wedding. We did it for them, I guess."

"Can I ask you a funny question?"

"Sure."

"Why don't you both have the same last name?"

It was Maria who answered me. "You know, Meg, I had the name Abbott all my life. Maria Abbott did things that I was proud of. I won a music award in high school, and I was Maria Abbott. I was elected to Phi Beta Kappa in college, something I worked hard for, and I was Maria Abbott. When I realized I wanted to marry Ben, I also realized that I didn't want to stop being Maria Abbott. Ben could understand that. There's no law that says a wife must take her husband's name. So I didn't. Someday you may feel the same way about Meg Chalmers."

Right now I know there's no one I would rather be than Meg Chalmers. It's a funny thing about names, how they become part of someone. I thought suddenly of the little boy Will Banks, years ago, who sat in a room angry and sad, and carved WILLIAM on the closet floor.

"Hey," I said. Funny I hadn't thought to ask before. "The baby. What are you going to name him? Her? It?"

Maria groaned. "Ask any other question, Meg. *Don't* ask what we're going to name him her it. We can't decide. We fight about it all the time. We scream at each other. It's *awful.*"

Ben said, "I've quit worrying about it. I figure the baby is going to arrive and before it does anything else, it's going to shake hands all around and say, 'Hi. I'm — — —.' That's the only way we're going to know what its name is."

Then he jumped up, bounded through the living room, and opened a door. "But look! This is where it will be born!" I looked through the living room and saw an empty room beyond, very clean, its walls freshly painted white, with a brass bed alone in the center.

"And this is where it will sleep," said Maria, smiling, touching the cradle with her bare foot, so that it rocked slightly.

"And this is what it'll wear!" said Ben proudly, reaching into the drawer of a partly sanded pine chest, and pulling out a tiny blue nightgown. The drawer was filled with little folded things.

104

"This is what it'll eat!" grinned Maria, cupping her hands around her breasts.

"And —" Ben stood still suddenly, in the middle of the living room. "Meg, come. I want to show you something." He took my hand, and I followed him out the back door, picking up my photographs on the way. It was almost lunchtime.

Ben took me past the garden where the peas were thriving against the wire trellises, across the newly cleared space where he'd been pulling up alders, past the little wooden bird feeder that Maria filled with seeds each morning. Behind a clump of young pine trees, he had pulled out brush and exposed part of a rock wall that had been there, I knew, for more than a hundred years. The sunlight filtered down through the nearby woods into the little secluded space; he had cut the grass there, and it was very soft, very green, very quiet.

He put his arm over my shoulders and said, "This is where we'll bury the baby, if it doesn't live."

I couldn't believe it. I pushed his arm off me and said, "*What?*"

"You know," he said firmly, "sometimes things don't work out the way you want them to. If the baby dies, Maria and I will bury it here."

"It's not going to die! What a horrible thing to say!"

"Look, Meg," Ben said, "you can *pretend* that bad

things will never happen. But life's a lot easier if you realize and admit that sometimes they do. Of course the baby's probably going to be just fine. But Maria and I talk about the other possibility, too. Just in case; just in case."

I turned away from him and left him standing there. I was so angry I was shaking. I looked back; his hands were in his pockets, and he was watching me.

I said, "Just in case you're interested, Ben Brady, I think you're an absolutely rotten person. That baby doesn't deserve you for a father."

Then I walked home, and on the way home I was sorry I had said it, but it was too late to go back.

8.

Molly is in the hospital again, and it's my fault.

Why can't I learn when to keep my mouth shut? I'd already said something I regretted, to Ben, and hadn't had the nerve to go to him and apologize. It was just a week later that I blew it with Molly.

She was lying on her bed, in her nightgown, even though it was eleven in the morning. She's gotten so darn lazy, and my parents don't even say anything to her about it. That's partly why I was mad at her, to begin with, because she was still in her night-gown at eleven in the morning.

She was grouchy and mad, too. I'm not sure why. I think mostly it was because school had just ended, before she'd even had a chance to go back. Tierney McGoldrick hardly ever calls her anymore. She doesn't know it, but toward the end of school he started dating a red-haired senior girl. At least I was smart enough not to tell Molly *that*.

But there she was, lying on her bed, grumbling about how awful she looks. I am so sick of hearing Molly talk about how she looks. Her face is too fat. Her hair is too thin. To hear her talk, you'd think she was really a mess, when the truth is that she's still a billion times prettier than I am, which is why I'm sick of listening to her.

I told her to shut up.

She told me to drop dead, and before I dropped dead, to pick up my sneakers from her side of the room.

I told her to pick them up herself.

She started to get up, I think to pick up my sneakers and throw them at me, and when she swung her legs over the side of the bed, I suddenly saw what they looked like.

"Molly!" I said, forgetting about the sneakers. "What's wrong with your *legs?*"

"What do you *mean*, what's wrong with my legs?" No one had ever criticized Molly's legs before; in fact, even I have to admit that Molly's got nice legs. She held up her nightgown and looked down.

Both of her legs were covered with dark red spots. It looked like a lot of mosquito bites, except that they weren't swollen.

"Does it hurt?"

"No," she said slowly, looking puzzled. "What could it be? It wasn't there yesterday; I know it wasn't."

"Well, it's there now, and it sure looks weird."

She pulled her nightgown down to cover her legs. Then she got into bed and pulled the covers up around her. "Don't tell anyone," she said.

"I will, too. I'm telling Mom." I started out of the room.

"Don't you *dare*," Molly ordered.

I'll be darned if I'll take orders from Molly. Anyway, I really thought my parents ought to know. I went downstairs and told Mom that there was something wrong with Molly's legs; she jumped up with a frightened look and went upstairs. I stayed out of it after that, but I listened.

I heard Mom and Molly arguing. I heard my mother get my father from the study. Then more arguing with Molly. I heard my mother go to the upstairs phone, make a call, and go back to Molly.

Then Molly crying. Yelling. I had never in my

life heard Molly like that before. She was screaming, "No! I won't! I won't!"

Things quieted after a few minutes, and then my father came down. His face was very drawn, very tired. "We have to take Molly back to the hospital," he told me abruptly, and without waiting for me to answer, he went out to start the car.

Mom came downstairs with Molly. She was in her bathrobe and slippers, and she was sobbing. When they were by the front door, Molly saw me standing all alone in the living room. She turned to me, still crying, and said, "I hate you! I hate you!"

"Molly," I whispered, "please don't."

They were in the car and ready to leave when I heard my mother call to me. I went outside, letting the screen door bang behind me, and walked over to the car. "Molly wants to tell you something," Mom said.

Molly was in the back seat, huddled in the corner, rubbing her eyes with the back of her hand. "Meg," she said, choking a little because she was trying to stop crying, "tell Ben and Maria not to have the baby until I get home!"

"Okay," I nodded. "I'll tell them." As if they had any control over it! But I would tell them what Molly said, just because Molly asked me to. At that point I would have done anything in the world for Molly.

I went back upstairs, picked up my sneakers and put them in the closet. I made Molly's bed. The pussy willows were still there, in their little vase. The photographs of Will were back on the wall, and the two of Molly and her flowers were with them now. The chalk mark was still there, faded, but there. It was a nice room, except that an hour before, Molly had been in it, and now she wasn't, and it was my fault.

I went down to the darkroom, gathered up the photographs of Maria I'd been working on, and walked across the field to their house.

Will Banks was there, having lunch with Ben and Maria. They were all sitting outside at the picnic table, eating the entire crop of peas. There was a huge bowl of them in the middle of the table, and they were each eating from it with their own spoons, as if it were the most normal sort of lunch in the world.

"Hey, Meg!" Ben greeted me. "How's it going? Have a pea. Have *two* peas!"

He fed me two peas from his spoon; they were the tenderest, sweetest peas I've ever eaten. I sat down on the bench beside Will, and said, "Molly's back in the hospital, and she says please don't have the baby until she comes home. I know that's a dumb thing to say," and then I started to cry.

Will Banks put his arms around me and rocked

111

me back and forth as if I were a baby. I cried until his shirt collar was wet clear through, saying "It's my fault, it's my fault, it's my fault" over and over again. Will said nothing except "There. There."

Finally I stopped crying, sat up straight, blew my nose on the handkerchief Will gave me, and told them what had happened. No one said very much. They told me, of course, that it wasn't my fault. I knew that already. Ben said, "You know, sometimes it's nice just to have someone to blame, even if it has to be yourself, even if it doesn't make sense."

We sat there quietly for a minute, and then I asked if I could borrow Maria's spoon. She wiped it on her napkin and gave it to me, and I ate all the peas that were left in the big bowl. There were *pounds* of peas, and I ate them all. I have never been so hungry in my life.

The three of them watched in amazement while I ate all those peas. When I was finished, Maria started to giggle. Then we all started to laugh, and laughed until we were exhausted.

It is so good to have friends who understand how there is a time for crying and a time for laughing, and that sometimes the two are very close together.

I took out the photographs of Maria. Will had seen them, of course, because we'd worked on them together. He is as able in the darkroom now as I am, but our interests are different. He is fascinated by the technical aspects of photography: by the chemicals, and the inner workings of cameras. I don't care so much about those things. I care about the expressions on people's faces, the way the light falls onto them, and the way the shadows are in soft patterns and contrast.

We looked at the pictures together, and talked about them. Ben was much like Will, interested in the problems of exposure and film latitude; Maria was like me: she liked seeing how the shadows curved around the fullness of the baby inside her, how her hands rested on the roundness of her middle, how her eyes were both serene and excited at the same time.

"Meg," she said, "Ben and I were talking about something the other night, and we want you to think it over and talk about it with your parents. If you want to, and if they don't mind, we'd like you to photograph the birth of the baby."

I was floored. "Golly," I said slowly, "I don't know. It never occurred to me. I mean, I don't want to intrude."

But they were both shaking their heads. "No," Ben said. "It wouldn't be an intrusion. We wouldn't want just anyone there, and of course you'd have to be careful to stay out of the way and not to touch anything sterile. But you're special, Meg; you're close to us. Someday Maria and I would like to be able to look back at that moment. We'd like the baby, someday, to be able to see it, too. You're the one who can do it, if you want to."

I wanted to, desperately. But I had to be honest with them, also. "I've never seen a baby being born," I said. "I don't even know much about it."

"Neither have we!" Maria laughed. "But we'll prepare you for that part. Ben will show you our books, and explain everything in advance so that you'll know exactly what to expect when the time comes. Only, Ben," she added to him, "I think you'd better do it *soon*, because I don't know how much longer we have. The calendar says two weeks, but there are times when I wonder if it might be sooner."

I promised to talk to my parents, and Ben said he would, too. Suddenly I thought of something. "What if it's born at night?" I asked. "There won't be enough light. I could use a flash, I suppose, but —"

Ben held up one hand. "Don't worry!" he said. He cupped his hands into a megaphone and held them against Maria's stomach. Then he spoke to the baby through his hands: "Now hear this, kid. You are under instructions to wait until Molly comes home. Then come, but do it in daylight, you hear?

"That'll do it," Ben said. "Maria and I are determined to have an obedient child."

114

Before I left, I took Ben aside and spoke to him alone. "I'm sorry, Ben, for what I said that day."

He squeezed my shoulders. "That's okay, Meg. We all say things we're sorry for. But do you understand now what I was talking about that day?"

I shook my head and answered him seriously, honestly. "No. I think you're wrong, to anticipate bad things. And I don't understand why you even want to think about something like that. But I'm still sorry for what I said."

"Well," Ben said, "we're friends, anyway. Hang in there, Meg." And he shook my hand.

Will walked me home across the field. He was very quiet. Halfway home, he said, "Meg, you're very young. Do you think it's a good idea, really, being there when that child is born?"

"Why not?"

"It might be very frightening. Birth isn't an easy thing, you know."

"I know that." I dislodged a small rock with one toe and kicked it through a clump of tall grass. "For pete's sake, Will, how can I learn if I don't take risks? You're the one who taught me that!"

Will stopped short and thought for a minute. "You're absolutely right, Meg. Absolutely right." He looked a little sheepish.

I looked around the field. "Will, what happened

115

to all those little yellow flowers that were here last month?"

"Gone until next June," he told me. "They've all been replaced by July's flowers. Molly's goldenrod will be in bloom before long."

"I *liked* those little yellow ones," I said grumpily.

" 'Margaret, are you grieving over Goldengrove unleaving?' " Will asked.

"What?" I was puzzled. He never called me Margaret; what was he talking about?

He smiled. "It's a poem by Hopkins. Your father would know. 'It is the blight man was born for, It is Margaret you mourn for,' " he went on.

"Not me," I told him arrogantly. "I *never* mourn for myself."

"We all do, Meg," Will said. "We all do."

That was three weeks ago. July is almost over. Molly isn't home yet. The baby hasn't been born, so I suppose it's following Ben's instructions and waiting for her. I've studied the books on delivering babies with Maria and Ben, and I'm ready to do the photographs. My parents don't mind. When I asked them, they said "Sure" without even discussing it. They're very preoccupied. I know why, finally.

It was a few nights ago, after supper. My dad was smoking his pipe at the kitchen table. The dishes were done; Mom was sewing on the quilt, which is almost finished. I was just hanging around, talking too much, trying to make up for the quiet that had been consuming our house. I even turned the radio on; there was some rock music playing.

"Hey, Dad, dance with me!" I said, pulling at his arm. It was something silly we used to do sometimes, back in town. My dad is a *terrible* dancer, but sometimes he used to dance with Molly and me in the kitchen; it used to break my mother up.

He finally put down his pipe and got up and started dancing. Poor Dad; he hadn't gotten any better since the last time we did it, and I think I have, a little. But he's pretty uninhibited, and he tried. It was dark outside; we had eaten late. Mom turned on the light, and I could see on the kitchen walls some of the drawings of wild flowers that Molly had been doing, that she had hung here and there. Dad and I danced and danced until he was sweating and laughing. Mom was laughing, too.

Then the music changed, to a slow piece. Dad breathed a great sigh of relief and said, "Ah, my tempo. May I have the pleasure, my dear?" He held out his arms to me and I curled up inside them. We waltzed slowly around the kitchen like people in an old movie until the music ended. We stood facing each other at the end, and I said suddenly, "I wish Molly was here."

My mother made a small noise, and when I looked over at her, she was crying. I looked back at

117

Dad in bewilderment, and there were tears on his face, too, the first time I had ever seen my father cry.

I reached out my arms to him, and we both held out our arms to Mom. She moved into them, and as the music started again, another slow, melancholy song from some past summer I couldn't remember, the three of us danced together. The wild flowers on the wall moved in a gradual blur through our circling and through my own tears. I held my arms tight around the two of them as we moved around in a kind of rhythm that kept us close, in an enclosure made of ourselves that kept the rest of the world away, as we danced and wept at the same time. I knew then what they hadn't wanted to tell me, and they knew that I knew, that Molly wouldn't be coming home again, that Molly was going to die.

9.

I dream of Molly again and again.

Sometimes they are short, sunshine-filled dreams, in which she and I are running side by side in a field filled with goldenrod. She's the old Molly, the Molly I knew all my life, the Molly with long blond curls and her light laugh. The Molly who runs with strong tan legs and bare feet. She runs faster than I can, in my dream, looks back at me, laughing, and I call to her, "Wait! Wait for me, Molly!"

She holds out her hand to me, and calls, with her

hair blowing around her, streaked with sun, "Come on, Meg! You can catch up if you try!"

I wake up; the room is dark, and her bed is empty beside mine. I think of her somewhere in a hospital I have never seen, and wonder if she is dreaming the same dream.

Sometimes they are darker dreams of the same field. I am the one, in this darker dream, who has run faster; I have reached some misty destination, a dark and empty house, where I stand waiting for her, watching her from a window as she runs. But the flowers in the field have begun to turn brown, as if summer is ending too soon, and Molly is stumbling; it is she who is calling to me, "Meg, wait! Wait! I can't make it, Meg!" And there is no way I can help her.

I wake from this dream, too, in a dark and empty room from which the sound of her breathing in the next bed has gone.

I have a nightmare in which a baby is born, but is old, already, at birth. The baby looks at us, those of us who are there, with aged and tired eyes, and we realize with horror that his life is ending at the very moment of its beginning. "Why? Why?" we ask, and the baby doesn't answer. Molly is there, and she is angry at our asking; she shrugs coldly and turns away from us. Only she knows the answer, and she won't share it with us, although we plead with her.

120

I wake terrified that it is real.

I told my father of the dreams. When I was a very little girl and had nightmares, it was always my father who came to my room when I cried out. He used to turn on the light and hold me; he showed me that the dreams weren't true.

Now he can't. We sat on the front steps in the evening, and I blew the gray fuzz of dying dandelions into the pink breeze as the sun was setting. The fears that come into my room in the night seemed far away, but Dad said, "Your dreams come out of what is real, you know. It helps, some, to think about what they mean. That you and Molly are going to be separated, even though you don't want to be. That you want to know why, why life sometimes ends too soon, but no one can answer that."

I crushed the stem of a dandelion in my hand. "It doesn't help, understanding why I have nightmares. How can it help? It can't make Molly better.

"It isn't fair!" I said, the way I said it so often when I was a little girl.

"Of course it isn't fair," Dad said. "But it happens. It happens, and we have to accept that."

"And it wasn't fair that you and Mom didn't tell me!" I said, looking for someone to blame for something. "You knew all along, didn't you? You knew from the very beginning!"

121

He shook his head. "Meg, the doctors told us that there was a chance she would be all right. They have these medicines that they try. There is always a chance something will work. There was no way that Mom and I could tell you when there was a chance."

"Then isn't there *still* a chance?"

He shook his head slowly. "Meg, we can hope for it. We *do* hope for it. But the doctors say there isn't, now. The medicines aren't working for Molly now."

"Well, I don't believe them."

He put his arm around me and watched the sun setting.

Then he said, in his quoting voice, " 'We are such stuff as dreams are made on, and our little life is rounded with a sleep.' That's Shakespeare, Meg."

I was furious. "What did *he* know? He never knew Molly. And why *Molly?* Dad, I'm the one who always got into trouble! I'm the one who threw up on my own birthday cake, who broke the window in kindergarten, who stole candy from the grocery store. Molly never did anything bad!"

"Meg," he said. "Meg. Don't."

"I don't care," I said angrily. "Someone has got to explain to me *why.*"

"It's a disease, Meg," he said in a tired voice. "A horrible, rotten disease. It just happens. There *isn't* any why."

"What's it called?" Better to know what your enemy is before you confront it, Will had told me once.

Dad sighed. "It's called 'acute myelogenous leukemia.'"

"Can you say that three times fast?" I asked him bitterly.

"Meg," said Dad, putting his arms around me and holding me so tight that his voice was muffled, "I can't even say it once. It breaks my heart."

Mom and Dad go back and forth to the hospital in Portland. They don't take me. I am too young, according to the hospital rules, to visit, but I don't think that's the reason. I think they don't want me to have to see Molly dying.

I don't argue with them. All the times I've argued with them in the past: to be allowed to see a certain movie, to drink a glass of wine with dinner, to sit in the back of one of Dad's classes at the university, listening. "I'm old enough! I'm old enough!" I remember saying. Now I don't argue, because they know and I know I'm old enough; but I'm scared. The dreams and the emptiness at home are enough; it takes all the courage I have to deal with those. I'm afraid to see my own sister, and grateful that they don't ask me to come.

When she's at home, my mother stitches on the quilt and talks about the past. Every square that she fits into place reminds her of something. She remembers Molly learning to walk, wearing the pale blue overalls that are now part of the pattern of the quilt.

"She used to fall down on her bottom, again and again," my mother smiled. "She always jumped back up laughing. Dad and I used to think sometimes that she fell on purpose, because it was funny. Molly was always looking for things to laugh at when she was a baby."

"What about me? Do you remember *me* learning to walk?"

"Of course I do," Mom said. She turned the quilt around until she found the piece she was looking for, a flowered pattern of blue and green. "This was a little dress. It was summer, and you weren't yet a year old. You were so impatient to do the things that Molly could do. I remember watching you in the back yard that summer. You were very serious and solemn, pulling yourself to your feet, trying to walk across the grass alone.

"You'd fall, and never take time to cry, or laugh, either. Your forehead would wrinkle up as you figured out how to do it right, and tried again."

"I'm like Dad."

She smiled. "Yes, you are, Meg."

"And Molly is more like you. I always thought that was an easier way to be."

Mom sighed and thought about it for a minute. "Well," she said, "it's easier for the little things, to be able to laugh at them. It makes life seem pretty simple, and a lot of fun.

"But you know, Meg," Mom said, smoothing the quilt with her fingers, "when the big, difficult things come, people like Molly and me aren't ready for them. We're so accustomed to laughing. It's harder for us when the time comes that we can't laugh."

I realized that it was the first time I had ever seen my mother not able to shrug things off with a quick smile and an easy solution. And I knew that, hard as it was for me, with my helplessness, my anger, and the dreams that came like faceless prowlers into my sleep and filled me with fear, it was worse for Mom.

"Dad and I are here, Mom," I said uncertainly, "if that helps."

"Oh, Meg," she said, and hugged me. "I don't know what I'd do without you and Dad."

10.

It was five in the morning when Ben called on the third of August. Mom was in Portland, staying with friends who live near the hospital where Molly was; she and Dad were taking turns being there. It was Dad who got me up when Ben called.

I threw on my jeans and a sweater and sneakers, grabbed the camera in a big hurry, and headed across the field. It was going to be a beautiful day. The sun was coming up, very red, so that even the yellow goldenrod looked pink. The baby had obeyed Ben's instruction and elected to come in daylight. It would be a, well, a semi-obedient baby; it wouldn't wait any longer for Molly to come home. Maybe it understood the realities of things better than the rest of us.

When I knocked at their door, Ben called for me to come on in. "I can't open it!" he called. "I'm sterile!

"I mean, I'm sterilized. Or something," he explained when I went inside and met him in the living room. He was wearing a long, white, wrinkled shirt backwards, and holding his hands up carefully so that he wouldn't touch anything.

"We blew the timing, I guess," he said, looking apologetic. "Or the book was wrong. Everything's happening faster than it was supposed to. Remember in the book, Meg, about the first stage of labor, which lasts a long time? I figured that was when we'd all be hanging around, planning what we'd do next!

"I don't know what happened. Maria just woke up about an hour ago and said she felt funny. And now, I don't know, I feel as if we ran a stoplight and ought to go back and do it again the way we were supposed to.

"I mean, I think it's going to be born right away! And I've forgotten everything the book said. I'm running around holding my sterile hands in the air, afraid to turn the pages of the book to find out what it said about the second stage. *Maria's* fine. But I feel so stupid, Meg!" He stood there, looking helpless.

I could sympathize with how he felt, because suddenly I felt panicky, and forgot how the camera worked.

"Is that Meg?" called Maria. She sounded astonishingly healthy for someone who was about to have a baby any minute. Ben went back in the room where she was, and motioned for me to follow.

She was on the bed, with her head propped up on a pillow. It didn't bother me that she was naked. We had talked about things like that enough, the three of us.

It bothered me a little that she was so cheerful. I thought something must be wrong; it wasn't supposed to be easy, having a baby. But Maria looked happy and full of energy. It was only Ben and I who were pale and scared.

I lifted my camera and photographed Maria smiling. The instant I had the camera in my hands, things felt comfortable. The light was good; the settings fell into place as I manipulated them; everything was okay.

Ben had a stethoscope, and he listened through Maria's abdomen to the baby. I could see that he experienced the same thing; when he picked up the simple instrument, he felt in control of things again. It was the helplessness that scared us both. "Listen!" Ben said, and handed the stethoscope to me.

I put the camera down. I listened where he told me to and could make out the rapid, strong heartbeat of the baby. It was full of energy and life; I smiled, hearing it, and nodded in response to Maria's questioning eyes.

Then, as I watched, she closed her eyes and began to breathe rapidly. I photographed her again, and turned the camera toward Ben. He was leaning over, watching carefully. I photographed the intentness of his face as he waited and watched, not touching her; she bent her knees and arched her back slightly. There was no sound in the room but her breathing, and I could see the strain move through her whole body.

"Look," Ben whispered to me. I moved to the foot of the bed, and could see, as the passage widened, taut, almost shaking with the action of the laboring muscles, the top of the baby's head. I could see its dark hair.

Then it disappeared, withdrawing like a mittened fist pulled back into a sleeve. Maria relaxed, opened her eyes, and sighed. Ben moved up near her head and talked quietly to her. "Everything's fine," he said gently. "I can see the head. It'll be soon, very soon." He smiled at her, and I photographed their heads together, and realized they had forgotten I was there.

Maria closed her eyes again and drew a deep, loud breath. Ben moved quickly again to the foot of the bed; I stood back and watched. Then I remembered the camera, moved farther from the bed, and photographed her whole body as she lay poised, gathering herself, her chin up, mouth open and gasping, waiting. Suddenly she groaned and lifted her whole body from the bed.

"Take it easy, take it easy," Ben was murmuring. He leaned forward and touched the baby's head carefully, guiding it as it moved from her body. I came closer and photographed his strong hands holding the tiny head like the shell of an egg. The face was toward me, flat and motionless, its features nothing more than lines like a hastily drawn cartoon: the straight line of a motionless mouth, two slits of swollen, tightly closed eyes, and the tiny, squashed curve of a nose. Maria relaxed again. Ben stood very still, his hands still gently around the head, and the small, flattened face was as immobile as the painted face of a plastic toy.

"Once more," he told Maria. I don't think she heard him at all; her whole being was clenched tight, and then she gasped as the rest of the little body slid toward Ben.

And still the only sound was Maria breathing. I was shooting pictures but I didn't even hear the click of the shutter, just the long, quiet, exhausted breaths.

Then, the cry of the child. Ben was holding it there in his two hands, rubbing it between them. He rubbed its narrow, grayish back; finally, the incredibly small arms and legs moved a little, like a sleeper startled from a dream, and it wailed briefly. Maria smiled at the sound and lifted her head to see. Ben grinned at her and said, "It's a boy. I told you it would be a boy."

He lay the baby on her stomach, waited a moment, and then tied the cord in two places and cut carefully between them. The baby was free of Maria now, but it squirmed against her as if it wanted to stay close. Its face, in those few moments, had changed from bluish-gray to pink, and like a sponge dipped in water, a shape had grown from the flatness of it. The tiny nose had risen into a soft and perfect curve; the thin line of mouth had become a moving, searching thing, and a tongue came from between the lips, tasting the air; the eyes opened and closed, blinking and squinting; the forehead drew up into wrinkles as the head turned against Maria's skin. She reached down with one hand, touched it gently, and smiled. Then she closed her eyes and rested again.

131

"Meg?" Ben handed me a soft white towel from the pile of things he had on a table beside him. "Take the baby for a few minutes, would you, while I finish up here?"

I put my camera on the floor in the corner, wrapped the towel around the baby, and lifted it away from Maria. It was so tiny, so light. I pushed the towel away from the little face, and held it down so Maria could see. She smiled at me, murmured, "Thank you," and I took the baby into the living room.

I held him for a moment in the open front doorway of the house. The sun was golden now, and the dew was already evaporating from the tall grass and flowers in the field. The birds were awake. "Listen," I whispered to the baby, "the birds are singing to you." But he was asleep, his fingers relaxed and warm against my chest.

I sat in the rocking chair and moved slowly back and forth, trying with the soft, steady rhythm of the chair to make up for the abrupt and agonizing journey he had just had. I thought of the overwhelming force that had gripped Maria's whole being at his birth, and the startled, almost painful way that he had moved as he felt his way to life outside her body. I was shaken more than I had anticipated by the awesomeness of the transition.

With one hand I took a corner of the towel and wiped his face, which was still stained from his delivery. As the towel touched him, he gave a surprised jerk and opened both eyes; his fingers fluttered. Then he fell asleep again, breathing softly. The corners of his mouth moved briefly into what seemed to be a momentary smile, and he made a little sound with his lips as he slept.

"Ben?" I called softly.

"Yes? Everything okay? I'm almost through."

"Everything's fine. He says to tell you he's happy."

Ben came out of the room where Maria was, wiping his hands on a towel. He leaned over me, looked down at the baby, and grinned. "He says he's happy? I *told* you he'd tell us his name."

I gave the baby to Ben, went in the bedroom to get my camera, and kissed Maria on the cheek. She was covered with a blanket, and sleeping. I left the three of them there by themselves, and went back home to where my father was waiting.

And they did name him Happy. Happy William Abbott-Brady. When Will Banks heard that, he was a little taken aback at first. "Happy William?" he asked in surprise. "What kind of name is *that?*" Then he thought for a moment. "Well, there's a flower called *Sweet* William. *Dianthus barbatus,* actually. So I suppose there's no reason why a boy can't be named Happy William. So long as he lives up to it, of course."

Suddenly I wanted to be the one to tell Molly.

I had been afraid to see Molly, and now I wasn't. There isn't any way to explain that. The only thing that had happened was that I had watched Maria give birth to Happy, and for some reason that made a difference.

Dad drove me to Portland, and on the way he tried to tell me what it would be like at the hospital. "You have to keep reminding yourself," he said, "that it's still Molly. That's the hard thing, for me. Every time I go in her room, it takes me by surprise, seeing all that machinery. It seems to separate you from her. You have to look past it, and see that it's still Molly. Do you understand?"

I shook my head. "No," I said.

Dad sighed. "Well, I'm not sure I do either. But listen, Meg — when you think of Molly, how do you think of her?"

I was quiet for a minute, thinking. "I guess mostly I think of how she used to laugh. And then I think of how, even after she got sick, she used to run out in the field on sunny mornings, looking for new flowers. I used to watch her, sometimes, from the window."

"That's what I mean. That's the way I think of

134

Molly, too. But when you get to the hospital, you'll see that everything is different for Molly now. It will make you feel strange, because you're outside of it; you're not part of it.

"She'll be very sleepy. That's because of the drugs they're giving her, so that she'll feel comfortable. And she can't talk to you, because there's a tube in her throat to help her breathe.

"She'll look like a stranger to you, at first. And it'll be scary. But she can hear you, Meg. Talk to her. And you'll realize that underneath all that stuff, the tubes and needles and medicines, our Molly is still there. You have to remember that. It makes it easier.

"And, Meg?" He was driving very carefully, following the white line in the center of the curving road.

"What?"

"One more thing. Remember, too, that Molly's not in any pain, and she's not scared. It's only you and I and Mom, now, who are hurting and frightened.

"This is a hard thing to explain, Meg, but Molly is handling this thing very well by herself. She needs us, for our love, but she doesn't need us for anything else now." He swallowed hard and said, "Dying is a very solitary thing. The only thing we can do is be there when she wants us there."

135

I had brought the little vase of pussy willows with me. I shifted them on my lap, and reached over and squeezed Dad's hand for a minute.

Mom met us at the hospital; the three of us had lunch together in the first-floor coffee shop. We talked mostly about Happy.

"I was the first one to hold him, Mom," I told her. "I think he smiled at me."

Mom looked as if she was remembering something. She started to speak, stopped and was silent for a minute, and then said what she had been thinking. "I remember when Molly was born. It's a very special time."

She told me that Molly was awake, that she knew I was coming, that she wanted me there. Then they took me upstairs.

She looked so small. For the first time in my life I felt older, bigger than Molly.

But not more beautiful. I would never feel more beautiful than Molly.

Her hair was completely gone. All those long blond curls were no longer part of Molly; the translucent skin of her face and head were like the fine china of an antique doll against the white pillow of the hospital bed. Above her, labeled glass bottles and plastic bags dangled from a metal rack; through the tubes that led from them to the veins in Molly's left arm, I watched the solutions drip slowly, like tears. The tube that entered her throat was held firmly in place with clean adhesive tape against her skin. I tried to separate all those things from Molly in my mind. Even though pain was knotted inside me like a fist, I saw the way the lashes of her closed eyes were outlined on her cheek in perfect curving lines; I followed with my eyes the moving, blurred patterns of sunshine from the window on her bed, as the leaves of the trees outside moved and swept the sun across her hands and arms.

"Molly," I said. She opened her eyes, found me there, and smiled. She waited for me to talk to her.

"Molly, the baby is born."

She smiled again, very sleepily.

"It's a boy. He was born in the brass bed, the way they wanted. He came very quickly. Ben was all set to wait for hours, but Maria kept laughing and saying, 'No, Ben, it's coming right away!' And it did. Ben picked him up and put him on Maria's stomach, and he curled up and went to sleep."

She was watching me, listening. For a moment it was as if we were home again, in our beds, talking in the dark.

"Then Ben gave him to me, and I carried him to the doorway and showed him that the sun was coming up. I told him the birds were singing to him.

"Will came over later and brought them a big

bouquet of wild flowers. I don't know the names —
you would, though. All yellow and white.

"Ben and Maria and Will all said to tell you they
love you."

She reached out and took my hand and squeezed
it. Her hand was not as strong as Happy's.

"Ben and Maria asked me if I would make
another copy of the picture of you holding the
Queen Anne's lace. They want to hang it on the
wall in the living room."

But she wasn't listening anymore. She had turned
her head to one side and closed her eyes. Her hand
slipped gently out of mine and she was asleep again.
I put the little vase of pussy willows on the table
beside her bed, where she would see it when she
woke up. Then I left her there alone.

On the drive home, I told my father, "Will Banks
said a line from a poem to me once. He said, 'It is
Margaret you mourn for,' and I told him I never
mourn for myself. But I think he was right. So much
of my sadness is because I miss Molly. I even miss
fighting with her."

My father pulled me over close to him on the seat
of the car and put his arm around me. "You've been
great through all of this, Meg," he said. "I'm sorry I
haven't told you that before. I've been busy
mourning for myself too."

Then we sang the rest of the way home. We sang

138

"Michael, Row Your Boat Ashore," mostly off-key, and we made up verses for everybody. We sang "Dad's boat is a Book boat," "Mom's boat is a Quilt boat," "Meg's boat is a Camera boat," "Ben and Maria's boat is a Happy boat," and "Will's boat is a House boat," which struck us both as much funnier than it really was. Finally, we sang "Molly's boat is a Flower boat," and when we finished that verse, we were turning down the dirt road to home.

Two weeks later she was gone. She just closed her eyes one afternoon and didn't ever open them again. Mom and Dad brought the pussy willows back for me to keep.

11.

Time goes on, and your life is still there, and you have to live it. After a while you remember the good things more often than the bad. Then, gradually, the empty silent parts of you fill up with sounds of talking and laughter again, and the jagged edges of sadness are softened by memories.

Nothing will be the same, ever, without Molly. But there's a whole world waiting, still, and there are good things in it.

It was September, and time to leave the little

house that had begun to seem like home.

I answered the knock at the front door and then went upstairs to the study. Dad was sitting at his desk, just staring gloomily at the piles of paper-clipped pages that he had arranged in some order on the floor.

"Dad, Clarice Callaway is at the door with some man. She says she hates to bother you at such a bad time, but."

"But she is going to do it anyway, right?" He sighed and got up. At the front door I heard Clarice introducing him to the man who was standing there holding a briefcase and looking impatient and annoyed. Dad brought them inside, asked Mom to make some coffee, and the three of them sat down in the living room.

I went back to the darkroom where I was trying to pack. I was going to have a darkroom in town; Dad had already hired a couple of his students to build the shelves and do the plumbing and wiring in what had been a maid's room, many years ago, on the third floor of the house there. It would, in fact, be a larger, better equipped darkroom than the one I'd had all summer, so it wasn't that that was making me depressed. And Will Banks had almost completed work on the darkroom that he was building for himself, in what had been a pantry of his little house. So my going away wasn't going to

141

mean the end of Will's interest and enthusiasm or skill, and it couldn't have been that that was making me feel sad as I packed up my negatives and chemicals and tools. I guess it was just that we wouldn't be doing it together anymore, Will and I.

It is hard to give up the being together with someone.

I sealed the packing boxes with tape, wrote "Darkroom" on them, and carried them to a corner of the kitchen. There were other boxes there already; Mom had been packing for several days. There were boxes marked "Dishes," "Cooking Utensils," and "Linens." We'd been living like campers all week, eating from paper plates, finishing up the odds and ends in the refrigerator, making meals from the last few things in Mom's little garden.

There was a box marked "Quilt." Two nights before, my mother had snapped off a thread, looked at the quilt in surprise, and said, "I think it's finished. How can it be finished?" She turned it all around, looking for some corner or spot that she'd forgotten, but every inch was covered with the neat, close-together rows of her tiny stitches. She stood up and laid it out on the big kitchen table. There they were, all those orderly, geometric patterns of our past, Molly's and mine. All those bright squares of color: in the center, the pale pinks and yellows of

142

our baby dresses; farther out, in carefully organized rows, the little flowery prints and the bright plaids of the years when we were little girls; and at the edges, the more subdued and faded denims and corduroys of our growing up.

"It really is," she said slowly. "It's all done." Then she folded it and put it in the box.

Now I could hear her serving coffee in the living room. There was an argument going on. I could hear the quick, angry voices of the visitors, and suddenly I heard my mother's soft voice say, "That's not *fair*," the way I had so often said the same thing to Molly.

There was silence in . the living room for a moment after Mom said that. Then I heard my father say, "There's no point in our continuing to discuss this. Let's go down the road to see Will. You should have gone to see him first, Mr. Huntington."

Dad came into the kitchen to use the phone. "Will?" he said. "Your nephew is here. Can we come down?"

Dad grinned as he listened to the reply. I could imagine what Will was saying; I had never heard him say a good word about his sister's son.

"Will," said Dad on the phone. "*You* know that, and *I* know that. Nevertheless, we have to be civilized. Now calm down. We'll be there in a few minutes."

After he hung up, he said to me, "Meg, run over

to Ben and Maria's, would you? Tell them you'll stay with Happy if they'll meet us at Will's house to talk to his nephew from Boston."

When he went back into the living room, I heard Clarice Callaway say, "I haven't finished my coffee."

And I heard my father reply, "Clarice, I hate to inconvenience you, but." I could tell from his voice that it gave him a lot of satisfaction, saying it.

I loved taking care of Happy. That was another thing I hated about moving back to town, that I wouldn't have a chance to watch him grow bigger and learn things. Already he was holding his head up and looking around. The newborn baby part of him was already in the past, after only a month; now he was a little person, with big eyes, a loud voice, and a definite personality. Maria said he was like Ben, with a screwball sense of humor and no respect for propriety. Ben said he was like Maria: illogical, assertive, and a showoff. Maria whacked Ben with a dish towel when he said that, and Ben grinned and said, "See what I mean?"

I just thought he was Happy, not like anyone else but himself.

When Ben and Maria came back from Will's, I asked them what was going on. Maria rolled her eyes and said, "*I* don't know. Craziness, that's what's going on."

Ben was roaring with laughter. "Meg, I have to show you something." He went to the closet and got the box with the album of wedding pictures.

"I've already seen them, Ben. I know you're married. I told my father so. Clarice can't still be worrying about *that.*"

"No, no, *look,* dummy," said Ben. He flipped through the heavy pages of colored photographs until he found the one he wanted. It was of a crowd of wedding guests, middle-aged people, drinking champagne. In the center of the crowd, looking terribly proper and at the same time a little silly from the champagne, was Will Banks' nephew.

"It's Martin Huntington!" Ben was practically doubled up, laughing. "I couldn't believe it. I walked into Will's house, and there was this jerk with a lawyer suit on, holding a briefcase, and he looked at me with my jeans and my beard, as if he didn't want to get too close for fear of being infected with some disease. And when I realized who he was, I held out my hand — you should have been there, Meg — and said, 'Mr. Huntington, don't you remember me? I'm Ben Brady.'"

"How do you know *him?*" I asked.

"He's been a junior partner in my father's law firm for years," laughed Ben. "Oh, you should have seen it, Meg. He stood there in Will's living room with his mouth open, and then he said in that pompous way he has, 'Well, Benjamin. I, ah, of course had no idea that, ah, it was you living in my family's house. Ah, of course, this does, ah, add a certain element of, ah, awkwardness to these proceedings.'

"'Proceedings!' Can you imagine, calling a discussion in Will Banks' living room 'proceedings'? That's so typical of Martin Huntington. I can't wait to tell my father!"

"But what's going to happen?"

Ben shrugged. "I don't know. But I'm going to call my father. I know what I'd like to have happen. I'd like to buy this house from Will, if my dad will lend me the money for a down payment. I'd like Happy to grow up here. How about that, Hap? Hey, Maria, doesn't that kid ever stop eating?"

Maria was nursing Happy. She grinned at Ben. "He's gonna take after his old man," she said.

Back home, my parents were in the living room drinking the reheated coffee. The rug was rolled up, and the curtains were gone from the windows. Little by little the house was being emptied of everything that had been ours.

"Ben wants to buy the house," I told them. "And they'd live here always." I sighed, kicked off my shoes, and brushed away the pieces of dead leaves that were stuck to my socks and jeans. Everything in the field seemed to be dying.

146

"Well, that's terrific!" said my father. "Why are you looking so glum?"

"I'm not sure," I answered. "I guess because we're leaving. Next summer everything will be the same for *them,* but what about us?"

Mom and Dad were quiet for a minute. Finally Dad said, "Listen, Meg. This house will still be here next summer. We *could* rent it again. But Mom and I have talked about it, and we're just not sure."

"There are so many sad memories for us here, Meg," my mother said quietly.

"By next summer, though," I suggested, "maybe it would be easier. Maybe it would be fun to remember Molly in this house."

Mom smiled. "Maybe. We'll wait and see."

The three of us stood up; Mom headed for the kitchen, to finish the packing there. Dad started up the stairs to his study.

"You know," he said, stopping halfway up the staircase. "At one point in the book, I wrote that the use of coincidence is an immature literary device. But when Ben walked into Will's living room today and said, 'Mr. Huntington, don't you remember me?,' well —"

He stood there thinking for a moment. Then he started talking to himself.

"If I rearranged the ninth chapter," he muttered, "to make it correspond to —" He walked slowly up

147

the rest of the stairs, muttering. At the top of the stairs he stood, looked into the study at the piles of pages, then turned and called down to us triumphantly, "Lydia! Meg! The book is *finished!* It only needs rearranging! I didn't realize it until now!"

So the manuscript was packed, too, and in great bold capital letters, Dad wrote on the box, "BOOK."

The next day, the moving van came. Will Banks, Ben, and Maria, holding Happy, stood in the driveway of the little house, and waved good-bye.

It was the end of September when my father came home after his classes one day and told me, "Meg, comb your hair. I want you to go someplace with me."

Usually he doesn't notice or care if my hair is combed, so I knew it was someplace special. I even washed my face and changed from sneakers into my school shoes. I grabbed a jacket — it was getting chilly: the kind of September air that smells of pumpkins, apples, and dead leaves — and got into the car. Dad drove me to the university museum, the big stone building with bronze statues in front of it.

"Dad," I whispered as we went up the wide steps, "I have seen the Renaissance collection a thousand times. If you're going to make me take that guided tour *again*, I'll —"

"Meg," he said. "Will you please hush?"

The lady at the front desk knew Dad. "Dr. Chalmers," she said, "I was so sorry to hear about your daughter."

"Thank you," said my father. "This is my other daughter, Meg. Meg, this is Miss Amato."

I shook her hand, and she looked at me curiously. "Oh," she said, as if she were surprised. Didn't she know that Dad had another daughter? "*Oh*," she said again. "The photography exhibition is in the west wing, Dr. Chalmers."

I hadn't even heard about a photography exhibition. Not surprising, because I'd been so busy, fixing up the new darkroom, and getting ready for school. I had a sudden sinking feeling as Dad and I walked toward the west wing.

"Dad," I said, "you didn't submit any of my photographs to an exhibition, did you?"

"No," he said, shaking his head. "I would never have done that without asking your permission, Meg. Someday you'll do that yourself."

The huge white-walled room was filled with framed photographs on each wall. The sign at the entrance to the room was carefully lettered in Gothic script: *Faces of New England.* As I walked around the room, I recognized the names of many of the photographers: famous names, names I had seen in magazines and in books of photographs that I had taken from the library. The photographs were all of people: the old, gaunt faces of farmers who live on the back roads; the weathered, wrinkled faces of their wives; the eager-eyed, sunshine-speckled faces of children.

And suddenly there was my face. It was a large photograph, against a white mount, framed in a narrow black frame, and it was not just the coincidence of a stranger who happened to look like me; it was my face. It was taken at an angle; the wind was blowing my hair, and I was looking off in the distance somewhere, far beyond the meticulously trimmed edges of the photograph or the rigid confines of its frame. The outline of my neck and chin and half-turned cheek was sharp against the blurred and subtle shapes of pine trees in the background.

I knew, though I had not known it then, that Will had taken it. He had taken it in the village cemetery the day we buried Molly there and heaped her grave with goldenrod.

There was something of Molly in my face. It startled me, seeing it. The line that defined my face, the line that separated the darkness of the trees from the light that curved into my forehead and cheek was the same line that had once identified Molly by its shape. The way I held my shoulders was the way she had held hers. It was a transient thing, I knew, but when Will had held the camera and released the shutter for one five-hundredth of a second, he had captured it and made permanent whatever of Molly was in me. I was grateful, and glad.

I went close to read what was written below the photograph. The title was "Fringed Gentian"; on the other side was his signature: *William Banks.*

"Dad," I said, "I have to go back. I have to see Will. I promised him."

My father took me back on the weekend. I remembered, in the car, what a long trip it had seemed last winter, when we went for the first time to the house in the country. Now the distance seemed short. Perhaps it is part of a place becoming familiar that makes it seem closer; perhaps it is just a part of growing up.

There was Will, with his head inside the open hood of his truck. He stood up straight when we drove in, wiped his hands, and chuckled, "Spark plugs."

"Will, I came so you could show me the fringed gentian. I'm sorry I forgot."

"You didn't forget, Meg," he told me. "It wasn't time until now."

My father waited at Will's house while we walked across the fields. Almost all of the flowers were gone. Ben and Maria's house was closed up tight and empty, although the curtains Maria had made still hung at the windows. They had gone back so that Ben could complete the last course for his master's degree at Harvard.

"They'll be back," said Will, watching me look at the house, with its paint still new and its garden still tidy and weeded, even though the vegetables were gone. "The house is theirs now. Maybe next summer you can help Happy learn to walk."

Maybe. Maybe there would be another summer filled with flowers and the laughter of a little boy whose life was still brand-new.

Will went right to the place on the side of the woods where the spruce tree was beside the birches. I had forgotten the spot that he had pointed out months before, but this was his land; he knew it like his life. He pushed aside the underbrush and led me to the place where he knew the gentians would be growing. It was very quiet there. The ground was mostly moss, and the sunlight came down through the tall trees in patches, lighting the deep green here and there in patterns like the patchwork of a quilt.

The little clump of fringed gentians stood alone, the purple blossoms at the tops of straight stems that grew up toward the sunlight from the damp earth. Will and I stood and looked at them together.

"They're my favorite flower," he told me, "I suppose because they're the last of the season. And because they grow here all alone, not caring whether anyone sees them or not."

"They're beautiful, Will," I said; and they were.

" 'It tried to be a rose,' " Will said, and I knew he was quoting again, " 'and failed, and all the summer laughed: but just before the snows there came a purple creature that ravished all the hill; and summer hid her forehead, and mockery was still.' "

"Will," I said, as we turned to leave the woods, "you should have been a poet."

He laughed. "A truck mechanic would have been more practical."

I fell a little way behind him as we walked back across the field, wanting to capture every image in my mind. Even the goldenrod was gone. The tall grasses had turned brownish and brittle, like the sepia tones of an old and faded photograph. In my mind, in quick sequences as if a film were stopping and starting, I saw Molly again. I saw her standing in the grass when it was green, her arms full of flowers; with the wind in her hair, with her quick smile, reaching for the next flower, and the next. The floating pollen drifted in patterns through the sunlight around her, as she looked back over her shoulder, laughing.

Somewhere, for Molly, I thought suddenly, it would be summer still, summer always.

Across the field I saw the little house that had been our house. And ahead of me I saw Will. I watched as he walked toward home, pushing the grass aside with his heavy stick, and realized that he was leaning on it as he walked, that he needed its support. Walking through the rocky field wasn't as easy for him as it was for me. I understood then what Ben had told me once, about knowing and accepting that bad things will happen, because I understood, watching him, that someday Will would be gone from me too.

I ran to catch up. "Will," I said, "do you know that the picture of me is hanging in the university museum?"

He nodded. "Do you mind?"

I shook my head. "You made me beautiful," I said shyly.

"Meg," he laughed, putting one arm over my shoulders, "you were beautiful all along."